THE PHYSICS OF BLOWN SAND AND DESERT DUNES

by

R. A. BAGNOLD, F.R.S.

CHAPMAN & HALL
11 NEW FETTER LANE, LONDON EC4

First published June 26th 1941
Reprinted four times
Reprinted 1973
Softcover reprint of the hardcover 1st edition 1973

Published by Chapman & Hall Ltd
11 New Fetter Lane, London EC4P 4EE
ISBN-13: 978-94-009-5684-1 e-ISBN-13: 978-94-009-5682-7
DOI: 10.1007/978-94-009-5682-7

Distributed in the U.S.A. by
Halsted Press, a Division of
John Wiley & Sons, Inc. New York

PREFACE TO 1954 REPRINT

THE completion of the original manuscript of this book coincided with the beginning of World War II and with my own departure on military service in the Middle East. The number of copies which it was possible to print in 1941 was, for obvious reasons, small. And by the time many of those interested had returned to their normal pursuits the edition had become exhausted. The decision of the publishers to print a second edition will therefore, it is hoped, be welcomed.

Considerable re-writing would have been possible, but for several reasons I have retained the original text, subject to a few minor corrections. As regards the first half of the book time has not altered or appreciably extended the experimental facts concerning the movement of sand by wind. When at some future date the subject matter may come to be re-written, I feel it should be in the form of an entirely new book dealing much more generally with the movement of any kind of solid grains in any fluid, that of sand in air or in water being covered as special cases. Though my recent experimental work has lain in this direction the time is not yet ripe for such an enterprise.

As regards the second half of the existing book which deals with full-scale dunes and other sand forms, few if any new facts have emerged. Further progress here must, I think, be in the nature of surmise only, until local wind, and possibly temperature, records taken over fairly long periods are available for the very near vicinity of dunes of various types, and until our knowledge of the meteorology of deserts is more thorough than at present. The sandy regions of the world are economically unimportant; and were it not for the recent oil developments in the Middle Eastern deserts and for the nuisance caused to these vast operations by blown sand and dunes there would be little hope of the required data being collected. Under present conditions we may, however, look forward with some confidence to a start being made on sound and well-organized lines.

But intriguing though the shapes and movement of desert dunes may be, the physics of wind-blown sand has a potentially wider interest much nearer home. On the first page of the Introduction, written fourteen years ago, I referred to the wider problem of the transport of granular material of any kind by fluids in general, to the case of its carriage by liquids, both in rivers and, industrially, through pipes, and to the greater difficulties of observation in this case. These difficulties have been so great that research on lines conventional to hydraulic engineers has advanced very little our knowledge of the basic principles involved. There is, however, an essential unity underlying the internal dynamics of the flow of all fluids, whether gases or liquids, and this unity must extend to the interaction between the fluid flow and the movement of grains within it. Clearly, therefore, the difficult hydraulic problem should be approached by viewing it in as wide a perspective as possible. If by so doing we can find general relationships or physical laws which hold good in very different parts of the field of view, these must provide the clues by which the difficult hydraulic problem may be solved.

In the case of wind-blown sand the grains are some 2,000 times as heavy as the fluid. In that of water-driven natural sand the immersed weight of the grains is only one and a half times the weight of the fluid. Since no really intermediate pair of substances exist a big difference in the behaviour of the grains in the two fluids is only to be expected. It is possible in the laboratory to go much further. We can make an artificial sand which is only just heavier than water. Or more simply we can load water with, say, common salt till it is only just lighter than a sand made of crushed plastic—Perspex or polystyrene. In this way we can experiment with a granular material whose immersed weight is only a few thousandths of that of the fluid. Under these conditions the grains take a minute or more to settle a few inches to the bed. Yet at this opposite extremity of the scale of relative density many of the experimental difficulties met with in the case of natural sand in water are found to disappear. Curiously enough much of the same technique is applicable as was used in the case of wind-blown sand. Experimenting on these lines one finds that some phenomena barely detectable in one case become grossly exaggerated in the other, and vice-versa, but that several quite simple relationships are common to both these extreme cases.

The results of this work is approaching the stage of publication. From them a fairly clear picture is emerging of the general principles of the fluid transport of solids. But at the same time it is becoming apparent that in the intermediate and much more economically important case the real simple picture may long remain obscured from direct vision by practical experimental difficulties. Our knowledge of some aspects of it may have to remain indirect, derived from the two extreme cases.

One of these is the case of wind-blown sand. Being simple, cleanly and easily dealt with experimentally without elaborate apparatus, it seems likely to become an essential stepping stone to knowledge which is yearly more needed both by industry and by engineers.

R. A. B.

July, 1953

CONTENTS

CHAPTER 3

WIND-TUNNEL OBSERVATIONS

CHAPTER 4

THE SURFACE WIND

CHAPTER 5

THE EFFECT OF SAND MOVEMENT ON THE SURFACE WIND

CHAPTER 5

THE EFFECT OF SAND MOVEMENT ON THE SURFACE WIND —*continued*

PAGE

CHAPTER 6

CONFIRMATORY MEASUREMENTS IN THE DESERT

CHAPTER 7

THRESHOLD WIND SPEED AND SIZE OF SAND GRAIN

CHAPTER 8

SUMMARY OF THE PHYSICS OF GRAIN MOVEMENT

CHAPTER 8

SUMMARY OF THE PHYSICS OF GRAIN MOVEMENT—*contd.*

PART II

SMALL-SCALE EFFECTS. GRAIN SIZE DISTRIBUTION. SURFACE RIPPLES AND RIDGES

CHAPTER 9

GRADING DIAGRAMS

CHAPTER 10

GRADING CHANGES IN NON-UNIFORM SAND

CHAPTER 11

SURFACE RIPPLES AND RIDGES

PART III

LARGE-SCALE EFFECTS. SAND ACCUMULATION. DUNES. INTERNAL STRUCTURE, ETC.

CHAPTER 12

CONDITIONS FOR THE GROWTH OF A SAND SURFACE

CHAPTER 13

SAND SHADOWS AND SAND DRIFTS. GENERAL FACTORS ON WHICH DUNE SHAPE DEPENDS

CHAPTER 13

SAND SHADOWS AND SAND DRIFTS. GENERAL FACTORS ON WHICH DUNE SHAPE DEPENDS—*continued*

CHAPTER 14

THE BARCHAN DUNE

CHAPTER 15

THE LONGITUDINAL OR SEIF DUNE. THE WHALEBACK

CHAPTER 15

THE LONGITUDINAL OR SEIF DUNE. THE WHALEBACK —*continued*

CHAPTER 16

THE INTERNAL STRUCTURE OF SAND DEPOSITS

CHAPTER 17

'SINGING SANDS'

PLATES

INTRODUCTION

THE NATURE OF THE PROBLEM

THIS book results from an attempt to explain on a basis of experimental physics some of the many strange phenomena produced by the natural movement of sand over the dry land of the Earth.

The subject is but one aspect of a far wider problem which is still very imperfectly grasped—the transport of solid particles of any kind by fluids in general. Here the difficulty has been, and still is, that no one branch of science has attempted to deal with the problem as a whole, or to co-ordinate the vast amount of piecemeal work by students of different outlook in many unrelated fields.

The carriage of silt by rivers has received a great deal of attention from engineers. But owing to the difficulties of direct measurement, to the expense and labour of conducting full-scale experiments, and to a failure to find agreement as to the basic quantities upon which a theoretical edifice may be built, the published results are far from satisfactory. Little has emerged except empirical formulae; and these are rarely capable of reliable application to conditions other than those under which they were evolved.

The drifting of snow is of direct interest to transport authorities in many countries, to meteorologists engaged in the study of rainfall, to ski-runners and to mountaineers. Yet no means has been found whereby the precipitation can be gauged, or the rate of drift related to the strength of the wind.

In the industrial world the sorting and grading of crushed material by fluid elutriation is yearly becoming of greater importance, and air-blast is used extensively for the carriage of grain, coal dust, &c. But here again our knowledge of the fundamental relations between particle size and movement on the one hand and the fluid velocity on the other is still very scanty and rests on no theoretical basis.

Stimulated by the spectacular and intriguing effects of wind on dry sand in the desert—sand storms, ripples, dunes, and sand seas—many travellers and geomorphologists have attempted to describe and to classify these effects. But till recently no effort has been made to investigate the process of wind action on sand as a problem of aerodynamics, amenable to direct and precise measurement. In fact it is only within the last few years that a tardy realization of the great economic losses caused by wind erosion has directed any serious attention to the movement of silt and sand by wind.

In this case, both experiment and field observation are particularly easy and cheap ; and a basic knowledge of the mechanism involved appears at last to be within sight. I feel, therefore, that some account of the experimental work leading up to this result may be of interest to those engaged on the other aspects of the general problem.

It is, however, to the geologist and the geomorphologist that the subject of blown sand and dune formation is of the most direct importance. The geologist finds vast beds of sandstone and loess covering wide areas of the earth's crust. He accepts many of them as having been most probably laid down in the dry state. But the interpretation, from the structure of the deposits, of the conditions under which the deposition took place he cannot regard as complete until he fully understands the nature of the interaction between the wind and the grains composing them. Nor can the geomorphologist rest content, in his study for its own sake of the shape and movement of sand accumulations, until he knows *why* sand collects into dunes at all, instead of scattering evenly over the land as do fine grains of dust, and *how* the dunes assume and maintain their own especial shapes.

Sand dunes occur in two distinct habitats ; along the coasts of seas and rivers, on the one hand, and on the barren waterless floors of deserts, on the other. It is unfortunate that owing to their relative accessibility a far greater amount of study has been devoted to the former than to the latter ; for coastal dunes, because of their more temperate habitat, are much modified in form by the presence of vegetation. This, as we shall see, profoundly modifies the character of the wind which blows over them. Moreover, and this often applies too to the dunes on the borders of deserts, the mere fact of their accessibility permits the feet of animals and of men to interfere seriously with both the structure and the natural movement of their surfaces. The result is a general formlessness; in so much that the average mind associates a sand hill with something essentially chaotic and disordered.

But now, owing to the development of motor transport, it is possible to study in the further interiors of the great deserts the free interplay of wind and sand, uncomplicated by the effects of moisture, vegetation, or of fauna, and to observe the results of that interplay extended over great periods of time.

Here, instead of finding chaos and disorder, the observer never fails to be amazed at a simplicity of form, an exactitude of repetition and a geometric order unknown in nature on a scale larger than that of crystalline structure. In places vast accumulations of sand weighing millions of tons move inexorably, in regular formation, over the surface of the country, growing, retaining their shape, even breeding, in a manner which, by its grotesque imitation of life, is vaguely disturbing to an imaginative mind. Elsewhere the dunes are cut to another pattern—lined up in parallel ranges, peak following peak in regular succession like the teeth of a monstrous saw for scores, even hundreds of miles, without a break and without a change of direction, over a landscape so flat that their formation cannot be influenced by any local geographical features. Or again we find smaller forms, rare among the coastal sand hills, consisting of rows of coarse-grained ridges even more regular than the dunes. Over large areas of accumulated sand the loose, dry, uncemented grains are so firmly packed that a loaded lorry driven across the surface makes tracks less than an inch in depth. Then, without the slightest visual indication of a change, the substance only a few inches ahead is found to be a dry quicksand through which no vehicle can force its way. At times, especially on a still evening after a windy day, the dunes emit, suddenly, spontaneously, and for many minutes, a low-pitched sound so penetrating that normal speech can be heard only with difficulty.

These are some of the phenomena of desert dunes, and no satisfactory explanation of any one of them has so far been forthcoming.

The geomorphologist, aware of the vast periods of time during which his processes have acted, is rightly doubtful of the ability of the physicist and the chemist to imitate them usefully in their laboratories. He is, in consequence, generally averse to the experimental method of research. It seemed to me, however, that the subject of sand movement lies far more in the realm of physics than of geomorphology; and if any advance were to

2

be made in our knowledge of it, it must in the first instance be approached via the study of the behaviour of a single grain in a stream of wind.

After much desert travel, extending over many years, during which sand storms of varying intensity were frequently encountered, I became convinced that the movement of sand (as opposed to that of dust) is a purely surface effect, taking place only within a metre of the ground; and that large-scale eddy currents within the air stream play no appreciable part in maintaining the grains aloft. If this is true it is clearly possible to reproduce in the laboratory the complete phenomena of sand-driving, together with all the small-scale surface effects, such as ripples and the like, associated with it. The possibility of such an investigation under controlled conditions was first suggested to me by the experiments of Harding King [1] with a wooden trough laid on the sand in the open. Here, though of course the wind strength was not under control, it was found possible to produce various ripple forms by placing sands of different size-grading over the floor of the trough.

It appeared to me, therefore, that a research into sand-dune formation should best be divided into two stages. The first stage should comprise laboratory work with a suitable wind tunnel, by means of which an insight would be gained into the physics of the action of the air stream on the sand grains and of the reaction of the sand grains on the air stream. The applicability of the laboratory results to real conditions in the open would of course depend on the truth of the above underlying assumption. But if, subsequently, a series of quantitative predictions concerning the wind velocity and its distribution, and the rate of sand movement caused by it, based on the laboratory work, were to be corroborated by careful measurements during sand storms in the desert on a far larger scale, then there would be very strong grounds indeed for regarding both the assumption and the results based on it as being true. Such corroboration has already been obtained.

When this first stage has been reached; that is, when it is understood just how sand is picked up from, transported over, and accumulated upon, a flat surface of ground, and when the magnitude of the resistance is known which the sand movement exerts on the wind, it will be possible to proceed to stage two. This would be a purely aerodynamical investigation into the

[1] Harding King, W. J. (1916). *Geogr. J.*, 47, p. 189.

movement of an air stream over and round the curved surfaces of the accumulations which would then be taken as having risen out of the flat surface into the third dimension. Here experiments on a suitably small scale would be subject to the well-known 'model rules' by which in all problems in fluid dynamics a change of scale must be accompanied by a change of velocity and/or a change in the density of the fluid.

But stage two of the investigation is still for the future. This book is concerned mainly with stage one—the movement of sand over a flat or nearly flat surface; and the bulk of the book is based on facts brought to light during my own wind-tunnel experiments carried out in 1935 and 1936, and on subsequent verifications made in the Libyan Desert in 1938. Chapters are, however, devoted to a description of the observed morphology of actual sand forms in the field, and to a discussion of such of their features as can be explained qualitatively by a knowledge of sand movement in general.

Though the book is concerned with sand and wind, much of the matter in the chapters dealing with the movement of the grains can be applied equally well to dry granular snow, and the latter will for this reason rarely be found to receive special mention. As regards the less closely allied subject of sand movement in water, I have pointed out in appropriate places what appear to be the important differences as well as the similarities between the two phenomena.

Since this appears to be the first time an attempt has been made to deal in book form with the movement of sand in air, I trust that I may be excused in part at least both for weaknesses in the arrangement of the book and for the serious omissions which must inevitably be found. I am conscious that the references I have given to previous work on the subject constitute but a meagre list; but, confronted with a large, scattered, and somewhat diffuse literature, I have confined myself as far as possible to those works which deal with precise measurement and experimental verification. At the same time I gratefully acknowledge that in the course of my own research work many useful ideas have been suggested to me by a large number of other more descriptive writings.

In the matter of the presentation of the subject I have been faced with the difficulty that many of those to whom the book may be of interest may be discouraged by the prospect of a mathematical treatment. Since, however, the descriptive method has, in spite of a prodigious literature, failed to produce either qualitative explanations or useful data for mathematical explanations, the experimental method may perhaps be allowed its few mathematical symbols and its logarithmic diagrams if, in return, it yields a reliable groundwork of fact. The subject is very much a borderline one. As is usual with such subjects, the need to make the language reasonably intelligible to specialists in a large number of widely different fields of knowledge—geophysics, meteorology, aerodynamics, hydraulics, geology, geomorphology, &c.—necessitates a certain diffuseness of explanation which would otherwise be unwarranted.

I am much indebted to the authorities of the Imperial College of Science and Technology, London, for their kindness in allowing me the use of their laboratories; to Dr. C. M. White for his most valuable suggestions and advice; to Professor G. I. Taylor for his encouragement and help of many occasions; and to Dr. K. S. Sandford for reading through those parts of the present work which have a direct bearing on geology. I have to thank the Royal Geographical Society for their courtesy in allowing me to reproduce Figs. 1, 2, 3, 6, 15A, 19, 57, 58, and 62, and the Royal Society for Figs. 20, 22, 23, 24, 25, 26, 34, 38, 39, 40, 41, 42, 43, 44, 45 and 46. I would also like to acknowledge my gratitude to all those who in the past have been associated with me in those major expeditions into the remote desert which have supplied the practical knowledge of field conditions without which experimental laboratory work must remain inconclusive.

R. A. B.

PART I

THE PHYSICS OF GRAIN MOVEMENT

Chapter I

SAND AND DUST

I. THE ORDER OF SIZE OF SMALL PARTICLES. USE OF THE LOGARITHMIC SCALE

FIGURE I is intended to show approximately, in diagrammatic form, the relative sizes of material particles which are susceptible to the action of winds of normal speeds. They range from little

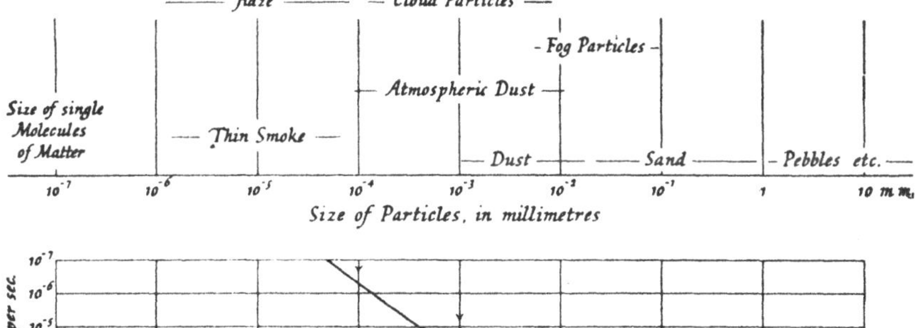

FIG. I.—RELATIVE SIZE AND RATE OF FALL OF SMALL PARTICLES

pebbles, on the large side, through sand grains and rain and fog drops to specks of dust and the tiny water droplets which constitute clouds. Thence, smaller and smaller, to the minute particles that form thin smokes and hazes. The estimated diameter of large molecules of matter is included for completeness.

The diameter of the largest particle in the diagram is seen to be some fifty million times that of the smallest. For such a diagram the ordinary linear scale is clearly unsuitable. If a linear scale (one in which 10 is added to 10 in the ordinary way to give the position of the succeeding division 20) had been used, 99 per cent. of the horizontal space in the diagram would have been occupied by the pebbles and the larger sand grains ; and all the rest of the material, all the vast range of small particles from sand grains to hazes, would have been squashed up into the last single millimetre of the scale.

The linear scale, since it was first cut on the wall of an Egyptian temple, has come to be accepted by man almost as if it were the one unique scale with which Nature works and builds. Whereas it is nothing of the sort. Its sole value lies in giving due prominence to the differences and sums of quantities, when these are what we want to display. But Nature, if she has any preference, probably takes more interest in the ratios between quantities ; she is rarely concerned with size for the sake of size.

For many purposes a far more convenient scale is one in which equal divisions represent equal multiples—one which multiplies 10 by 10 to make 100 rather than one which adds 10 to 10 to make 20. This point is stressed, because throughout the subject with which we are dealing the relations between one quantity and another are very often found to be of the logarithmic type ; so that we have the choice, in representing relations of this kind diagrammatically, between dealing with awkward logarithmic curves on a linear scale (with the added disadvantage of being limited in the extent of the scale) or exhibiting simple straight-line relations on an unlimited ratio scale such as that of Fig. 1. I shall use both scales indiscriminately, according to which is most suitable to the occasion.

It will be seen from the diagram that of the whole size range of 50,000,000 to 1, *sand* occupies but a tiny belt between 1 mm. and $\frac{1}{50}$ mm., or a ratio of 50 to 1. That is, the size range of sand grains occupies but one-millionth of the whole range of size of small particles which are affected by the wind. The truth of this statement depends, of course, on how we define sand ; and that, in turn, from the nature of the subject, depends on the relative behaviour of small particles in a wind. It is to this question that we must first turn.

2. THE DEFINITION OF GRAIN SIZE

If an object of any size, shape, or material is allowed to fall from rest through any fluid, whether air, water, or oil, its velocity will increase, at first with the acceleration of gravity, but thereafter at a decreasing acceleration till it reaches a constant value known as the *Terminal Velocity of Fall.* The reason is that the net force on the object is the resultant of the pull of gravity acting downwards, and the resisting force of the fluid acting always in a direction opposite to that of the motion. As the velocity of the motion increases, so does the resistance against that motion, till eventually the two are equal. No net force any longer acts on the object, which therefore moves at a constant speed.

The downward force of gravity depends on the volume of the object and its density. The resisting force depends on the area of frontage exposed to the fluid, on the shape of the object, and on its speed through the fluid. Hence, since natural solid particles are of irregular and haphazard shape, the individuals, even of a collection of particles or grains chosen to be all of the same average size, will not have the same rate of fall.

The first task is to find a convenient way of specifying the average size and shape of the grains of a given sample so that the average rate of fall of these specified grains can be calculated. Now a great deal of experimental work has been done on the behaviour of spherical objects in air and other fluids, and the fluid resistance of a sphere of a given diameter and a given density can be accurately calculated. The most useful method, therefore, of specifying our sand grains is to replace them by a collection of imaginary spheres of the same material and of such a diameter that they will behave in air in the same way as the *average* sand grain of the sample. We then have a simple workable material of identical grains completely specified by diameter and density; and, starting with any given initial conditions, we can calculate with confidence the subsequent paths of these ideal average grains through the air.

To obtain the diameter of a sphere which will be equivalent to a given sand grain, the mean dimensions of the grain are found by passing it through a series of sieves each having a known size of aperture which differs but slightly from that of the next in the series. The mean dimension is taken to be that midway between the size of the aperture of the sieve through which the grain will just pass and of that of the next sieve which will retain it.

This mean diameter is then multiplied by a suitable shape-factor. For desert sand this factor can be taken as 0·75.

The value of this factor can be found very simply by experiment. A small shower of mixed sand of all grain sizes is allowed to fall from a known height on to a slowly rotating disc covered with sticky paper, from a hopper which is made to open by a trigger operated by a cam on the disc. By this means the beginning of the fall is made to correspond in time with the passage of a fixed zero radius on the disc below. The exact time of fall

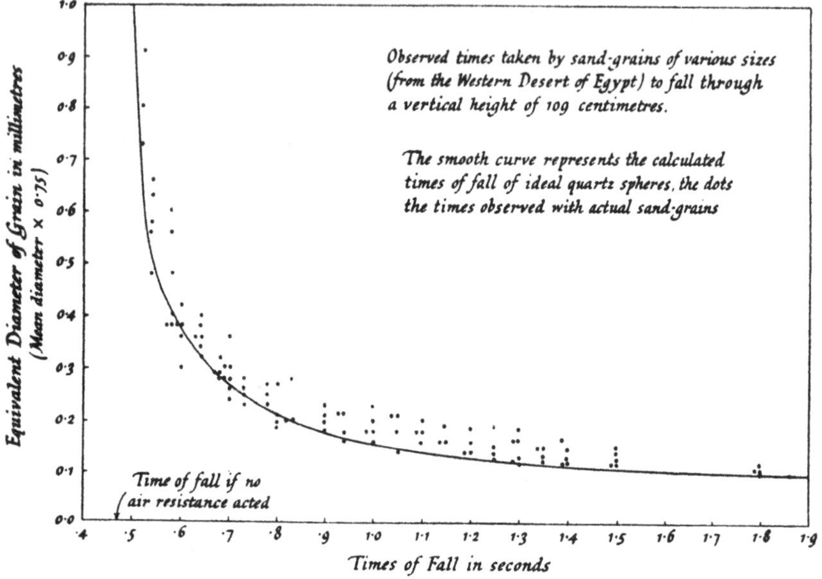

FIG. 2.—EXPERIMENTAL DETERMINATION OF THE SHAPE-FACTOR

can then be measured by the angle between the zero radius and the radius passing through any required grain (which is held in position by the sticky paper). The continuous curve in Fig. 2 gives the calculated time of all of quartz spheres of various diameters given by the scale on the left. The dots show the measured times of fall of actual sand grains whose measured diameters have been multiplied by a shape-factor of 0·75 to reduce them to their corresponding *equivalent diameters*, as explained above. The figure shows fairly well the degree to which sand grains of the same general size may be expected to vary as regards their wind resistance. It also shows the degree of closeness with which one can calculate the wind resistance and the rate of fall of a real grain of a given size.

The above is but a very brief reference to the subject of grain size and rate of fall. In contrast to our imperfect knowledge of the general effect of the presence of numerous particles on the motion of a fluid, a really formidable amount of detailed work has been devoted both to the rate of fall of individual particles through a fluid at rest, and to the measurement of the size of small particles. An excellent bibliography of original papers on the subject is given in a paper by Heywood [1]; and the whole subject is treated of at length by Krumbein and Pettijohn.[2]

3. THE SUSPENSION OF SMALL PARTICLES. THE DISTINCTION BETWEEN SAND AND DUST

Returning to Fig. 1; in the lower part will be found given the rates of fall of the various kinds of particles shown in the upper part, the velocities being measured downwards. Owing to the enormous range of velocities, a logarithmic scale is again necessary. It will be observed that the smallest particles, those constituting the thin smokes and hazes, do not fall at all. This is because they are so susceptible to displacement by collisions with molecules of air that the very feeble downward pull of gravity is counter-balanced by the dispersive tendency of the jostling they receive from the air molecules.

The velocity of the wind is never constant. The short-period variation of speed, or the gustiness, is due to the internal movements of the air. As these movements, or eddies, circulate haphazard about axes in all directions, there are internal air currents which move upwards and downwards as well as those which move forwards, backwards, and sideways relatively to the general direction of the wind. Close to the ground the upward and downward components of the eddy velocity have been found to be less than the components in other directions. Though the ratio of the upward eddy velocity to the mean velocity of the wind is very variable, an average figure of $\frac{1}{5}$ for this ratio is probably not far out. If, therefore, there are solid particles in the air whose terminal velocities of fall are less than $\frac{1}{5}$ of the mean velocity of the wind, some of these particles may be carried upwards and may remain for a time in partial suspension. On the other hand,

[1] Heywood, H. (1939). *Proc. Inst. of Mechanical Engineers*, 140.
[2] *Manual of Sedimentary Petrology*, 1938. (Appleton Century.)

larger particles with greater terminal velocities will remain on or near the ground.

Now it will be shown later that when sand is being driven by the wind, the grains rarely rise higher than 1 metre above the ground, and that the average height is much less—of the order of 10 cm. And it will also appear that the wind velocity, as measured at this height, which is just strong enough to set the grains on the ground in motion, is in the neighbourhood of 5 metres/sec., or 11 miles per hour. Taking as a rough estimate the value of $\frac{1}{5} \times 5 = 1$ metre/sec. as the maximum upward velocity of the internal movement of this wind, we see from Fig. 1 that sand grains having this velocity of fall have a diameter of about 0·2 mm. We might therefore expect that at somewhere about this size there should be a noticeable change in the character of the distribution of small loose particles existing on the Earth's surface.

This is found to be the case. When samples of natural sand are analysed by sifting, it is found that, in general, grains of one diameter predominate, and that the weights of sand of diameters both larger and smaller fall off rapidly as the diameter departs from the 'peak' value. And in the finest wind-blown sands the predominant diameter is never less than 0·08 mm. Usual values, depending on the locality, lie between 0·3 and 0·15 mm.[1]

We can thus define the lower limit of size of sand grains, without reference to their shape or material, as that at which the terminal velocity of fall becomes less than the upward eddy currents within the average surface wind. Particles of smaller size tend to be carried up into the air and to be scattered as dust.

The upper limit of sand size is that at which a grain resting on the surface ceases to be movable either by the direct pressure of the wind or by the impact of other moving grains.

Any substance consisting of solid non-cohesive particles which lie within these limits of size may be classed as 'sand'. Such substances all possess one peculiar characteristic: alone of all artificial or natural solids they have the power of self-accumulation—of utilizing the energy of the wind to collect their scattered components together into definite heaps, leaving the intervening country free of grains. They can do this in the open, unsheltered by wind-breaks other than those of their own making; and the heaps, or dunes, can retain their identity and can move about from place to place.

[1] Udden, J. A. (1898). Augustana Library Publications, No. 1. Wentworth C. (1932). *Univ. Ia. Stud. Phys.*, 14.

4. THE COMPOSITION OF NATURAL SAND. THE PREVALENCE OF QUARTZ

The relative prevalence of any material on the Earth's surface depends upon (1) the abundance or otherwise of the source from which it is derived, (2) the rate at which it is formed, and (3) the rate at which it is destroyed or transformed into something else. Consider, for instance, the case of dry snow which, according to the definition just given, is but a special form of 'sand', and which may display all its characteristics. Its source, water, is abundant; and it is formed rapidly and in great quantity in suitable climates. Yet, as dry snow, it exists in very limited amount. This is because, being unstable, it is so soon changed into firn-ice, water, or vapour. In addition, its tiny crystals, being brittle and easily cracked by impact, tend to be reduced to powder or dust when driven along the surface.

As rocks are degraded by the action of water and weather into smaller and smaller particles, fragments which are either soft, brittle or easily soluble pass rapidly down the scale of size. These have but a short life as sand grains, and do not contribute much material to the existing sand of the Earth's surface.

Thus, in order that a substance may be present as sand in large quantities, it must satisfy the following requirements; its mother substance must be, or have been, plentiful; it must be one which resists the action of chemical weathering, of solution, and of abrasion, and it must be tough enough to resist fracture by the impact of other grains during transport.

Of all natural substances, crystalline silica (quartz) complies best with these requirements; and it is of quartz that the bulk of sand grains are composed.

Quartz is not the only material, however, which occurs in the form of sand. Sands which are predominantly quartz often contain grains of other materials, and under special conditions, near a plentiful source of supply, sands are found which are composed entirely of other substances—e.g. of broken sea shells, magnetic iron-ore, flint, &c. But as regards their behaviour in a fluid, whether air or water, neither the composition of the grains, nor their shape, are found to have any considerable effect on the character of the accumulations produced. Grain size is far more important: for though the weight of a grain of a given size may vary with the material in a ratio of two to one, this variation in weight will be offset by a change of only the cube root of two, or 1·26, in the size.

Since quartz so greatly predominates in the sands found on the Earth's surface, the experimental work on which much of this book is based has been done with quartz sand. But the results in nearly all cases can be applied without change to other sands.

5. THE ORIGIN AND FORMATION OF SAND GRAINS

It is generally accepted by geologists that the bulk of the quartz sand grains found in the earth's crust, whether occurring free on the surface or in sandstones and other sedimentary rocks laid down long ago, have originated from the disintegration of quartz-bearing rock followed by some process of mechanical abrasion. But apart from the fact that certain quartz-rich rocks—e.g. granites—contain ready-made quartz particles of suitable size, there seems to be no unanimity as to what process is mainly responsible for having reduced the grains to their present size and shape.

Of the possible processes we have dry weathering on the one hand, and the mechanical action of water and frost on the other. In the case of a relatively insoluble and chemically inert substance such as quartz, the only kind of dry weathering available appears to be temperature splitting. But though there is plenty of evidence that the violent temperature changes experienced by surface rocks in desert regions can and do cause rocks and large stones to split, there is little or no evidence that this process extends to fragments smaller than 1 cm. in diameter. For the stresses set up depend on the temperature differences within the body of the material, and the material does its best to reduce these differences by the conduction of heat from the hotter to the colder parts. Though the surface may be exposed to rapid and violent changes of air temperature, the maximum possible rate of change is not unlimited. Hence the smaller the body the more easily can its internal adjustment of temperature keep pace with the externally applied changes. In the case of such small particles as sand grains it is extremely unlikely that any temperature splitting could ever take place in Nature.

Nor does it seem possible to account for any appreciable reduction in grain size by the action of the wind. Here again a definite limit is set to the mechanical pressure which a *rounded* grain can ever experience. The maximum conceivable pressure is that which is set up momentarily by the direct impact of a flying grain against a hard, unyielding rock face. This maximum pressure depends, for any one material, on the velocity of impact and on the diameter of the grain. The velocity is limited to that of the wind, and the pressure falls off rapidly the smaller is the grain diameter. Grains smaller than a diameter considerably exceeding that of a sand grain merely bounce off after impact like steel balls, without any sign of shattering.

Turning to water and ice as the agents whereby quartz fragments have been reduced to the size of sand grains, we have an abundance of direct evidence, in the beds of rivers and glaciers, and on sea beaches, that the process can and certainly does go on. It consists, clearly, in a violent grinding and crushing of the smaller fragments between bigger ones.

On the evidence available, therefore, it seems reasonable to suppose that the vast majority of the existing sand grains have been reduced, either recently or in long-past ages, to something very near to their present size by the action of water and perhaps to a lesser extent by that of ice. From the fact, however, that the grains of fluvial and marine sands are in general sharper and less rounded than those found in desert dunes, it is possible that wind action has an appreciable effect on the *shape* of the grains once they have been reduced to such a size that the wind can move them.

GENERAL REFERENCES

DESIO, A. (1931). *Missione a Cufra.* Vol. II

GAUTIER, E. F. (1908). *Sahara Algérien.* Vol. I. (Paris)

GIBBS, W. F. (1924). *Clouds and Smokes.* (J. & A. Churchill, London)

DUNNON, R. G. (1928–9). *Trans. Inst. Mining and Metallurgy*

TWENHOFEL, W. H. (1926). *Treatise on Sedimentation.* (Baillière, Tindall & Cox, London)

Chapter 2

THE BEHAVIOUR OF SAND GRAINS IN THE AIR

1. THE PHENOMENON OF SAND-DRIVING

A POPULAR misconception exists regarding sand storms, due to a failure to distinguish sand from dust. When, in any arid country, after a spell of calm weather, a strong wind begins to blow from a new direction, the air becomes charged with a mist of small particles. Where the surface is alluvial, with little or no sand on it, such as in Iraq or the country round Khartoum, the dust rises in dense clouds to a height of several thousand feet and the sun is obscured for a long period. This is obviously a dust storm, though it is often wrongly designated by the possibly more thrilling and cleanly term ' sand storm '. Owing to their feeble terminal velocity of fall the very small dust particles are raised and kept aloft by the upward currents of the wind's internal movement, as described in Chapter I (3).

On the other hand, in an erosion desert, the only free dust consists of those fine rock particles which have been loosened by weathering since the last wind blew, and have therefore not been carried away. In such country the wind produces for the first hour or so a mist consisting of both dust and sand. Later, although the wind may have shown no signs of slackening, the mist disappears. But the sand still continues to drive across country as a thick, low-flying cloud with a clearly marked upper surface. The air above the sand cloud becomes clear, the sun shines again, and people's heads and shoulders can often be seen projecting above the cloud as from the water of a swimming-bath. Where the ground is composed of coarse grains, pebbles, or large stones, the top of the cloud may be 2 metres above it, but it is usually less. Where the surface consists of fine sand, such as that of a dune, the height of the sand cloud is noticeably lower.

The bulk of the sand movement takes place considerably nearer the ground than the visible top of the cloud. Evidence of this is given by the effects of the sand blast on posts and rocks projecting from the ground ; the erosion is greatest at ground level, and is usually inappreciable at a height of 18 inches. Except in broken country, the sand cloud seems to glide steadily over the desert like a moving carpet, and the wind is comparatively gustless. When the wind drops the sand cloud disappears with it. This is a true sand storm.

On the borders of the desert and the sown land, sand storms may be accompanied by dust from the cultivation, so that their true nature is not apparent. Plumes of finer particles carried upwards by revolving wind eddies here distract the attention from the steady forward-moving sand cloud beneath, and give a false impression that all the solid matter is conforming to the turbulent movement of the wind. Even when the sand cloud is free from dust, as over a dry sand beach or in the interior of denuded desert, the actual movement of the sand within the cloud is very difficult to see. The individual grains are too small and travel too fast for the eye to follow their motion.

The first problem with which we are confronted is therefore to discover how it is that large massive grains a millimetre or more in diameter are encountered, often very painfully, at a height exceeding a metre above the ground. How are they kept aloft?

Since the only known upward force which might maintain these large sand grains in the air against the downward pull of gravity is that of the air itself, and since, as we have seen, this is not sufficiently strong, unless an abnormal turbulence is assumed, for which there is no evidence, we are driven to conclude that the grains are not kept aloft at all. An alternative hypothesis is that they move like ping-pong balls; that, having received a supply of energy from the forward pressure of the wind, their acquired horizontal velocity is converted into an upward one by impact with the ground. If the ground were covered with hard projections, pebbles or the like, whose faces were inclined at various angles, and if the balls were resilient and elastic, they would bounce high into the air. The pressure of the wind would drive them onward till, on sinking to the ground, they would bounce upwards once more. If, on the other hand, the ground were to be composed of a mass of other similar balls resting loosely on one another, the action when impact with the surface took place would be rather different. We can imagine the impacting ball splashing into the loose mass of surface balls, possibly forming a little crater and itself becoming buried, but ejecting in the process one or two other balls upward into the air. These would not rise so high as in the former case of the hard surface owing to the energy lost in disturbing the surface, but they would gather speed as they were driven down-wind till they in their turn hit the surface.

In order to ascertain whether this hypothesis can be applied to actual sand grains, we must examine the behaviour of such grains when they move rapidly through the air at speeds considerably higher than their terminal velocities, and also how far the elastic properties of real quartz grains will allow them to bounce off pebbles and rocks as suggested.

2. SUSCEPTIBILITY OF THE GRAINS TO WIND FORCES

When a body moves through the air, it is acted on, as has already been mentioned, by two forces; the force of gravity downwards, and a force due to the resistance of the air in a direction opposite to that of the relative motion. When these two forces are equal, the body moves with constant velocity. If the force of gravity is the greater, the body is accelerated; if less, its velocity is retarded. The ratio of these two forces under any given conditions is therefore of considerable importance. I have called it the *susceptibility*. It varies, for grains of one average shape, according to the size of the grain and its velocity.

Unfortunately, within the range of size and velocity with which we have to deal, the force of the air resistance or *drag* cannot be defined by any mathematical expression. Values for it can, however, be found for spheres from existing experimental data, and the susceptibility calculated therefrom. Fig. 3 shows the susceptibility of smooth quartz spheres of various diameters in terms of their relative velocities through the air. An explanation of the calculation is given in Appendix I at the end of this chapter.

In Fig. 3 the terminal velocity of fall is that corresponding to unit susceptibility; i.e. when gravity is equal to the air drag. The enormous value attained by the susceptibility in the case of very small grains should also be noticed. For instance, if a grain of 0·03 mm. is suddenly projected into a stream of air flowing at 15 metres per second or 33 miles per hour, the force of the air on the grain is 500 times the weight of the grain. Tiny dust grains therefore conform very closely to the movements of the air stream in which they happen to be carried. They collide with solid objects comparatively rarely, being checked as they approach, and diverted with the stream as it flows round the obstruction. Microscopically they are for this reason much sharper than the larger sand grains and show few signs of rounding.

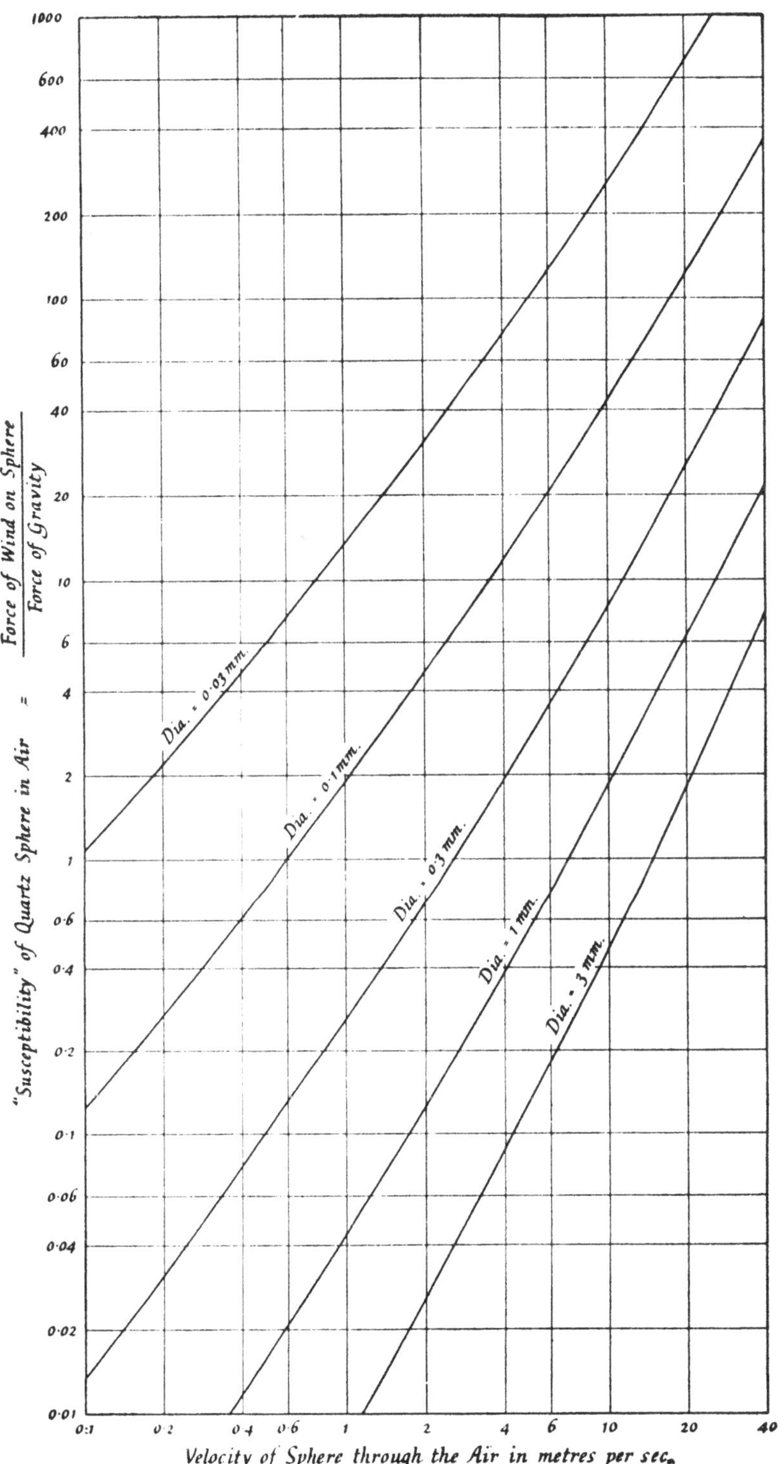

FIG. 3.—SUSCEPTIBILITY OF QUARTZ SPHERES

3

A simple example of how the susceptibility diagram is used to calculate the vertical motion of sand grains through still air is given in Appendix II to this chapter. When the direction of motion is inclined to the vertical, the problem of tracing the path of the grain is more complicated. The method which I have used

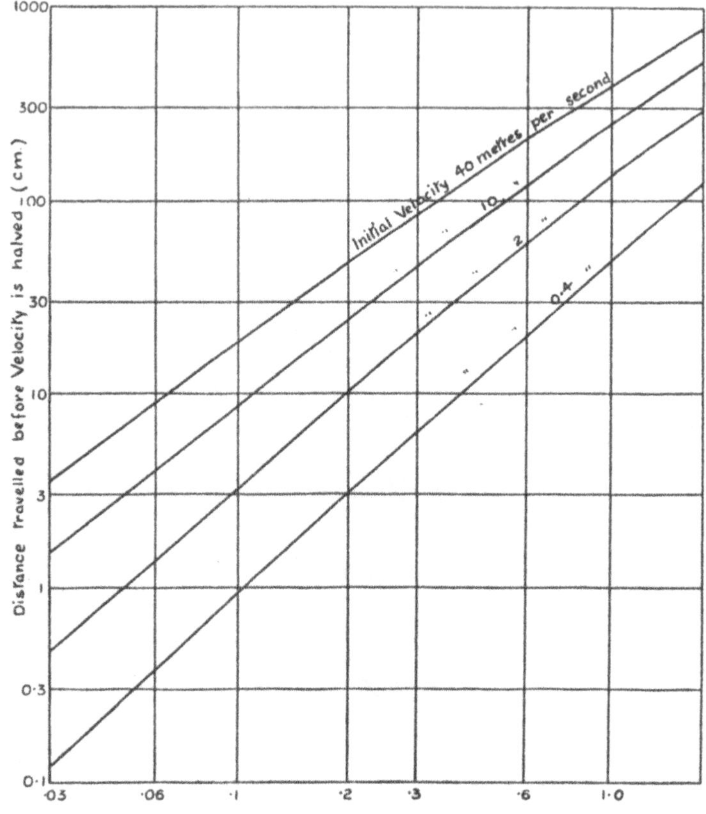

FIG. 4.—RELATIVE DISTANCES IN WHICH GRAIN SPEEDS ARE REDUCED TO HALF VALUE BY THE AIR DRAG

will be found described in a previous paper.[1] In both cases the method is approximate only, and resembles that used in ballistics for calculating the trajectory of a projectile.

An idea of the effect of the air drag on sand grains of various

[1] Bagnold, R. A. (1936). *Proc. Roy. Soc. A.*, 157, p. 617.

sizes can be gained from Fig. 4. This diagram gives the horizontal distances travelled (neglecting the effect of gravity) by sand grains through still air before their initial velocities are reduced to half-value by the air drag. It will be seen, for instance, that a grain of 0·1 mm. diameter initially moving through the air at 10 metres per second (22 miles per hour) will halve its speed in a distance of 9 cm., whereas a grain of 1·0 mm. diameter will travel 2·5 metres before doing so.

3. EXPERIMENTAL VERIFICATION OF THE APPLICATION TO REAL GRAINS OF CALCULATIONS BASED ON THE BEHAVIOUR OF EQUIVALENT SPHERES

In the example worked out in Appendix II a grain of sand of diameter 0·4 mm. (equivalent spherical diameter 0·3 mm.) is supposed to rise vertically from the ground after bouncing, at an initial speed of 14 metres per second or 31 miles per hour. If there were no air, i.e. if gravity alone acted on the grain, it would rise to a height of 10 metres, and the rise would take 1·4 seconds. Owing to the air drag, it only rises 1·6 metres and takes only 0·4 second to do it.

Having calculated the height to which grains of this size should rise if they left the ground at various initial speeds, it was of interest to find by actual experiment how nearly the calculations could be applied to real sand grains. For this purpose I used a spring gun of special design compressible in four stages, giving four known velocities at the end of its stroke. A small collection of sand grains of mean diameter 0·4 mm. (measured by sieve aperture) was placed on the top of the plunger of the gun, which was pointed vertically upwards. On releasing the trigger, the grains were shot upwards with a known initial velocity. In a good light, against a black background, the shower of grains, invisible while moving fast, appear suddenly to the eye at the moment they are stationary at the top of their rise. The height attained by the bulk of the grains can be estimated fairly well. The maximum height reached by the grains whose shape produced a minimum air drag was found by holding a sheet of oiled glass over the gun at increasing heights, till no more were caught on the oiled surface. Considering the variation in grain shape and the difficulty of ensuring that the motion was not assisted by an upward current of air produced by the rise of the gun's plunger, the agreement between calculation and experiment was good.

4. THE PATHS TRACED BY SAND GRAINS THROUGH THE AIR

Suppose that the grain rises vertically into moving instead of into stationary air. The drag is no longer vertically downwards, but remains in a direction opposite to that of the relative motion of the grain through the air. We must now be very careful to distinguish between two motions of the grain; that relative to the ground and that relative to the air. The grain, once it has risen into the air stream, travels down-wind relatively to the ground, increasing its forward speed until the latter approaches that of the wind (but to an observer moving along with the wind the grain appears to travel back-wards through the air, at first at the same speed as the ground, and then more slowly, as the drag of the air checks it).

The grain meanwhile has risen, reached the top of its path, and begun to fall. It falls more slowly than it has risen because the air drag is now acting partly upwards against gravity. If it has risen to a considerable height its forward velocity in relation to the ground is, by the time it strikes the ground, very nearly that of the wind, and its downward velocity is very nearly that of its terminal velocity of fall. Hence it must hit the ground at an angle β with the horizontal, which is given approximately by—

$$\tan \beta = \frac{\text{terminal velocity of grain}}{\text{velocity of the wind}}$$

If the grain has an equivalent diameter of 0·3 mm., and the wind, for example, blows at 12·5 metres per second or 28 miles an hour, $\tan \beta = 2{\cdot}7/12{\cdot}5$, whence $\beta_{\text{max.}} = 12\frac{1}{4}^\circ$.

When the initial velocity of rise is small and the grain path low (up to a height of a few cm.) the grain may only reach a forward speed of half that of the wind before it hits the ground. But on the other hand neither has it had time to reach its terminal velocity of fall. The angle in impact β therefore remains remarkably constant over a very wide range of conditions. It may be taken as lying between 10° and 16°.

Some typical grain paths are shown in Fig. 5.

5. EXPERIMENTS ON THE BOUNCING PROPERTIES OF QUARTZ GRAINS

Let us suppose that at the point where the grain in the above example strikes the ground there lies a pebble whose surface at the point of impact is inclined at such an angle that the grain rebounds vertically upwards. Its velocity just

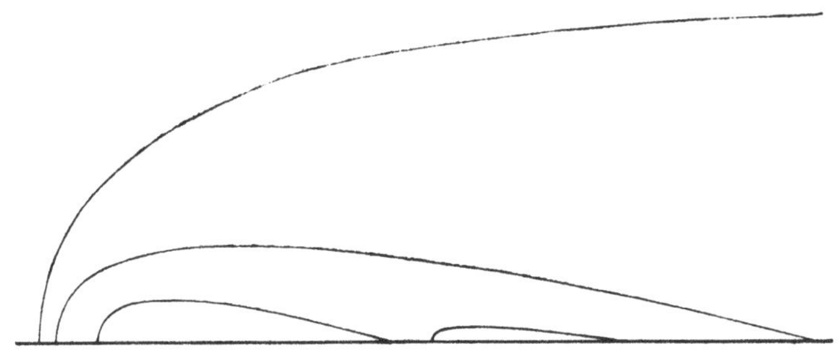

FIG. 5.—TYPICAL GRAIN PATHS

before impact was 12·5 metres per second horizontally and 2·7 vertically downwards, so that the total velocity of impact was $\sqrt{(12{\cdot}5^2 + 2{\cdot}7^2)} = 12{\cdot}8$ metres per second. If the grain were spherical and perfectly elastic it would—the pebble being assumed immovable and also perfectly elastic—rebound with no reduction in velocity. It would rise high into the wind, whose pressure would, as before, give it a forward velocity and make it describe another curved path.

We must now find out experimentally how nearly real sand grains conform to these ideal conditions. If we superimpose a fictitious horizontal velocity, equal and opposite to that of the wind, on all external objects, ground, air, and sand grain, the relations between them remain unaffected. But to the stationary observer everything will appear as if he were moving along with the wind. The ground will be rushing backwards, and the sand grain will drop on to it almost vertically through still air. The moving ground under still air can by this artifice be represented experimentally by the edge of a horizontal rotating disc, and pebbles and other objects gummed to its surface will imitate various types of ground. If sand is dropped vertically on to the edge of the disc as it turns, the grains, as they hit the fast-moving pebbles, are driven off in various trajectories. (In this experiment it should be remembered that the trajectories are not the same as the real paths relative to the ground, but represent the backward travel of the grain through the air, as seen by an imaginary observer moving with the wind.) The height reached by the grain at any instant, being at right angles to the fictitious superimposed velocity, remains the same as the real height reached if the ground were stationary and the air moving over it.

In one series of experiments the grains were captured on

vertical strips of sticky paper hung at different distances from the point of impact. In others they were allowed to fall to the ground and were collected on sheets of oiled glass, which with proper lighting picks out even the smallest particles very clearly. Since the falling grains encountered the moving pebble faces in a haphazard manner, they rebounded into the air at all angles, and from the highest and furthest positions at which grains were captured it was possible to trace the outline in space of the limiting trajectories followed by the grains. A set of these limiting positions is shown in Fig. 6 by dotted circles.

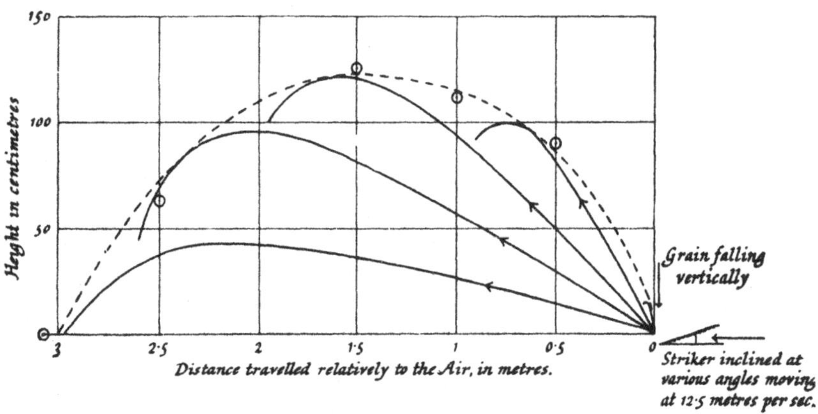

FIG. 6.—COMPARISON OF CALCULATED AND OBSERVED LIMITING PATHS OF GRAINS ON REBOUND AFTER IMPACT WITH GROUND PEBBLES (STILL AIR AND MOVING GROUND)

For the same known initial velocity of impact a set of *calculated* trajectories of equivalent spheres was traced out, on the assumption that resilience was perfect and that the spheres rebounded into the air with velocities equal to those of impact.

The calculated trajectories are also shown in Fig. 6, and the dotted line enclosing them gives the theoretical limit at which grains should be found. The agreement between theory and experiment is not quite as close as it looks, because the calculated curves were for spheres equivalent to the average sand grain, whereas the measurements show the limiting positions of the exceptional grains which travel furthest. Still, these measurements show that at least some grains are, in fact, almost perfectly resilient, and do follow fairly closely the paths calculated from general aerodynamical data.

It may seem at first sight that although this idea of impact and bounce is reasonable enough in the case of such a resilient substance as quartz, it is unlikely to hold good for grains of softer material. This objection would certainly be valid for larger bodies, for the intense local stresses set up at the points of impact would, even in the case of quartz, be greater than the material could stand. Local crumbling or wholesale splitting would take place, and the velocity of rebound would thereby be much reduced. But for the same velocity of approach it can be shown that the impact stresses set up in very small particles such as sand grains are much less intense. Indeed, it is a matter of common observation that little grains of even such a fragile material as dry snow will bounce into the air without breaking when they are driven by the wind against a rock or a wall. The bouncing of hail-stones is still more noticeable.

6. SALTATION

Summarizing, the results of laboratory experiments show that, of a sample of quartz sand whose grain diameter is determined by sifting, a fair idea of the behaviour of the grains can be gained from the calculated motion of a smooth sphere of a certain equivalent diameter. This equivalent diameter for average desert sand is equal to 0·75 times the measure grain diameter. When a flying grain, on reaching the ground, strikes the hard surface of a pebble or rock, it may bounce off it with almost perfect resilience, and may reach a height as great as that of the observed top of the sand cloud during sand-driving. When the grain, having risen into the air on rebound, is acted on by the wind, it moves in a curved path whose flatness is quite sufficient to give the impression to the eye of an unsupported horizontal flight. It strikes the ground at a flat angle of between 10° and 16°, depending on the size of the grain, its height of rise, and the speed of the wind.

It seems physically possible, therefore, that the phenomenon of sand-driving can be explained by this bounding motion of the grains. In his classic paper on the movement of sand under water, Gilbert [1] described the same type of motion, and called

[1] Gilbert, G. K. (1914). U.S. Geological Survey, Prof. Paper 86.

it *saltation*. Once the grains have begun to rise from the surface, their motion in air and water appears to be essentially the same and differs only in degree. In water the height of rise is but a few grain diameters, whereas in air it is several hundred or thousand grain diameters, and the range down-stream is correspondingly greater.

I shall use the name 'saltation' for the motion of sand in air, but without prejudice to the question of whether or not the mechanism which causes the grain to jump from the surface is the same in the two fluids. In air it is certainly the impact of a grain with the surface; but this is rarely so in water.

Appendix I

CALCULATION OF THE SUSCEPTIBILITY

THE resisting force p offered by an object to a stream of fluid flowing past it with relative velocity v is given by

$$p = c \times \tfrac{1}{2}\rho a v^2$$

where ρ is the density of the air (I have taken this as $1{\cdot}22 \times 10^{-3}$ for air of medium humidity at 15° C.), a is the cross-sectional area of the front of the object exposed to the flow, and c is the resistance coefficient.

Unfortunately c is not constant except under special conditions, nor, except for very small particles (smaller than those with which we have to deal), is it given by any mathematical expression. Practical values of it have had to be found by experiment.

The special conditions under which objects of similar shapes have the same resistance coefficient is expressed by

$$\frac{\text{Linear dimensions of object} \times \text{Relative velocity}}{\text{Kinematic viscosity of fluid}} = \text{Constant}$$

The value of this expression is known as the Reynolds Number. As long as the Reynolds Number is constant, c remains the same, even though the factors within the Reynolds Number vary between themselves. It is therefore usual to give the experimental values for c in terms of the Reynolds Number. The kinematic viscosity varies with the fluid, its temperature and pressure. I have taken it as 0·146 cm.^{2}/sec. for air at 15° C. and 760 mm. pressure. At 40° C. and the same pressure it is 0·167. In the case of a sphere, the linear dimension is taken as the radius. The Reynolds Number of an ideal sphere is therefore taken as $vr/0{\cdot}146$, and to find the theoretical air resistance it is merely necessary to look up the experimental value of c corresponding to this particular Reynolds Number.

The range of magnitudes with which we are concerned are as follows:

Sand grains of radii $r = 0{\cdot}001$ to $0{\cdot}1$ cm.
Relative velocity of grain and wind $v = 10$ to 2×10^3 cm./sec.
Reynolds Numbers between 10^{-2} and 10^3.

Between these limits of Reynolds Number the resistance coefficient increases rapidly, for a given grain size, as the Reynolds Number *Re* decreases. For values of Re below 10^{-2} the resistance follows Stokes Law, c is calculable and is equal to $12/Re$. For values of Re between 10^3 and 10^5 c remains nearly constant. Sand phenomena therefore occupy a particularly complicated region of the velocity-resistance relation, an incalculable region between Stokes Law on the one hand, and a constant value on the other. A further complication must also be noted. It has been found that a smooth body has, by virtue of its smoothness, a different value of c for a given Reynolds Number, from that of a sharp-cornered body of the same dimensions. There are thus two sets of experimental curves connecting the Reynolds Number with the resistance coefficient c, and it is probable that very small sand grains should be classed as sharp rather than smooth.

The Susceptibility S is obtained by

$$S = \frac{p}{mg}$$

$$\text{and } p = c \times \tfrac{1}{2}\rho a v^2$$

which, for a sphere of diameter d, is $\frac{\pi}{8}c\rho d^2 v^2$. m for a quartz sphere of density σ is $\frac{\pi}{6}\sigma d^3$. Hence

$$S = \frac{3\rho v^2 c}{4g\sigma d}$$

Putting $\rho = 1{\cdot}22 \times 10^{-3}$ and $\sigma = 2{\cdot}65$

$$S = 3{\cdot}51 \times 10^{-7}\frac{cv^2}{d}$$

The required values of c for smooth spheres were taken from the table given by Prandtl in *The Physics of Solids and Fluids* (Ewald, Poschl, and Prandtl), where the subject of fluid resistance is very clearly summarized.

Appendix II

CALCULATION OF GRAIN MOTION

AS a simple example of the use of the susceptibility diagram in tracing the theoretical motion in air of quartz sand grains, or rather, of their equivalent spheres, we may take the case of an average sand grain of mean diameter 0·4 mm. (equivalent spherical diameter 0·3 mm.) shot vertically upwards into still air with an initial velocity of 14 metres per second, or 31 miles per hour. Here both the force of gravity and that of the air resistance act downwards. The grain will be retarded till it ceases to rise, and will then fall. The retardation due to gravity is equal to g; and since the ratio of the two forces is the susceptibility S, the retardation due to the air drag is gS; so that the total retardation at any instant is $g(1 + S)$; but it is continually changing in value.

It is required to find the maximum height to which it will rise, and the time taken. (If the air were not present, the height h of rise would be given by the simple expression $h = v^2/2g$. Putting $v = 14$ and $g = 9{\cdot}81$, we have $h = 10$ metres. Under the same condition the time of rise would be given by $t = v/g$ and would thus be 1·43 seconds.)

We start by splitting the upward motion up into a series of short periods of time such that the grain's velocity is reduced by an equal amount, say 2 metres/sec. during each period. If the periods are reasonably short we can assume without much error that the retardation is constant through the period, so that the susceptibility S can be taken as approximately that corresponding to the average velocity. Thus, for the first period the velocity drops from 14 to 12 metres/sec.; the average velocity is 13 metres/sec., and the susceptibility (found from the appropriate curve on Fig. 3) is 12. The retardation is therefore $9{\cdot}81\ (1 + 12) = 127{\cdot}5$. From the usual kinematical relation for constant retardation $u^2 - v^2 = 2\alpha\mathrm{L}$ (where u and v are the initial and final velocities respectively, and L is the distance travelled), we have, putting $u = 14$ and $v = 12$, $\mathrm{L} = 0{\cdot}202$ metres. The duration of the period is given by $u - v = \alpha t$, whence $t = 2/127{\cdot}5 = 0{\cdot}0157$ seconds. Similarly, for the next period, $u = 12$, $v = 10$, and S for the new average velocity of 11 metres/sec. is 9; whence $\alpha = 98{\cdot}1$, $\mathrm{L} = 0{\cdot}224$ metres, and $t = 0{\cdot}0204$ seconds. We can complete the calculation in tabular form as follows—

Period	14 to 12	12 to 10	10 to 8	8 to 6	6 to 4	4 to 2	2 to 0
$u^2 - v^2$	52	44	36	28	20	12	4
Average velocity	13	11	9	7	5	3	1
S	12	9	7	4·5	2·7	1·2	0·28
$\alpha = 9{\cdot}81(1 + S)$	127·5	98·1	77·6	53·4	35·8	21·4	12·4
2α	255	196·2	155·2	106·8	71·6	42·8	24·8
L	0·202	0·224	0·232	0·262	0·280	0·280	0·160
t	0·0157	0·0204	0·0258	0·0375	0·0559	0·0935	0·1610

REFERENCES

EWALD, POSCHL, AND PRANDTL. *Physics of Solids and Fluids.* (Blackie)
BAGNOLD, R. A. (1935). *Geogr. J.*, 85, p. 342

Chapter 3

WIND-TUNNEL OBSERVATIONS

1. THE DESIGN OF A SPECIAL WIND TUNNEL FOR SAND EXPERIMENTS

BEFORE proceeding to the results of the experimental work done in sand moving under controlled conditions through a wind tunnel, it may be of interest to describe shortly the final form of the tunnel with which the work was carried out. The design had to fulfil a number of special requirements, and as no previous experimental work on the subject had been published, a satisfactory arrangement was only evolved after several unsuccessful designs had been tried out.

Plate 1 shows the general lay-out. The inside section was 1 foot square. The floor and roof were of $\frac{3}{16}$-inch plywood, and the sides of glass. Air was sucked in through the bell-mouth A by a fan B, 18 inches in diameter, placed at the top of the box C, in which the outgoing sand was allowed to settle. The bottom of this box consisted of a hopper with sloping sides which conducted the used sand down into a collecting box D. The wind speed through the tunnel could be controlled partly by varying the motor speed and partly by opening or closing a by-pass shutter in the top of the box C.

A suction tunnel has several advantages for this class of work over one in which air is blown in from the intake end. The entering air is undisturbed by the rotating fan, so that no honeycomb is necessary to smooth out the fan eddies. There is also the great practical advantage that the negative pressure inside the tunnel keeps all removable doors and lids pressed against their seats. This applies too to sealing devices for preventing air leaks at the joints.

Several attempts were made to economize space by using centrifugal separators at the down-wind end to collect the sand, but the added air resistance was found to absorb so much fan power that the idea was abandoned in favour of a simple settling box of large size. The box used measured $4 \times 3\frac{1}{2} \times 5$ feet high, and with this it was found that except at the highest wind speed used, no appreciable quantity of sand was drawn up through the fan.

The tunnel proper was made in 3-foot sections. Early work was attempted with a short tunnel of but two sections, owing to the space available being limited. But it was soon apparent that stable conditions of equilibrium flow of wind and sand could not be attained unless the tunnel were far longer. More sections were added till, in its final state, it extended to 30 feet. On many occasions even then the need was felt for an extra 20 feet, but owing to the cumulative effects of air leakage into the interior

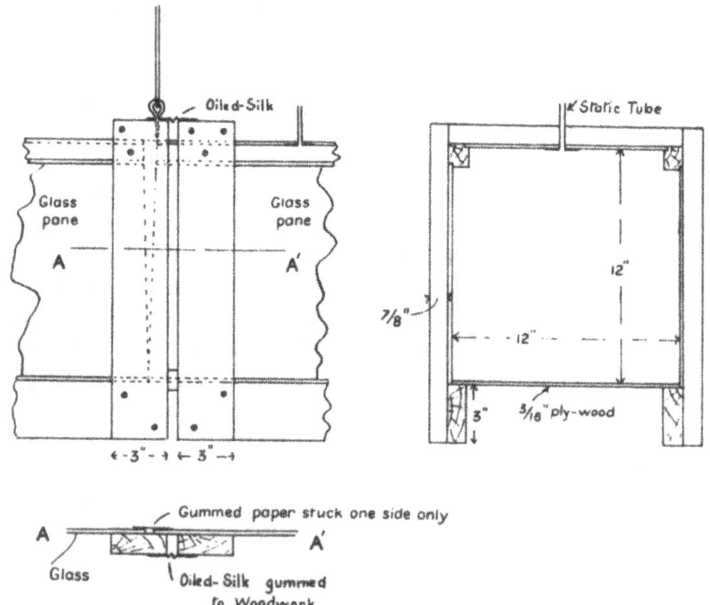

FIG. 7.—DETAILS OF THE JOINTS BETWEEN TUNNEL SECTIONS

due to the big difference of pressure between the inside and outside, this would have necessitated a complete re-design.

As suggested in Chapter 2 (1), the supposed bounding motion of the grains should differ in character according to whether the ground surface consists of hard immovable projections such as pebbles, &c., or of loose sand of similar grain size to that in motion. A precise study of this latter case of a loose sand bed was particularly needed, since it was clearly associated with the fundamental problem of the cause of the accumulation of sand on existing sand surfaces. On this account it was important that the design of the tunnel should allow of accurate measurements being made of the weight of sand in motion through the tunnel under a wind of known strength, and of small changes which might occur in the level of the surface sand at different points along the floor during the sand movement.

For this purpose the whole tunnel was suspended from spring balances attached to the joints between the sections. The joints themselves, though air-tight, were made flexible to allow of changes in the weight of the sand bed in one section taking place without affecting the balance readings of the adjoining sections. Details of the joint construction are shown in Fig. 7. By means of the spring balances the removal or deposition of one ounce of sand over an area of 3 square feet could be detected.

In order to make the sand movement along the tunnel as continuous as possible, a stream of sand could be made to pour in at the up-wind end through a mechanically controlled regulator from a sand reservoir. This reservoir was also hung from a spring balance, so that the rate in inflow could be measured accurately.

2. METHOD OF OPERATION

The general procedure during an experiment was as follows: Sand was first spread evenly over the tunnel floor with a special rake to a depth of 1·5 cm. A note was then made of the readings of all the spring balances. The fan was started with or without the simultaneous starting of an incoming stream of sand from the reservoir. During the run observations were made on (*a*) the wind velocity at a series of heights from the sand surface upwards, (*b*) the fall of static air pressure from section to section along the tunnel, (*c*) the actual paths traced out by the grains in saltation. This was done both visually and photographically. After a period varying according to the strength of the wind from 2 to 45 minutes, the run had to be stopped owing to the appearance of bare patches of wood floor caused by removal of sand from the bed. The spring-balance readings were again taken, and such details noted as the wavelength of the ripples formed on the surface.

Since all the sand which had passed any given section of the tunnel must have come either from the reservoir or from the sand bed somewhere up-wind, the algebraic sum of the changes in the readings of all the balances up-wind of the point considered must give the total weight of sand which had passed the point. This weight, divided by the duration of the run, gave the average rate of sand flow past the point. At the same time the actual changes of weight of the various sections of the tunnel gave immediately the local accumulation or removal of sand on the bed to the nearest ounce. Thus the bulk movement of sand along the tunnel was determined with considerable accuracy.

3. OBSERVATION OF THE GRAIN PATHS. METHOD OF ILLUMINATION

The paths of the individual grains was observed by means of an intense beam of light which was made to shine downwards through a narrow longitudinal slot in the tunnel roof. Both the interior of the tunnel and the background of the further wall were made dark, so that when looking horizontally through the glass front wall, nothing could be seen except an illuminated strip in the centre of the sand bed parallel to the length of the tunnel. The comparatively few flying sand grains which passed through the length of the beam above this narrow strip shone out very vividly. The after-image retained in the eye caused their paths to stand out against the dark background like a skein of silver threads. The number of paths seen at once depended of course on the narrowness of the beam, and if the latter was too broad it was impossible to pick out individual paths from a confused mass of bright lines. The same experiment can be done in the open air in bright sunlight by erecting a black vertical screen parallel to the direction of the sand-driving wind, and above it an opaque roof with a long slot in it through which, at a convenient time of day, the sun can throw a narrow beam.

For photography the beam must be very intense. As the tiny disc of light which constitutes the instantaneous image of a single grain moves across the photographic plate, the effective exposure time is that during which this disc is passing over any fixed point on the plate ; i.e. the time taken by the grain to move a distance equal to its own diameter. If the grain is travelling at 10 metres per second (22 miles per hour), and has a diameter of 0·25 mm., it will pass its own diameter in 0·25/10,000 = 1/40,000 second.

Several unsuccessful attempts were made to obtain photographs of the grain tracks (which were easily visible to the naked eye). Fig. 8 illustrates the simple and inexpensive method which was finally found to give satisfactory results. The upper diagram

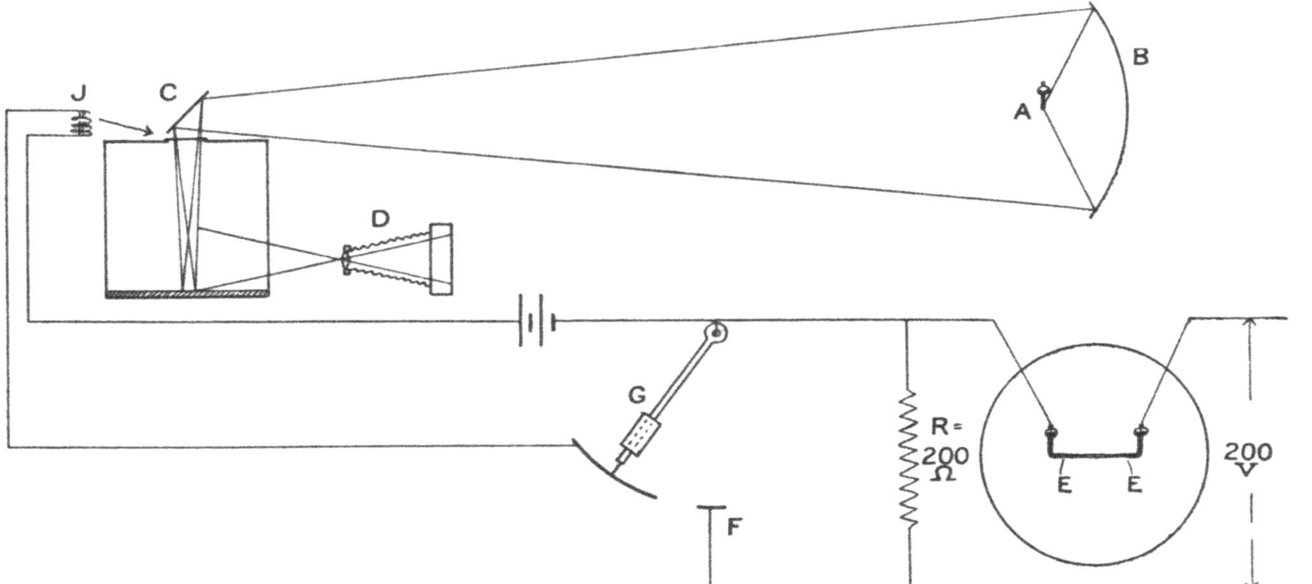

FIG. 8.—METHOD OF ILLUMINATION OF MOVING GRAINS

gives the general arrangement. Light from the source A was focussed as well as possible on the floor of the tunnel by a 24-inch parabolic searchlight mirror B (obtained from surplus war stock) directed downwards through a glass window in the roof by the plane mirror C. The source was an explosive mercury arc contained in a capillary tube of Pyrex glass, shown in the lower diagram. The arc was 3 cm. long and 1 mm. in diameter, and gave a very convenient illuminated wedge within the tunnel, about 1 cm. thick and 18 cm. long. The electric circuit was arranged as shown. The resistance R was adjusted to give a steady current of about 1 amp. through the mercury column in the tube. This was sufficient to maintain a feeble continuous arc for purposes of focussing and adjustment. This arc was kept steady by restrictions in the tube at E.E. By a trigger arrangement not shown, the falling arm G opened the shutter of the camera D (set to any desired exposure from $\frac{1}{100}$ to $\frac{1}{25}$ sec.) just before it made contact with F. A solenoid J placed above the glass window in the roof just within the light beam and energized by an auxiliary low-tension battery was made to hold against the under side of the glass a bright steel ball. The arc was lighted in the first instance by a spirit lamp held under the middle of the arc tube, long enough to boil the mercury and so break the continuity of its liquid column.

At the required moment the arm G was allowed to fall. In falling it first broke the auxiliary solenoid circuit, and let drop the steel ball. It then opened the camera shutter. Finally it made momentary contact with F and short-circuited the resistance R, causing current at 200 volts to surge through the mercury vapour. The duration of the short-circuit was controlled by the height from which the arm G fell. The resulting intense flash of light lit up both the flying sand grains and the falling ball so that they appeared together as streaks on the photographic plate. The duration of the flash could thus be calculated from the travel of the ball while it was illuminated (its velocity being known from the distance it had fallen). From the then known duration of the flash the lengths of the grain streaks gave at once the velocity of the grains. Owing to the violence of the discharge through the tube it was not possible to keep it on for more than about $\frac{1}{50}$ sec. without destroying the tube. Since these experiments were done, a conveniently small high-pressure arc lamp has been placed on the market. Its continuous light may be sufficiently powerful to take the place of the above arrangement.

For the observation of ripples and other surface effects, a 1,000-watt lamp was made to shine down the tunnel from some distance beyond the mouth, so that the beam was nearly parallel with the sand surface. Surface undulations far too slight to be otherwise noticed were thus sharply defined by light and shadow.

4. SALTATION OVER A LOOSE SAND SURFACE, INITIATED BY GRANULAR IMPACT

To make the conditions as simple as possible, experiments were initially carried out with sand of nearly uniform grain size. All grains other than those between 0·3 and 0·18 mm. were removed by sifting. This particular grade was chosen because it forms a large proportion of the more mobile parts of desert sand dunes.

The sand was spread loosely but evenly over the tunnel floor to a depth of 1·5 cm., and a very gentle wind was turned on, whose speed was well below the threshold at which it was able to disturb the surface grains. An electric switch then started a small but steady stream of sand falling from the roof of the tunnel near its mouth. The grains fell diagonally through the wind like rain drops. On striking the ground they made little craters in the surface, and either ejected other grains or themselves rose a centimetre or so into the air. The wind carried these secondary grains forward a few centimetres before they in turn struck the ground. In doing so they might cause a few more grains to jump feebly, but the disturbance died away to nothing a short distance down-wind of the point where the primary stream hit the ground. It ceased altogether the moment the incoming stream was cut off.

At a rather greater wind speed, but still less than that required to start grain movement without the disturbance of the incoming sand stream, a sudden change took place. On switching on the sand supply, the jumping movement along the tunnel, instead of rapidly dying away down-wind from the mouth, continued on indefinitely; and further down the tunnel it appeared as a steady cloud. The movement ceased, as before, directly the stimulation at the tunnel mouth was stopped.

Two important ideas are suggested by this experiment—

(*a*) It is evident that below the critical wind speed the energy of the grains as they move feebly along the surface comes partly from their initial fall from the roof, and partly from the pressure of the wind upon them. But after the initial energy of the fall has been expended in disturbing the surface at each subsequent impact, the energy received from the wind is not sufficient to make up for the impact losses. Hence the movement dwindles to nothing. At the critical wind speed, however, the energy received from the wind by the average saltating grains becomes equal to that lost, so that the motion is sustained.

(*b*) The occurrence of a steady sand movement at wind speeds so small that the wind alone is incapable of disturbing the surface grains indicates that these, once the saltation is started, are jerked up into the air not by the direct action of the wind but by the impact of descending grains.

The critical threshold wind at which an initial disturbance of the sand becomes a continuous movement along the down-wind surface, plays an important part in the mechanism of sand movement in general. In papers already published I have called it the 'dynamic threshold', but I now think a more suitable name for it is the *impact threshold*. Its significance will be discussed in Chapters 5 and 7.

The speed at which the initial disturbance travels along the surface could be easily measured. The vertical illuminated beam was placed some distance—25 feet—down the tunnel, and by watching, control switch in hand, it was possible to time the first appearance of the saltation after the disturbance at the tunnel mouth had been started. It travels slowly; from a half to a third of the speed of the wind, depending on the height at which the latter is measured. The first signs of it could be seen in two ways; either by the appearance of the silver thread-like grain streaks in the light beam; or, if the surface was first pressed smooth with a sheet of glass, by the eruption in it of tiny impact craters.

5. SALTATION INITIATED BY DIRECT WIND PRESSURE

When the wind speed was increased above the impact threshold —the stimulating sand inflow being cut off—another critical wind speed was reached when the surface grains, previously at rest, began to be rolled along the surface by the direct pressure of the wind. The particular wind speed at which this happened was not so definite as in the case of the impact threshold, for the rolling started at different points in the tunnel according to the strength of the wind. For instance, even at the highest wind speeds no movement took place at the extreme up-wind end of the sand floor. It began at the down-wind end, and, as the wind was increased, the point of initial movement shifted further and further up the tunnel. This is to be accounted for by the fact that fully developed turbulence does not set in till the wind has travelled some distance from the tunnel mouth (see Chapter 4, Sections 3 to 5). The grains first start to roll when acted upon by the faster-moving air of the turbulent eddies.

I have previously called this the 'static' threshold wind speed, to distinguish it from the 'dynamic', but I shall take this opportunity to re-name it the *Fluid Threshold* (that at which sand movement starts owing to the direct pressure of the fluid only). A foot or so down-wind of the point at which the rolling began, the grains could be seen to have gathered sufficient speed to start bouncing off the ground; and over the remainder of the floor the 'sand cloud' effect of true saltation was maintained.

6. SALTATION AT HIGHER WIND SPEEDS

Both photographs and direct visual observation at greater wind speeds indicate that the grain movement is always of the same type, a saltation, or movement by bounds. The height of rise depends on the initial upward velocity with which the grain leaves the surface. The higher the grain rises, the longer it is exposed to the force of the wind, and the greater is the velocity with which it hits the ground; hence, in turn, the more violently is another grain ejected into the air.

Plate 2 shows three actual photographs of grain paths. The limited lengths of the paths correspond to the limited period of illumination. The fainter downward tracks are those of fast-moving grains near the end of their flight. More than one instance can be seen in (*a*) of an actual impact. The descending grain disappears into a little crater below the surface outline, and from the crater a slow-speed grain rises almost vertically. In another case a descending grain has clearly ricochetted off the surface and continued forward at a flat angle and without losing much speed. One instance can be seen in (*b*) of a rapidly spinning grain which appears as a dotted line, as the reflecting positions of the facets recur. Rotation does not seem to be the rule.

7. THE SURFACE CREEP

As can be seen from Plate 2, the grains in saltation strike the surface at a comparatively flat angle. A portion of the energy they have acquired from the wind is passed on to the grains that are ejected upwards to continue the saltation. The bulk of the energy is, however, dissipated in disturbing a large number of surface grains. This energy is ultimately all lost in friction between the surface grains, but the net result of the continued bombardment of the surface is that a slow forward creep takes place on the part of the grains composing it.

Individual grains are knocked onward by the blow they receive from behind. At low speeds they can be seen to move in jerks, a few millimetres at a time; but as the wind is raised, the distance moved lengthens and more grains are set in motion, till in high winds the whole surface appears to be creeping slowly forward.

Although there can be no exact distinction between the motion of the surface grains and of those grains in saltation whose paths through the air are very low, yet there exists a clear difference between the causes of these two kinds of sand motion. The grains in saltation receive their momentum directly from the pressure of the wind on them after they have risen into it. The grains

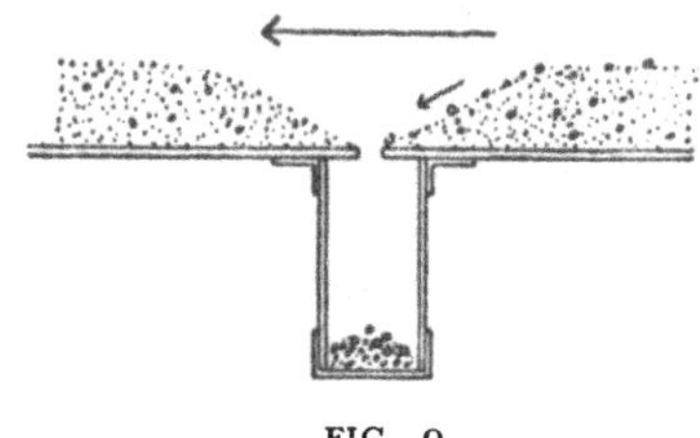

FIG. 9.

in *surface creep*, on the other hand, remain unaffected by the wind. They receive their momentum by impact from the saltation.

The amount of the surface creep, that is, the weight of surface sand which moves past a fixed mark in a given time, can be measured very simply by means of a ‘sand trap’. A narrow transverse slot, 1 to 3 mm. wide, was cut in the tunnel floor, and a closed container attached underneath. The grains in saltation passed over the little gap in the ground, but the surface grains, as they were knocked forward, tumbled over the crest of the sand slope and fell into the trap.

Of the total weight of sand which flows past a fixed mark per second, the surface creep accounts for between a quarter and a fifth. Though the saltation thus greatly preponderates, the surface creep plays a very important part in sand movement in air.

(*a*) It is the means of transport whereby those grains can be moved about whose weight is far too great to be shifted by the unaided pressure of the wind. A high-speed grain in saltation can by impact move a surface grain six times its diameter, or more than 200 times its own weight.

(*b*) In a normal sand of mixed size the grains in surface creep are on the average larger than those in saltation. Thus, owing to the different speeds of travel—a fraction of an inch a second in the case of the surface creep, as opposed to many feet per second in the case of the saltation—the surface creep is responsible for changes in the size-grading of sand deposits.

(*c*) The rippling of wind-blown sand is due to an unevenness of flow on the part of the surface creep, which causes alternate piling-up of the grains and denudation, like traffic blocks and intervening spaces on a road.

These effects will be referred to again in detail in subsequent chapters.

8. SURFACE RIPPLES

After the sand movement has gone on for a short time, the surface becomes uniformly rippled, the crests and troughs running nearly at right angles to the wind direction ; but since the ripples advance down-wind at a slightly greater rate in the centre of the tunnel floor, where the wind is strongest, than at the sides, the crests are generally curved backwards on each side. With sand of nearly uniform grain size the ripples are very flat and can only be detected by the shadows thrown in the troughs by a horizontal beam of light. In section they are nearly symmetrical.

As the sizes of the grains depart from uniformity the symmetry is reduced, the lee slopes becoming steeper. The height of the crest above the trough greatly increases and the ripples are much more noticeable.

The ripple length, or the distance from crest to crest, increases with the strength of the wind. For sand of nearly uniform grain size, between 0·3 and 0·18 mm. the ripple length was found to be 2·4 cm. at the lowest wind speed at which movement was possible (the impact threshold), and to attain a maximum of 12 cm. When the wind exceeded a certain speed the ripples flattened out and disappeared, leaving a smooth flat surface. The formation of surface ripples will be dealt with in greater detail in Chapter 11.

9. SALTATION OVER HARD GROUND

In the preceding sections we have noticed what happens when sand is driven over a bed consisting of grains of the same size as those in the sand cloud passing overhead. If the surface grains are larger, the impacts of the grains descending from the saltation assume in an increasing degree the character of bouncing

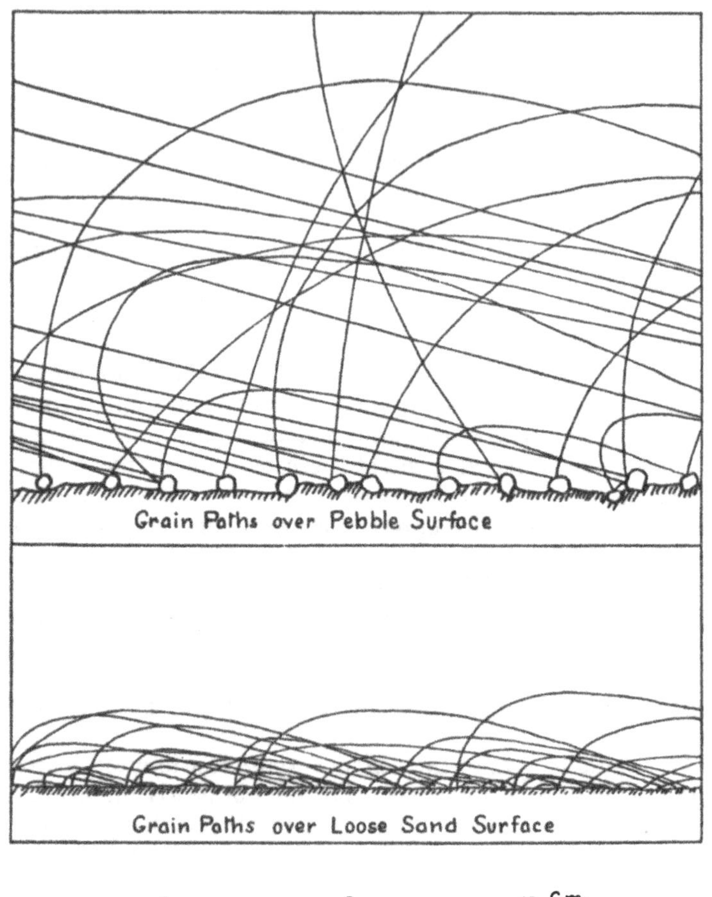

FIG. 10.—DIFFERENCE BETWEEN THE SALTATION OVER SAND AND OVER PEBBLES

rather than splashing. Less energy is dissipated in disturbing the surface and more is retained by the grains, which now tend to rebound after impact. As a result, (*a*) the sand cloud formed by the saltation rises to a much greater height, so that the average range of the grains down-wind, from impact to impact, is far longer; and (*b*) the surface creep ceases altogether when the grains on the ground are too big to be moved at all.

The difference in the behaviour of the saltation could be seen very clearly in the tunnel. For when the surface was of uniform fine sand the top of the cloud was but a few inches high, but when small pebbles were scattered over the surface the whole tunnel height became evenly filled with flying grains from floor to roof. The descending grains bounced violently off the pebbles, so that they rose to the roof and even rebounded off it. In fact, when a small hole was cut in the roof, grains could be seen to fly out of it (against the inrush of air caused by the suction in the tunnel) and rose a metre or more above the floor level whence they started.

The difference is shown diagrammatically in Fig. 10.

10. THREE POSSIBLE TYPES OF GRAIN MOTION: SUSPENSION, SALTATION, AND SURFACE CREEP

As we have already seen, sand grains are in general too large to be carried in true suspension. But the motion of the smallest sand grains may in a high wind approach to suspension, in that the upward wind eddies may check the descent of a grain and so cause it to remain in the air longer and to travel further before it again strikes the ground. A grain in true suspension, since it never comes in contact with the ground, must travel at the average forward speed of the wind and so cannot offer any appreciable obstruction to it.

Similarly the grains in surface creep, since they remain always on the ground and receive their forward momentum from the impact of other grains, also offer no extra resistance to the wind by virtue of their motion.

It is only the third type of grain motion, the saltation, which by alternate contact with the air and the ground removes momentum from the air and so opposes a special kind of resistance to the wind. But, as the great bulk of wind-driven sand moves by saltation, and as the motive power is supplied by the wind, a detailed examination of the behaviour of the wind near the ground can no longer be postponed.

REFERENCE

BAGNOLD, R. A. (1936). *Proc. Roy. Soc. A.*, 176, p. 594

Chapter 4

THE SURFACE WIND

1. THE MEASUREMENT OF WIND VELOCITY [1]

INSTRUMENTS for measuring the velocity of the wind can be divided into three kinds : (*a*) those in which the wind, by blowing on vanes or hemispherical cups, causes a frictionless shaft to rotate ; (*b*) non-moving instruments in which the measure of the velocity is obtained from the degree of cooling felt by an electrically heated wire placed in the air stream ; (*c*) non-moving instruments which measure directly the pressure which the wind exerts on an obstacle placed in its path. The moving-vane type of instrument is useful for recording the average wind velocity over long periods ; like the log-line at sea it measures the distance travelled by the fluid past the vanes between the times at which readings are taken. The non-moving instruments, when their readings have been converted into velocities, give the instantaneous values at the moment of reading, and are therefore more suitable for accurate experimental purposes. Owing to the necessary fineness of the wire the hot-wire type is very delicate, and is not likely to be of use for work in which the air contains large flying particles such as sand grains.

The simplest pressure instrument consists of a metal plate held at right angles to the wind by a spring (Fig. 11*a*). The greater the wind pressure on the plate the more it is deflected against the opposition of the spring. The amount of the deflection is read off a scale and converted into velocity by an appropriate calibration table.

In the *pitot tube* the metal plate is replaced by a column of stationary air contained in a tube whose open mouth faces the oncoming wind (Fig. 11*b*). The wind, in blowing against the mouth of the tube, increases the pressure of the stationary air within it. This increase of pressure is communicated through a pipe to a delicate gauge which may be situated at any convenient

[1] See Ower, E. (1933). *The Measurement of Air Flow.* (Chapman & Hall, London.)

distance away. The pitot tube has two outstanding advantages over all other types of wind instrument. Since the pressure in the tube is a fluid pressure (distributed evenly over all parts of the fluid boundary), the area of the orifice exposed to the wind is immaterial, and the tube can be made as small as we like. It is thus possible to measure very accurately the changes in velocity at different points close together and very close to the ground. By using a fine hypodermic syringe tube for instance, the wind velocity can be measured within less than a millimetre of the boundary surface over which it is flowing. The pitot tube is also very accurate; and the pressure, when read on a suitable gauge, can be converted into velocity by a simple alge-

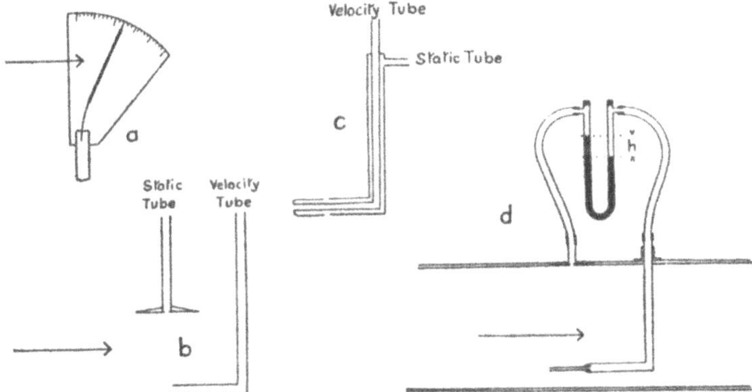

FIG. 11.—TYPES OF PRESSURE INSTRUMENT FOR MEASURING WIND VELOCITY

braic process, so that no calibration is necessary. Its only disadvantage is that for low wind speeds—less than say 10 feet per second—the pressures are very small and require a delicate micro-gauge for their measurement.

The pressure from which the wind velocity is calculated is not an absolute one. It is the excess of pressure in the fixed tube facing the wind over the static pressure within a tube whose mouth may be imagined to be moving along with the wind past the fixed one.

The measurement of this static pressure inside the wind needs some care. For instance, if we try to measure it with a barometer which is shielded from the wind within a closed box, the box must have some aperture whereby the outside pressure can be communicated to the space inside; and the air pressure registered by the barometer will vary according to whether the aperture is facing the wind, parallel to it, or in the lee of it. A barometer inside a house is susceptible to a strong wind, and reads differently according to the side of the house on which the windows are open.

In practice it is found that the static pressure is given correctly if the orifice to which the gauge or barometer is connected is a clean round hole in a smooth flat plate whose length is not less than twenty times the diameter of the hole, and whose plane is set parallel to the direction of the undisturbed wind (Fig. 11*b*). In a more convenient form the pitot itself consists of two concentric tubes; the inner tube is open-ended and faces the wind, while the outer one has small holes bored in its wall at some distance from the end. The annular space between the tubes is closed at the front end facing the wind, and has a nozzle at the back to which a pipe can be connected. This type is shown in Fig. 11*c*. It is useful for measurements in the open. Inside a wind tunnel, specially when it is required to measure the velocity very close to the ground or wall, it is best to use the separate velocity tube of Fig. 11*b*, and a static orifice flush with the wall. The mouth of the velocity tube can consist of a fine steel hypodermic tube 2 cm. long and 1 mm. bore. The arrangement is shown in Fig. 11*d*.

The simplest form of gauge or manometer is that shown in Fig. 11*d*. It consists of a U-tube containing a liquid. Alcohol is better than water since it more thoroughly wets the surface of the glass, and rises and falls more evenly in consequence. If one arm of the U is connected to the velocity tube and the other to the static tube, the difference in height between the two columns of the liquid, when multiplied by its density, gives at once the difference of pressure required.

The pressure difference to be measured may be very small. For a wind of 10 feet per second it is only 0·056 grams per sq. cm., which corresponds to a difference of level of 0·56 mm. of water, or 0·71 mm. of alcohol (the density of alcohol being 0·79). A manometer for measuring such pressures can be made very simply in the form shown in Fig. 12. Here the movement of the liquid is magnified by inclining one arm of the U at a flat angle. By making the other arm very wide—the surface of a small tank, in fact—the change of level of its surface can be neglected, so that the pressure differences can be read directly off a scale laid along the inclined arm. There are many possible modifications of the inclined-tube manometer, and other suitable types of gauge exist as well. For details the reader is referred to Ower's book cited in Section 1. A portable multiple instrument suitable for rapid measurements in the open is described in Chapter 6.

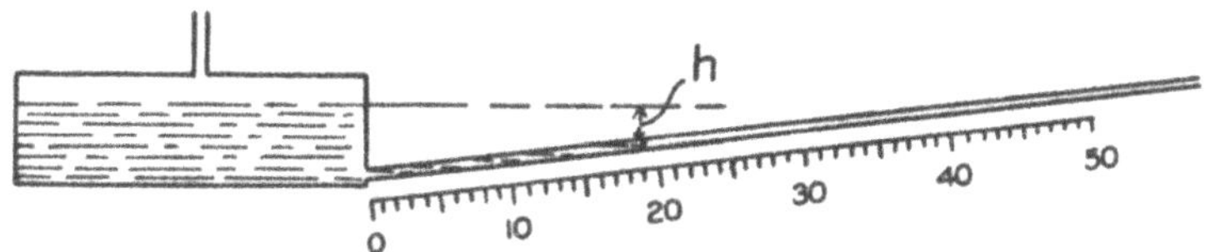

FIG. 12.—INCLINED-TUBE MANOMETER

Having found the pressure difference between the velocity and the static tubes of the pitot, the velocity of the air can be calculated immediately from a simple form of Bernoulli's Equation. Let the pressure in the velocity tube be p_1, that in the static tube p_2 and the density of the fluid ρ. Then the velocity v is given by

$$p_1 - p_2 = \tfrac{1}{2}\rho v^2$$

Hence, if we call p the pressure difference $p_1 - p_2$ we have

$$v = \sqrt{\frac{2p}{\rho}} \quad . \quad . \quad . \quad . \quad (1)$$

For air at normal temperature and pressure ρ can be taken as $1{\cdot}22 \times 10^{-3}$ grams/cm.^{3}. If v is measured in cm./sec., the pressure p is in dynes/cm.^{2}. If p is measured in grams per sq. cm., the acceleration $g = 981$ cm./sec.^{2} must be introduced in the numerator of the expression under the square root, so that in these units $v = 1265\sqrt{p}$. If h is the height of the liquid in cm. as read off the gauge, then σh can be substituted for p, where σ is the specific gravity of the liquid. For alcohol $\sigma = 0{\cdot}79$, so that

$$v = 1125\sqrt{h} \quad . \quad . \quad . \quad (1a)$$

Measurements in a wind tunnel of air velocities of the low values corresponding to those of a normal wind are rendered difficult by the unavoidable fluctuations of velocity caused by the varying slow movements of the air of the room at the tunnel mouth. For accurate work it is necessary to take several—perhaps eight—pressure readings, convert them into velocities as above, and take the mean of them.

2. THE SURFACE DRAG

Consider for a moment a column of air which is being sucked through a tunnel such as that described in the last chapter. The longer the tunnel or the smaller its cross-section, the greater must be the suction necessary to drive the air through it at a given speed. The tunnel walls offer a resistance to the passage of the air, and this resistance must be overcome by an excess of pressure at the up-wind end over the pressure at the down-wind end. That is, the static pressure falls progressively towards the down-wind end. Suppose there are two small static orifices in the tunnel wall at A and B (Fig. 13), and that these are connected in turn to one arm of a manometer, the other arm being

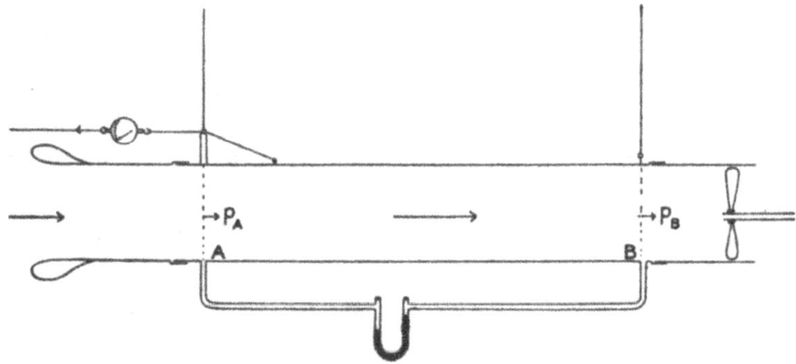

FIG. 13.—PRESSURE DROP ALONG A TUNNEL

left open to the atmosphere outside. We can then measure the static pressures at A and B relative to that of the atmosphere. Both will of course be lower. Over any cross-section the static pressure must be the same at all points from the wall to the centre (otherwise there would be a sideways flow of air across the tunnel). Therefore if the pressure per sq. cm. at A is multiplied by the area of the cross-section, we get the total force with which the whole column of air down-wind of A is being pushed along. Similarly the smaller pressure at B multiplied by the same area gives the backward force opposing the motion of the air up-wind of B. The difference between the two (which can be got simply by connecting the two arms of the manometer simultaneously to A and B) therefore gives the actual force which the resistance of the tunnel walls exerts on that part of the air column between A and B, and which opposes the flow.

If we isolate this part of the tunnel by sliding joints, so that it is free to move a little lengthwise, and attach a spring balance horizontally as shown in the figure, this actual mechanical force with which the tunnel is being pulled can be measured directly. The pull is quite appreciable. When the wind through the experimental tunnel, 30 cm. square in cross-section, blew at 11 metres or 36 feet per second, the pressure drop between two points 6·5 metres (21 feet) apart was 0·35 gm. per sq. cm. Thus the total lengthwise pull on the tunnel walls between the two points was $0{\cdot}35 \times 30^2 = 0{\cdot}3$ Kg.

The pull is transmitted from the fan blades to the tunnel by the frictional drag between the air and the walls. Each sq. cm. of the walls, roof and floor contributes its little quota. Assuming all the four faces of the tunnel interior have the same roughness, we can calculate the drag per sq. cm. of tunnel surface by multiplying the pressure drop by the tunnel cross-sectional area, and dividing by the total surface area of the interior. In the above example the drag per sq. cm. of surface was evidently

$$\frac{300}{4 \times 30 \times 650} \text{ gm.} = 3{\cdot}8 \text{ mgm.}$$

3. STREAMLINE AND TURBULENT FLOW

We must now enquire how this edgewise pull or shear is transmitted sideways through the tenuous body of the air from the centre to the walls. The wind velocity at the actual wall is zero, and it increases to a maximum at the centre. For slow wind speeds we can imagine the air to be divided up into a number of layers, each one moving a little faster than the one beneath it, so that it slips over it. If the molecules composing the air were all moving in straight-line paths parallel to the general forward motion, the layers would be entirely independent of one another, there would be no friction between them, and no drag could be transmitted to the walls.

But the molecules in all fluids are in constant rapid motion in all directions: hence molecules in a fast-moving layer are continually straying into the slower one next door, and vice versa. On the average, when a molecule in a fast layer strays into a slower one, it carries with it a momentum greater than that of the average molecule in the slower layer. The fast layer therefore loses momentum and the slow one gains it. This interchange, going on continuously, constitutes a steady force between one layer and the next; the fast layer is urging the slow one forward, and the slow one is dragging back the fast.

When the wind is feeble the general motion of the molecules is, apart from the above interchange, a steady drift in a direction parallel to the surface. Near the surface the velocity at any point is proportional to the distance of the point from it; and over the tunnel cross-section both the pressure drop and the drag on the walls are proportional to the average velocity of flow. Under these conditions the flow is said to be *streamline*, or *laminar*.

But when the wind exceeds a certain critical strength, depending on the size of the tunnel, the flow becomes quite different. It changes from streamline flow to *turbulent flow*. In place of the straying of single molecules from one layer to the next, we have a straying by whole groups of molecules. These, in the form of *eddies* of air rotating about axes in all directions, wander about inside the body of the wind. The molecules no longer progress steadily forward, but are carried hither and thither by the turbulence of the air. We cannot any more think of the air itself as being composed of thin layers sliding over one another. All we can picture is the space being divided up into layers, in each of which the *average* forward velocity of the air has some definite value which varies from layer to layer according to a definite law.

Since the shearing force or drag is now transmitted through the air to the walls of the tunnel by a transference of momentum by eddies rather than by individual molecules, the drag may be expected to be connected with the general velocity of flow by a different law. The drag, instead of varying directly with the velocity of flow now varies as the square of the velocity. Similarly the distribution of the velocity with the height above the surface is also different. The velocity at any point now varies not as the height, but as the logarithm of the height. Fig. 14*a* and *b* show the velocity distribution in the cases of streamline and turbulent flow respectively according to the height above the surface.

The word 'turbulent' is used in fluid dynamics to define the above particular kind of flow and to distinguish it from streamline flow. Whether the flow of a fluid in a tunnel or pipe is streamline or turbulent is not always apparent to the eye, for the scale or 'grain' of the eddies may be very small. The motion may seemingly be quite steady, and yet be turbulent in the above strict sense, in that it obeys the laws of turbulent motion and not those of streamline motion. In general the eddy diameter is small near the boundary surface, and becomes bigger as the boundary recedes ; but since the movement is haphazard a big eddy may stray temporarily close to the boundary. In the open big eddies make themselves felt as gusts.

A good idea of turbulent motion can be got by watching the water surface within a foot or so of the side of a moving ship. The eddies can be seen to get bigger and to rotate more slowly as the distance from the ship's side increases.

Before leaving the subject of turbulence, an important distinction must be noted between the normal wandering eddies,

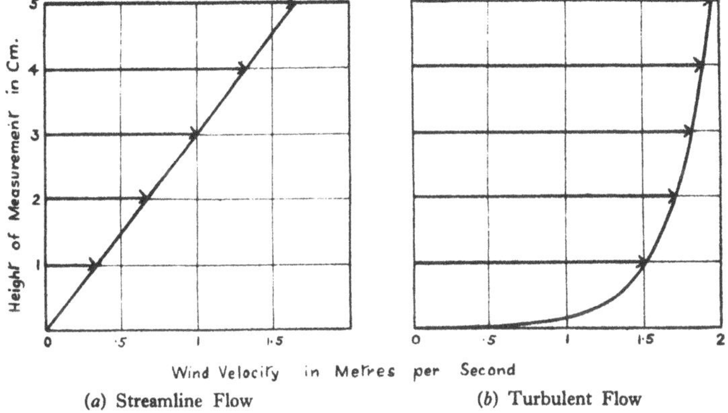

(*a*) Streamline Flow (*b*) Turbulent Flow

FIG. 14.—COMPARISON BETWEEN STREAMLINE AND TURBULENT FLOW NEAR A BOUNDARY SURFACE

often imperceptible, which are inseparable from the idea of turbulent flow, and those violent localized swirls which are found in the lee of an abrupt change of surface angle, such as the crest of a dune, the brink of a cliff, or an isolated rock. In the open the eddies wander about in a haphazard manner, and over a reasonable period of time the average velocity of the wind at all points is the same if measured at the same height above the ground. But near an obstruction the swirls of air caused by it do not wander at random. They originate at a definite place in the lee of the obstruction, and may be held there for some time before breaking off. They have a definite axis of rotation and a definite magnitude, and when they break away, they tend to follow the same path down-wind. Hence in the lee of an obstruction the average velocity of the wind is affected by the average direction and magnitude of the swirls.

4. THE TRANSITION CONDITION. THE REYNOLDS' NUMBER.[1]

In the design of ships and of aeroplanes much experimental work is done with models. The connection between the scale of the model and the relations which the measured pressures and velocities bear to their full-size counterparts was worked out many years ago by Osborne Reynolds. If the size of the model, or in the case of flow in a pipe, the diameter of the pipe, is l, and the velocity of flow is v, and if the state of the fluid is defined by a quantity ν called the ***kinematic viscosity***, then the general movement of the fluid will be similar and the pressures will be unchanged provided the relation lv/ν remains equal to a constant number *Re* known as the ***Reynolds' Number***. Thus if the size of the model or the diameter of the pipe is halved, the fluid will only behave in a similar manner if we correspondingly double the velocity of flow or change the state of the fluid by halving ν.

This condition for similar flow holds good even for a change of fluid—say, from air to water (with the obvious proviso that we are dealing with the flow below the free upper liquid surface, which in the case of a gas does not exist). ν varies somewhat with the temperature and pressure of the fluid, but for air at sea level it may be taken as 0·14 in C.G.S. units. For water it is only one-tenth of this value. Hence if the scale remains the same, the conditions of flow will be unaltered in a change from air to water provided the velocity is reduced to one-tenth of its former value.

The Reynolds' Number defines the behaviour of all fluids, including the transition from streamline to turbulent flow. It has been found that in a square tunnel or pipe, apart from exceptional cases where the boundary surfaces have been made particularly smooth and the intake has been very carefully rounded off, the transition occurs when the Reynolds' Number exceeds about 1,400. Thus turbulence sets in when the product $l \times v$ exceeds $1{,}400 \times 0{\cdot}14 = 200$ (for air). For the tunnel described in the preceding chapter, where $l = 30$ cm. the flow must be turbulent for all wind speeds above about 7 cm./sec. For the open atmosphere Brunt,[2] taking l as the distance between the ground and

[1] A very clear account is given by Ewald, Poschl, and Prandtl in *The Physics of Solids and Fluids*. (Blackie, 1930.)

[2] Brunt, D. *Physical and Dynamical Meteorology*. (Cambridge, 1934.) p. 209.

the tropopause, calculates that if the wind exceeds 1 metre per second the air movement must be turbulent, however steadily it may appear to blow. We need not therefore consider streamline motion any further.

The Reynolds' Number and the conditions for similarity of fluid flow have been touched upon because they must enter into any comparative discussion of sand movement in air and water, and also into the question of the possibility of investigating dune formation by means of models.

5. THE DISTRIBUTION OF WIND VELOCITY WITH HEIGHT

As stated above, the air movement with which we have to deal in this book is always turbulent, both in the wind tunnel and in the open. But in the case of the wind tunnel, measurements of wind velocity distribution should be made at points several tunnel diameters down-wind of the entrance, in order that the state of turbulence may have an opportunity of spreading throughout the air column (the room air as it enters the tunnel is almost still and therefore non-turbulent).

If a series of measurements of wind velocity are made at different heights above the surface, and the results plotted against a linear scale of height, the curve will be of the type already shown in Fig. 14*b*. In Fig. 15*a* two such curves are shown, each referring to a different wind strength. The velocity is not proportional to the height but to the logarithm of the height.

The curve is an awkward one from which to derive useful information. Owing to its flatness close to the ground, small changes there in its shape are almost impossible to detect. Moreover, distinctions between one kind of curvature and another being hard to recognize by eye, special features which are clearly exhibited by a mathematical equation are often not apparent when the equation is represented pictorially by a curve. On the other hand a straight line can always be recognized as such, it has a direction which can be readily measured, and it has a definite position with regard to the axes of reference.

In interpreting the meaning and discussing the significance of such a curve as that shown we are forced to choose between two alternatives. The mathematically minded can consider its equation without bothering about the graphical representation of it; the non-mathematician had best reduce the curve to a straight line by a suitable change in the type of scale used to plot the curve, and resolve to conquer his prejudice against a scale which happens not to be that of a tape-measure. Such a prejudice is quite unjustified, since a graph is in any case a fictitious contrivance. If, for instance, a measured velocity increases uniformly between two heights according to the ratio that one height bears to the other, there is no more fiction in using a ratio scale of height than there is in drawing a complicated curve. After all, neither the logarithmic curve nor the straight line really exist in the air.

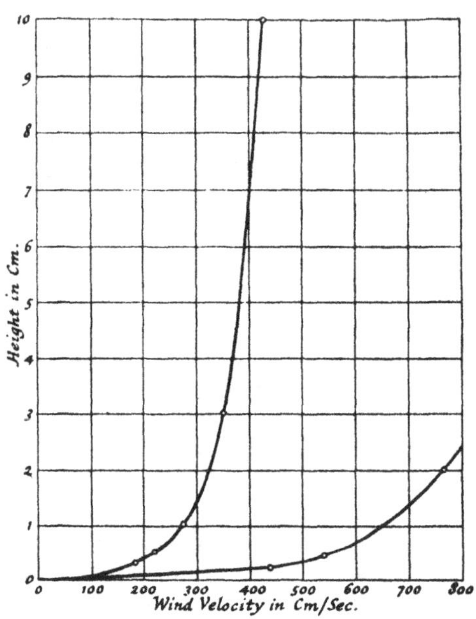

FIG. 15*a*.—VELOCITY DISTRIBUTION ON LINEAR AND LOGARITHMIC HEIGHT SCALES

In Fig. 15*b* the same measured values of velocity and height from which the curves of Fig. 15*a* were drawn have been plotted against a scale of log-height. In considering wind velocities near the ground we must henceforward regard as of primary importance not the actual magnitude of the height but the ratio of one height to another. The log-scale has no zero; smaller and smaller decimals are merely continued as far as we like on the opposite side of unity to the increasing multiples of ten.

The first point to be noticed in the figure is one which would have been impossible to detect if the log-scale had not been used.

By joining the plotted points by a straight line, and continuing this line till it meets the axis of zero velocity at O, we find that zero wind velocity occurs at a certain small but quite definite height above the surface.

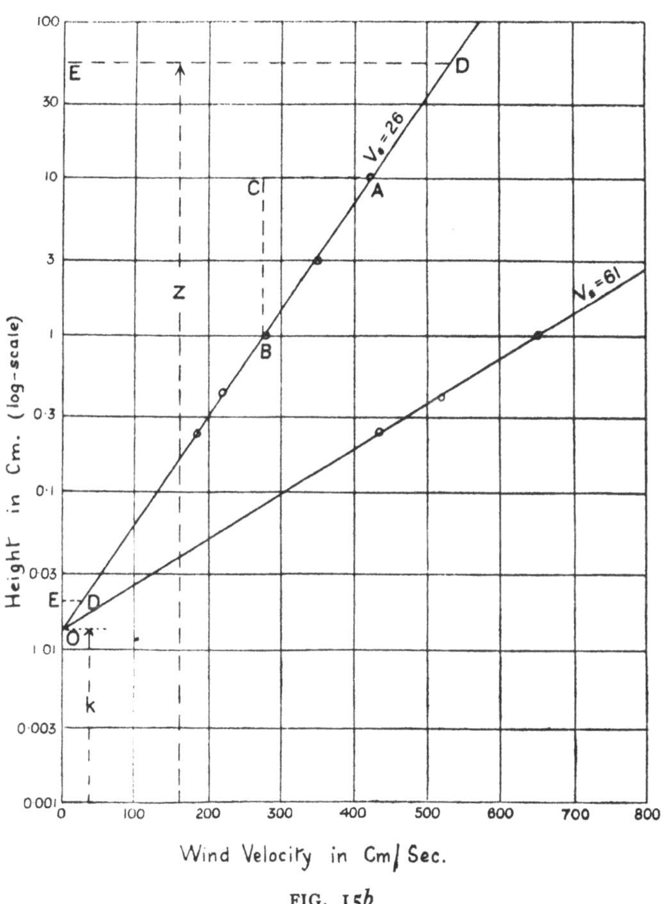

FIG. 15*b*

6. THE SURFACE ROUGHNESS

If now the wind is increased in strength and another series of velocity measurements taken, the plotted points are found to lie on another straight line which converges on the first to a zero of velocity at the same point as before. In fact, over any given uniformly rough[1] surface the velocities of all winds at all heights reasonably[2] near the ground can be represented by a group of straight lines which converge to a focus on the axis: and the height of the focus above the surface depends only on the roughness of the surface.

As a result of a detailed examination of this question, Prandtl found that the height of the focus is associated with the size of the irregularities which constitute the roughness. Suppose the surface consists of sand grains immovably fixed, or of boulders of even size scattered over the ground. It has been found that the height of the focus, which we will call k, at which the wind velocity is zero, is approximately equal to $\frac{1}{30}$ of the diameter of the grains or stones. This means that if, for example, the boulders are 30 cm. in diameter, the air from the ground on which they lie up to a height of 1 cm. is still, and the wind movement only begins at this level.

Knowing nothing at all about the surface, we can, by making measurements of wind velocity at two different heights above it, discover approximately the average size of the grains of which it is composed. In Fig. 15*b* the height k is seen to be 0·015 cm. Therefore the roughness is equivalent to an even layer of small pebbles of diameter $0{\cdot}015 \times 30 = 0{\cdot}45$ cm.

7. THE DRAG VELOCITY V_*. FOR STEADY WINDS BLOWING OVER FLAT SURFACES V_* IS ALSO EQUAL TO THE VELOCITY GRADIENT PERPENDICULAR TO THE SURFACE.

The same two velocity measurements will not only tell us about the character of the surface and its roughness. They will also give data from which can be found both the amount of the drag which the surface exerts on the wind and the wind velocity at any other height.

We saw in Section 1 of this chapter that the *direct* wind force

[1] For smooth surfaces, with which we are not concerned at present, the logarithmic relation between wind velocity and height very close to the surface has to be slightly modified. The distinction between 'rough' and 'smooth' surfaces is explained in Chap. 7 (1).

[2] With very gentle winds the simple logarithmic relation may be disturbed by temperature differences in the atmosphere; and at heights of many metres, far above the level in which sand movement takes place, there may be serious disturbances due to both temperature and barometric effects.

p per sq. cm., acting against an orifice exposed *at right angles* to the wind direction, is given by

$$p = \tfrac{1}{2}\rho v^2 \quad . \quad . \quad . \quad . \quad (2)$$

where v is the wind velocity at the level of the orifice. A similar relation is found to hold for the *shearing force or drag* per sq. cm. of ground surface *parallel* to the wind direction. If τ is the drag per sq. cm., then

$$\tau = \rho V_*^2 \quad . \quad . \quad . \quad . \quad (3)$$

where V_* is in this case a quantity which has the dimensions of a velocity but is at present merely a mathematical symbol for the expression $\sqrt{\frac{\tau}{\rho}}$. V_* is called the *drag velocity.*

Under steady wind conditions over flat surfaces V_* has, however, a very important physical significance. *V_* is directly proportional to the rate of increase of the wind velocity with the log-height.* And since the velocity and the log-height have a straight-line relationship, V_* is proportional to the tangent of the angle which this straight line or velocity ray makes with the height ordinate. The factor of proportionality is found to be 5·75.

In Fig. 15*b* the tangent of the angle of inclination of the velocity ray OD is the ratio of the distances AC to CB between any two points on the ray; and V_* is equal to $\frac{AC}{CB}$ divided by 5·75. For convenience we may choose the points A and B so that the height of A is 10 times that of B. The log-height CB is then equal to $\log_{10} 10 - \log_{10} 1 = \log_{10} \frac{10}{1} = 1$, so that in this case $V_* = \frac{AC}{5{\cdot}75}$.

Hence in order to find the surface drag τ it is only necessary to measure the wind velocity at any two convenient known heights, to plot these velocities on a graph against the log-height as in Fig. 15*b* and to draw a straight line through the resulting points. The velocity difference AC between any two levels of which one is 10 times the height of the other gives us $5{\cdot}75 V_*$: and thence $\tau = \rho V_*^2$.

On the other hand, if V_* and the roughness constant k are known, the wind velocity v at any height z is found as follows: The velocity v may be represented in Fig. 15*b* by any distance DE. By simple proportion $DE = \frac{AC}{CB} \times EO$, and this is equal to $5{\cdot}75\, V_* \times EO$. But EO is the difference $(\log z - \log k)$ between the log-heights at E and O. Hence, writing $\log z - \log k$ as $\log \frac{z}{k}$, we have

$$\left.\begin{aligned} v &= 5{\cdot}75 V_* \log \frac{z}{k} \\ \text{or} \quad v &= 5{\cdot}75 \sqrt{\frac{\tau}{\rho}} \log \frac{z}{k} \end{aligned}\right\} \quad . \quad . \quad . \quad (4)$$

where $V_* = \sqrt{\frac{\tau}{\rho}}$.

This simple but very important equation connects the fluid velocity v at any height z above the surface with the surface roughness constant k and the drag force τ per unit area of surface. It is due to Prandtl, and has been found experimentally to hold good near any straight rough surface, for any fluid, whether air, water, or oil, both in pipes and in the open, provided only that the state of flow is such that turbulence is fully developed.

The meaning of V_* should be clearly grasped, for it will enter largely into subsequent discussions. Defined as the drag velocity $\sqrt{\frac{\tau}{\rho}}$ it is also, when the flow is steady and straight, a measure of the *velocity gradient* of the wind; that is, of the rate of increase of velocity with the log-height. These two properties of V_* are really but two aspects of the same thing; for it is the change of velocity with the height that causes the shearing stress in the air and transmits it to the ground as the surface drag. If the wind velocity did not increase with the height there could be no surface drag (the velocity ray OD in Fig. 15*b* would in this case be vertical). The stronger the wind blows, the greater is the drag on the ground, and therefore the greater must be the inclination of the velocity ray away from the vertical.

V_* may be regarded as a property inherent in the wind at all heights near the ground. A knowledge of V_* and k completely defines the state of the wind (assuming we are sufficiently far away from the local effects of isolated obstructions, and that minor effects due to large temperature differences are neglected). k fixes the point O (Fig. 15*b*) at which the velocity rays cut the axis, and V_* determines the inclination of the ray. So it is possible to read off the velocity v at any required height.

The physical meaning of V_* as a velocity can be found by a consideration of the geometry of Fig. 15*b*. Since $V_* = \frac{AC}{5{\cdot}75} \times \frac{1}{CB}$, it follows that $V_* = AC$ when $CB = 1/5{\cdot}75$. But CB is the logarithm of the ratios of the heights z_A and z_B of the levels A and B. Hence V_* is the increase in the wind velocity between any two levels whose log-height differ by $1/5{\cdot}75$ or $0{\cdot}174$, and whose linear heights are therefore in the ratio $\log^{-1} 0{\cdot}174 = 1{\cdot}5$.

The particular figure of 5·75 for the factor of proportionality between V_* and the tangent of the angle of inclination of the linear velocity ray arises from Prandtl's theory of the 'mixing length'. This is the average distance through which a mass of fluid carrying momentum from one level to another is supposed to travel before its momentum is merged with that of the fluid in the new level. A concise account of the theory in English is given by Brunt.[1]

8. CHANGE OF WIND SPEED CAUSED BY CHANGE OF SURFACE TEXTURE

In order that the surface wind may continue to blow, against the frictional force of the ground drag, it must be steadily urged forward by the drag it in turn experiences from the faster-moving air above it. This upper wind receives its motive power from meteorological forces; and these in general act fairly uniformly over wide areas. If the surface is a plain of even roughness, the wind to a height of several metres at least is in equilibrium between the applied force from above and the retarding drag of the ground. The shear stress in it, and therefore its velocity gradient V_*, are constant from the ground upwards.

Now suppose that the wind in its passage suddenly encounters a change of surface texture. For example, let the average size of the surface irregularities on the up-wind side of the border of change be 3 cm. (pebbles), and that on the down-wind side be 3 mm. (coarse grit). At the border there is a sudden change in the level of zero wind velocity. Up-wind it was at a height $k_1 = 3/30 = 0{\cdot}1$ cm., and after we pass the border it falls to $k_2 = 0{\cdot}3/30 = 0{\cdot}01$ cm. This means that the wind at level O_1 which has been stationary is now allowed to move forward, owing to the reduced size of the obstructions. The new level of zero velocity is at O_2 (Fig. 16).

The air at greater heights also speeds up progressively as the

[1] Brunt, D. *Physical and Dynamical Meteorology*. (Cambridge, 1934.) pp. 232–5.

news of the change of ground conditions spreads upwards via the little eddies of turbulence. But since the meteorological forces higher up which are causing the wind are unaffected by the small local change of conditions at the surface, the shearing stresses which they are maintaining in the air below remain the same. This means that near the ground V_* must ultimately be the same as before. Hence the ultimate wind velocity distribution is represented by a ray parallel to the old one, but displaced to the right so that it passes through O_2 at the new height k_2.

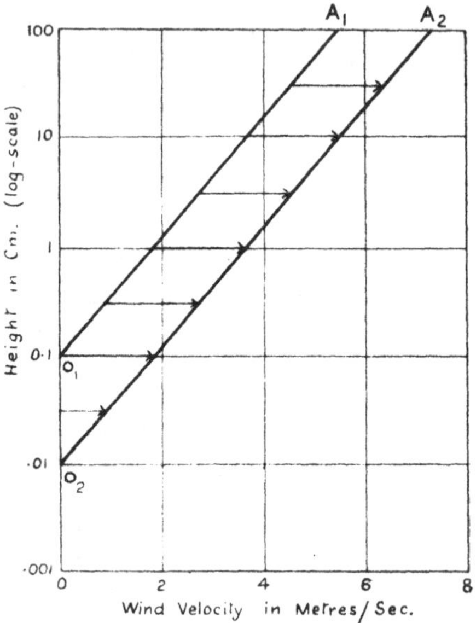

FIG. 16.—CHANGE OF WIND SPEED CONSEQUENT ON A CHANGE OF SURFACE ROUGHNESS

The velocity of the wind at all heights has been increased by the same amount—in this case 1·9 metres per second. Similarly if the roughness of the surface becomes greater instead of less, the whole wind is checked, but the velocity gradient is unaltered.

It appears therefore that in the open the velocity gradient V_* is a more stable and in many ways more important quality of the wind than its actual velocity at some particular height; for the latter changes according to the surface texture, whereas the former in the long run does not. There seems no reason why the above argument should not be applied to very large roughnesses such as trees, provided they are fairly evenly spaced and we deal only with the wind above their tops. It would not apply in the case of single isolated obstructions.

9. THE BOUNDARY LAYER

In the case of a change of ground surface such as that considered above it should be noted that although the velocity change in the wind must be instantaneous at ground level at the border, it takes time to travel upwards; so that at any height above the ground the change will not be fully developed until we reach a point some distance down-wind of the border.

The space next to the surface can therefore be pictured as occupied by a *boundary layer* whose thickness increases as the distance from the border becomes greater. Within the layer the change of velocity initiated at the border has been completed, but above it the air has not yet had news of the change of surface texture. At great distances down-wind the border layer occupies the whole space near the ground.

The thickness of the layer increases with the distance comparatively slowly. The thickness at any given distance is proportional to the change in the size of the surface roughness, and is independent of the velocity. Some recent figures indicate that if the change of roughness is δ, the ratio of the distance down-wind to the height of the boundary layer at that distance is 40 for a distance of $10^4\delta$ and 80 for a distance of $2{\cdot}4 \times 10^6\delta$. In the example given in the previous section δ was about 3 cm., so the boundary layer would have grown to a thickness of 1·2 metres in a distance of the order of 300 metres.

Immediately to leeward of a border across which the roughness increases in size, the velocity gradient just above the surface is greater than elsewhere, because the surface air has been checked and that just above has not. The drag on this part of the surface is therefore greater than elsewhere; but it decreases again to the general constant value further down. This higher drag can however be prevented from decreasing if the velocity of the air above is made to increase with the distance. This can be effected by making the air immediately to leeward of the border pass through a constriction in a pipe, or over a mound in the open. And if the windward profile of the mound conforms to a certain mathematical curvature,[1] the drag remains constant from the

[1] White, C. M. (1939), *Report to the International Union of Geophysics and Geodesy* (Washington).

texture border at the windward foot of the mound up to its summit. This has an important bearing on the profile of stream ripples in water and probably also on that of large-scale dunes in air.

Chapter 5

THE EFFECT OF SAND MOVEMENT ON THE SURFACE WIND

1. CHANGES IN THE VELOCITY DISTRIBUTION

WE can now examine the changes which occur in the wind when it blows over a *mobile* surface of loose sand; and compare the new velocity distribution with that which would be produced by the same sand if it were prevented from moving. It may be clearest to begin with the experiment by which these changes were discovered.

In the first instance a nearly uniform sand of average grain diameter 0·25 mm. was spread over the tunnel floor. Any artificial smoothness was obliterated by allowing a stream of wind to blow over it for a short time. By this means a normal surface of wind-blown sand was ensured; that is, it was not only pitted with tiny bombardment craters a few grain diameters in size, but was made to undulate in the usual flat transverse ripples. The surface was then 'fixed' by spraying with water-mist; the wind was turned on again, and a series of velocity readings taken at different heights. This was repeated for a number of different strengths of wind, and the resulting velocity rays are shown as dotted lines in Fig. 17. The rays converge, as can be seen in the figure, to a focus at a height k somewhat greater than $\frac{1}{30}$ of the grain diameter. (The height k actually corresponds more nearly with $\frac{1}{30}$ of the height of the little bombardment craters; which is what we might expect.)

The surface was now allowed to dry off so that it again became mobile, and the whole series of velocity measurements was repeated for greater and greater wind strengths, beginning below the impact threshold at which the sand movement started. The new velocity distributions of the wind are shown by the heavy continuous lines of Fig. 17. It will be seen that *the sand movement profoundly alters the state of the wind.* It was found that the wind could be increased in strength up to a distribution shown by the dotted line $V_* = 22$—the fluid threshold—without

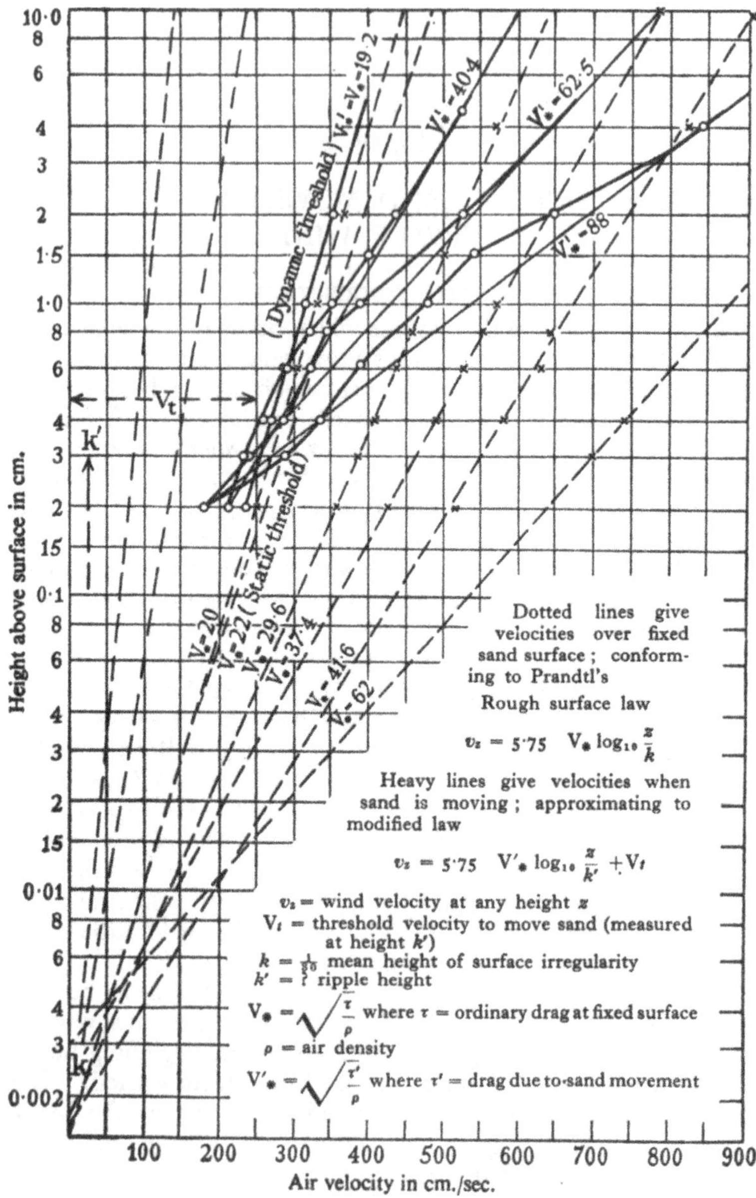

FIG. 17.—WIND VELOCITY DISTRIBUTIONS

any sand movement taking place. But once the movement had started at some point in the tunnel, the velocity of the wind close to the surface further down the tunnel immediately dropped to a lower value—the impact threshold—owing to the extra drag of the saltation. The distribution at the impact threshold is marked on the diagram $V_* = V'_* = 19{\cdot}2$.

Within 2 cm. of the surface the velocity distributions for higher wind strengths are no longer straight, but they approach to straight lines higher up, as has been verified by subsequent measurements in the open. Disregarding the kinks for the present, and considering the new velocity rays as straight lines (the thin continuous lines in the figure), it will be seen that *no matter how strongly the wind is made to blow*; i.e. no matter how great is the velocity gradient, *the wind velocity at a height of about 3 mm. remains almost the same.* Moreover at levels still closer to the ground the wind velocity actually falls as the wind above is made stronger.

As nearly as I have been able to measure, it appears, both from wind-tunnel experiments and also from measurements made in the desert up to a height of 1·8 metres, that, just as the velocity rays in the case of the fixed surface all converge to a focus at a height k, so, in the case of a moving sand surface, they also converge to a focus, though quite a different one.

In Fig. 18 the arrangement is shown for simplicity by straight lines only. The position of the new focus O' is determined by a certain height and a certain velocity. We will call the height of the focus k'. In Figs. 17 and 18 it is seen to be about 0·3 cm. It is probable that the height k' is associated with the height of the ripples which form on the surface, in a way somewhat analogous to that in which the smaller height k is associated with the smaller dimension of the granular texture of the surface. At all events k' rises from 0·3 cm. for uniform sand in which the ripple amplitude is very low, to about 0·8 cm. for a mixed sand, which produces ripples of considerable amplitude.

Over the fixed surface the focus is located for us as far as velocity is concerned: it lies on the line of zero velocity gradient, i.e. that at which the *air movement* first begins. In the same way the focus for the moving sand surface lies on the velocity gradient at which the *sand movement* first begins—the impact threshold.

This impact threshold gradient varies approximately as the square root of the grain diameter (see Chapter 7). The measure-

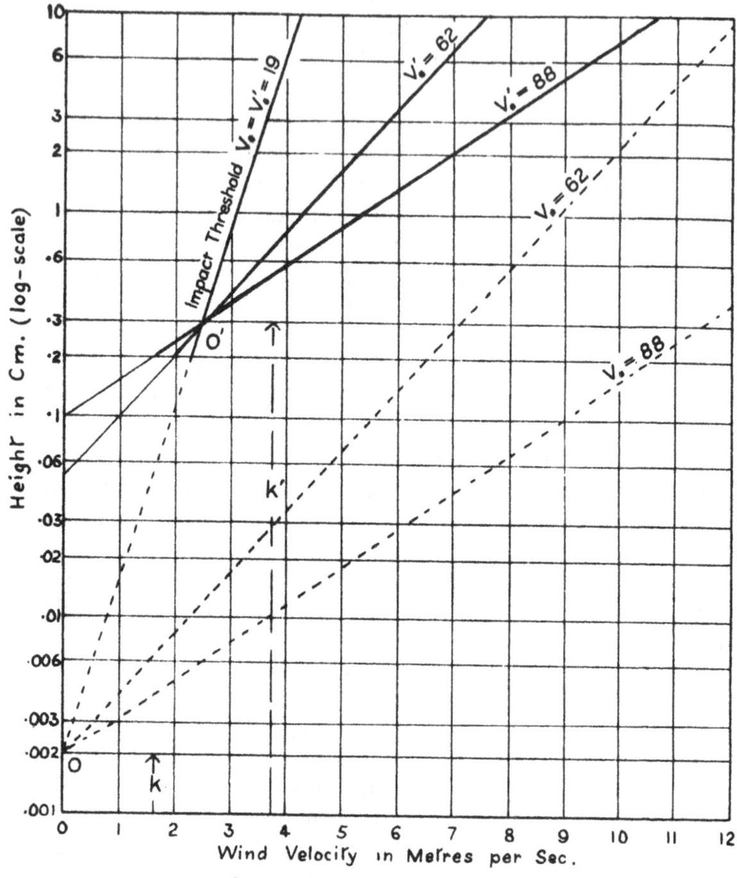

FIG. 18.—SCHEMATIC VIEW OF FIG. 17.

ments on which Fig. 17 is based were made with uniform sand of grain diam. 0·25 mm. For this size of sand the velocity gradient at the impact threshold is about 19 cm./sec. Thus from a knowledge of the average grain size we know the position of the point O′ on the diagram, and we know that during sand-driving the wind velocities at all heights are given by a series of straight lines passing through O′.

Mathematically, the wind velocity v at any height z above the ground during sand-driving can be expressed in terms of the velocity gradient by the following modification of equation 4 given in the preceding chapter:

$$v = 5{\cdot}75\ V'_{*}\ \log\frac{z}{k'} + V_t \quad . \quad . \quad . \quad (1)$$

where V_t is the threshold velocity as measured at the height k'.

As will be shown in Section 3, the rate at which sand is driven over the surface is a simple function of the wind velocity gradient[1] V_{*}. Thus by the above equation, or by its graphical counterpart of which Fig. 18 is an example, the rate of sand movement can be calculated from a knowledge of the measured velocity v at any height z of measurement.

As a practical example of the effect of the shift of the velocity curve brought about by the sand movement, suppose we have a wind with a measured velocity gradient $V_{*} = 62$ blowing over a plain of sand of grain diameter 0·25 mm. Suppose further that a shower of rain has fallen on an up-wind portion of the plain leaving the rest dry and mobile. Over the wetted surface on which the sand cannot move, the wind velocity at a height of 10 cm. is seen from the appropriate dotted line of Fig. 18 to be 12 metres, or 39 feet, per second. Further on, on the dry moving sand, the velocity at the same height has fallen to less than 8 metres, or 26 feet, per second. At a height of only 1 cm. above the surface the effect is more pronounced. The velocity falls from 8·8 to 4·3 metres per second.

Regarding it in another way, if we continued the line $V'_{*} = 62$ downwards through the focus, it will be seen to meet the ordinate of zero velocity at a height of 0·05 cm. Thus the state of the wind is the same as it would be if it blew over a fixed surface whose roughness corresponded to pebbles of diameter $0{\cdot}05 \times 30 = 1{\cdot}5$ cm. Similarly the state of the wind over a surface of moving sand when $V'_{*} = 88$ is seen to be the same as it would be over a fixed surface composed of stones of 3 cm. diameter. Since in reality there are no such solid fixed obstructions projecting upwards, it is clear that it must be the saltating sand grains, entangled so to speak in the air stream well above the surface, which are responsible for the effect; and that the stronger the wind blows the greater is the height above the surface at which they offer their maximum obstruction to the passage of the wind.

[1] Throughout the remainder of this book V_{*} will refer only to conditions when no sand movement is taking place, and V'_{*} will refer to the altered condition brought about by the sand movement.

2. THE CHARACTERISTIC GRAIN PATH

Considering only a sand of uniform grain size, we saw in Chapter 1 that owing to their varying shapes the individual grains exhibit differences in their behaviour in the air. For purposes of calculation, however, it was found possible to replace the heterogeneous collection of real grains by ideal spheres whose behaviour was the same as that of the average of the real grains.

We have now a similar problem, in that the saltating grains rise to different heights and travel different distances, even in the same wind. Using the same artifice it should be possible to replace the heterogeneous collection of grain paths, great and small, by an imaginary single path such that if all the sand grains in the saltation followed this path the effect of the saltation upon the wind would remain unchanged. Such a ***characteristic path*** would, for any given conditions of grain size and wind strength, be equivalent to the average real grain path.

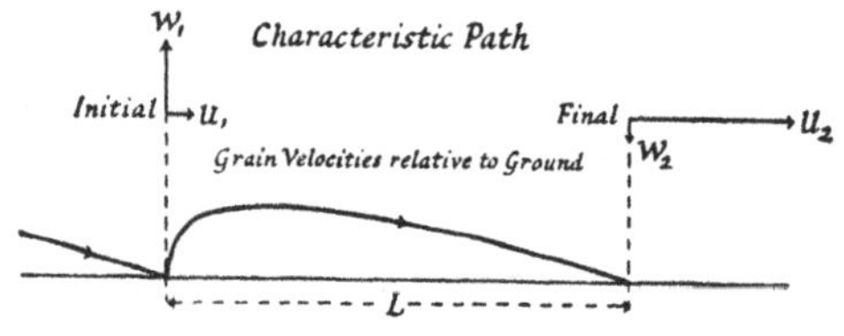

FIG. 19.—THE CHARACTERISTIC PATH

Since photography shows that the grains rise from the surface with a forward velocity small compared with that which they attain during the subsequent flight, it is convenient to assume as an approximation that our average or characteristic grain leaves the surface with an upward velocity which is initially vertical. With this assumption the subsequent path of the grain is completely defined by the value of the initial upward velocity w_1 (Fig. 19), and by the wind velocity distribution.

Calculation shows that the grain acquires the bulk of its forward momentum from the wind while it is travelling at a level very near that of the top of its path. That is, it exerts a maximum drag on the air at this height. Hence, for a given wind, if the characteristic path has any real meaning at all, we should expect that careful measurements of wind velocity would reveal a change in the velocity gradient at some definite height above the surface. Reference to Fig. 17 will show that there is clear evidence that this is indeed the case. There is a decided kink in each of the velocity curves. The widest part of the kink, i.e. the maximum departure from the straight-line relation, rises, as the wind gradient is increased, from about 0·6 cm. to 1·5 cm. The observed height of the kink in the wind velocity curves therefore throws valuable light on the height of the characteristic path.

This height may seem at first sight to be very low compared with the visually observed height of the sand cloud, which is ten times as great. But measurements of the relative weight of sand collected at different levels above the surface indicate that

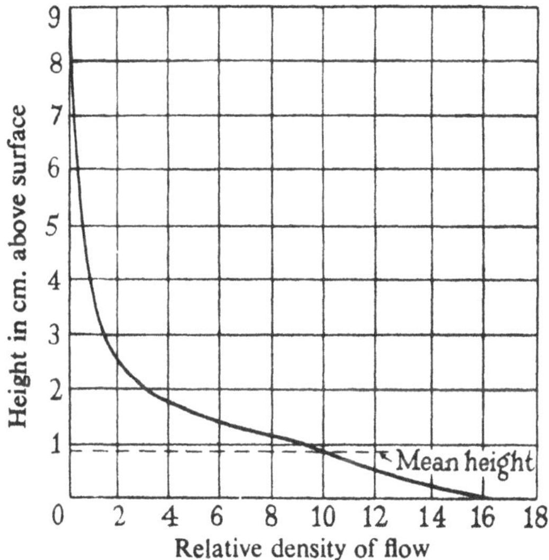

FIG. 20.—APPROXIMATE CURVE SHOWING DISTRIBUTION OF SAND GRAINS ACCORDING TO HEIGHT ABOVE THE SURFACE

the bulk of the movement does in fact take place very close to the ground. Fig. 20 shows how rapidly the movement falls off with the height. It also shows that the mean height of the grains corresponds closely with that of the kink in the velocity curves.

Assuming that the height of the kink in the wind velocity curve really is a physical manifestation of the average height to which the grains rise, we are tempted to look for a similar manifestation of their average *range* down-wind. By taking an arbitrarily chosen value for the initial velocity of rise w_1, it is possible to trace out mathematically the path which a grain will describe under the influence of a wind whose velocity is distributed according to one of the curves of Fig. 17. For each of these wind distributions a set of grain paths was traced out, each corresponding to a different value of w_1. By interpolation it was then possible to find the values both of w_1 and of the range l for a grain path whose height corresponded to that of the kink in each of the experimental velocity curves of Fig. 17. Below are comparative figures, for each wind gradient V'_*, for the calculated range l, and also for the measured distance between the actual ripples produced on the sand surface during the experiments of which Fig. 17 is the result.

V'_*	19·2	25·0	40·4	50·5	62·5	88	cm./sec.
Range (calculated)	2·5	3·0	5·4	8·0	11·6	27	cm.
Ripple length (measured)	2·4	3·0	5·3	9·15	11·3	—	cm.

This remarkable agreement between the range, as calculated theoretically from the evidence of the wind velocity measurements, and the wavelength of the real ripples, suggest strongly that the latter is indeed a physical manifestation of the length of the hop made by the average sand grain in its journey downwind. These experiments were done with sand of nearly uniform grain size. With mixed sands the kink in the velocity curves is not so clearly defined, presumably owing to the fact that grains of different sizes have different characteristic paths.

3. THE DRAG CAUSED BY MOVING SAND. RELATION BETWEEN WIND GRADIENT AND RATE OF SAND MOVEMENT

If a stationary sand grain rises from the surface with a horizontal velocity u_1 (Fig. 19) and strikes it again after travelling a distance l with a horizontal velocity u_2 all of which is lost on impact, the momentum extracted from the air will be $m(u_2 - u_1)$, where m is the mass of one grain. The loss will be distributed over the length l, so that the loss per unit length will be $\frac{m(u_2 - u_1)}{l}$. Similarly, if a mass q_s of sand in saltation moves along a lane of unit width and passes a fixed point in one second, the rate of loss of momentum by the air will be

$$q_s \frac{u_2 - u_1}{l} \qquad (2)$$

per second, per unit width of lane, per unit length of travel, i.e. per unit area of surface per second. The rate of loss of momentum is equivalent to a force; so that the expression $q_s\frac{(u_2 - u_1)}{l}$ is a measure of the resistance exerted on the air by every sq. cm. of surface due to the sand grains moving over it. And since, as we have seen, u_1 is small compared to u_2, we can as an approximation neglect u_1 and express the resisting force per unit area, or the drag τ', as

$$q_s\frac{u_2}{l} = \tau' \quad . \quad . \quad . \quad . \quad (3)$$

where τ' is the drag on the air due to the sand movement, and u_2 and l are respectively the final velocity and the range of the grains, all of which are supposed to follow the characteristic or average path.

Now, as we have seen in Section 7, Chapter 4, the fluid drag at or near a boundary surface can be expressed in terms of the velocity gradient of the fluid, so that we can replace τ by $\rho V_*'^2$ and write

$$q_s\frac{u_2}{l} = \rho V_*'^2 \quad . \quad . \quad . \quad . \quad (4)$$

u_2/l is merely a relation between two elements of a grain path, and has been found to approximate very closely over a wide range of values to g/w_1, where w_1 is, as before, the initial vertical velocity of rise of the grain at the beginning of its path. Hence we can write

$$q_s\frac{g}{w_1} = \rho V_*'^2$$

or

$$q_s = \frac{\rho}{g} V_*'^2 w_1 \quad . \quad . \quad . \quad (5)$$

The arbitrary assumption is now made that the initial velocity of ejection w_1 is proportional to the velocity gradient of the air V_*'. This seems reasonable, since the characteristic grain is supposed to be ejected from the surface by the impact of a similar grain whose final velocity is the mean of the velocities of all the real grains describing all possible paths in the sand cloud. Since these grains are exposed to the air stream at all heights, their mean velocity of impact is likely to be controlled by V_*', which defines the whole distribution of air speed. Thus it is assumed that

$$w_1 = BV_*' \quad . \quad . \quad . \quad . \quad (6)$$

where B may be regarded as an 'impact coefficient' which may vary according to the nature of the sand but should remain constant for any given sand. Hence we have

$$q_s = \mathrm{B}\frac{\rho}{g}V'^3_* \quad . \quad . \quad . \quad . \quad . \quad (7)$$

The value of B was found from the evidence given by the height and range of the characteristic path (for the uniform sand used) to be 0·8.

The total sand flow q consists of the saltation q_s, together with the surface creep q_c, and a small remainder q_0 which may be carried in suspension. Since the sand of the surface creep derives its forward momentum from the bombardment of the saltation and not directly from the wind, it contributes nothing to the drag exerted on the wind; and as the sand in true suspension (if any) travels at the same speed as the wind it also contributes nothing. Measurements both in the wind tunnel and in the open indicate that the surface creep q_c is approximately equal to a quarter of the whole sand flow q. Neglecting the effects of true suspension which, except perhaps in the case of a very dusty sand, appear to be very small indeed, we can therefore substitute $\frac{3}{4}q$ for q_s in the above expression, so that we have

$$q = \frac{4}{3} \times 0{\cdot}8\frac{\rho}{g}V'^3_* = 1{\cdot}1\frac{\rho}{g}V'^3_* \quad . \quad . \quad . \quad (8)$$

Since both q and V'_* are quantities easily measurable, we are now in a position to verify experimentally the foregoing theory. The following table gives the results which were obtained with uniform sand of average diameter 0·25 mm. q was measured directly by weighing the total quantity of sand carried through the wind tunnel by a wind whose gradient V'_* was measured at the same time.

V'_*	25	40·4	50·5	62	88
$q = 1{\cdot}1\frac{\rho}{g}V'^3_*$ (calculated)	0·0215	0·092	0·178	0·323	0·94
q (measured)	0·029	0·118	0·25	0·44	1·22
$\frac{q \text{ measured}}{q \text{ calculated}}$	1·35	1·28	1·4	1·36	1·3

q being expressed in gm. per cm. width of lane, per second.

It will be seen that the measured values of the sand flow

conform in a remarkable way the predictions based on the idea of the hypothetical 'characteristic path'. Not only are the theoretical values of the same order as the actual measured ones, but the ratio of the two is nearly constant over a fifty-fold range of values. That the sand flow as experimentally measured is rather larger than the theory suggests is probably due to the grains of the sand used not being identical in size. For though the sand was as uniform as possible, the grains ranged from 0·18 to 0·3 mm. in diameter; and as impact phenomena are concerned with masses, the variation in mass between the biggest and the smallest must have been at least 4·5 to 1. Thus considerable bouncing must have occurred, and the effect of this must have been to increase the initial upward velocity w_1 of the smaller grains which would bounce most; i.e. to increase the value of the impact coefficient B. Experiments with sand of the same mean grain size but of a wider size variation show that B does increase as the grain size becomes less uniform.

It also appears from experiments that for a given wind drag (a given value of the gradient V'_*) the rate of movement of a fine sand is less than that of a coarse sand. For grain diameters of the order of those found in dunes, i.e. between 0·1 and 1·0 mm., q appears to vary approximately as the square root of the grain diameter.

Introducing an empirical coefficient C, the actual measured rate of sand movement is given by the expression

$$q = C\sqrt{\frac{d}{D}}\,\frac{\rho}{g}\,V'^{3}_{*} \quad . \quad . \quad . \quad (9)$$

where D is the grain diameter of a standard 0·25 mm. sand, d is the grain diameter of the sand in question, and C has the following values:

1·5 for a nearly uniform sand,
1·8 for naturally graded sand, such as that found on dunes,
2·8 for a sand with a very wide range of grain size.

The above expression gives the important relation between the sand flow q (the weight of sand which moves along a lane of unit width past a fixed point in unit time) over a surface of loose sand, and the *gradient* V'_* of the wind which drives it. In C.G.S. units $\frac{\rho}{g}$ is equal to $1{\cdot}25 \times 10^{-6}$.

4. RELATION BETWEEN WIND VELOCITY AND RATE OF SAND MOVEMENT

Owing to the logarithmic relation between wind velocity and height, the expression giving the sand flow in terms of the *wind velocity as measured at a given height* is more complicated.

In Fig. 21 O′ is the common focus to which the wind velocity rays converge during sand-driving, and O′A is a ray representing any given velocity distribution. The focus O′ lies at a height k' above the surface, and A lies at the height z at which the wind velocity is measured. The actual levels GO′ and FCA in the figure are, as before, spaced on the paper at heights equal to $\log k'$ and $\log z$ respectively.

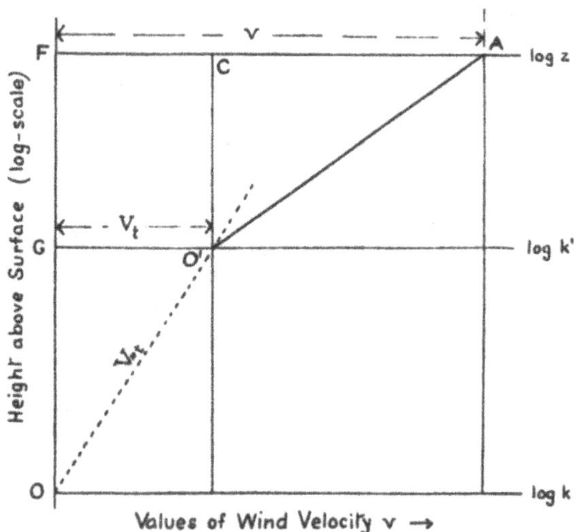

FIG. 21.—RELATIONS BETWEEN WIND VELOCITY, WIND GRADIENT, AND THRESHOLD VELOCITY V_t

The total wind velocity at the height z is represented by the distance FA. It will be seen that this velocity is the sum of a constant velocity FC = GO′, which is the threshold velocity as measured at the height k' for the particular sand considered, plus an increment CA whose value is determined by the inclination of O′A to the vertical, i.e. by the value of V'_*.

The threshold velocity GO′, which we will call V_t, can be found by drawing through O, whose height k is known from the size of the sand, a line OO′ inclined at the impact threshold wind gradient for the sand. For uniform sand of 0·25 mm. diameter k' is 0·3 cm. and V_t is 2·5 metres/sec. For an average dune sand of mixed grain size k' can be taken as 1 cm. and V_t as 4 metres/sec. (see Chapter 6).

Now from Chapter 4 (7), we have

$$V_* = \frac{CA}{CO'} \times \frac{1}{5{\cdot}75} = 0{\cdot}174\frac{CA}{CO'}$$

and since the distance CO′ is equal to $(\log z - \log k')$ or $\log \frac{z}{k'}$,

$$V_* = \frac{0{\cdot}174}{\log z/k'}.CA$$

For any one kind of sand and any standard height of measurement $\log z/k'$ is constant, and we can write

$$V_*^{\,3} = \alpha(AC)^3$$

where α is a constant equal to $\left(\frac{0{\cdot}174}{\log z/k'}\right)^3$.

Hence the sand flow q which, as we have seen, varies as the cube of V'_*, also varies *as the cube of the excess of wind velocity over and above the constant threshold velocity at which the sand begins to move.*

The total wind velocity v as measured at the height z is represented by FA, and CA is equal to $(v - V_t)$. So, from equation (9) of this chapter, we have

$$q = \alpha C \sqrt{\frac{d}{D}}\,\frac{\rho}{g}(v - V_t)^3 \quad . \quad . \quad . \quad (10)$$

Taking 1 metre as the standard height of measurement, and 1 cm. as a practical value for k', $\log z/k' = 2$ and $\alpha = 6{\cdot}58 \times 10^{-4}$. Assuming also that the sand is of average diameter so that $d/D = 1$, and that $C = 1{\cdot}8$, the sand flow q is given in terms of the wind velocity v by

$$q = 1{\cdot}5 \times 10^{-9}(v - V_t)^3 \quad . \quad . \quad . \quad (10a)$$

in C.G.S. units.

The curve of Fig. 22 gives the rate of movement of an average dune sand in metric tons per metre width of lane per hour, for winds of various strengths as measured at a height of 1 metre above the ground. This curve results from direct measurements in the desert, which closely confirm previous wind-tunnel figures. It shows the enormously rapid increase which takes place in the weight of sand moved when the wind rises appreciably above the threshold. For instance, a strong wind blowing at 16 metres

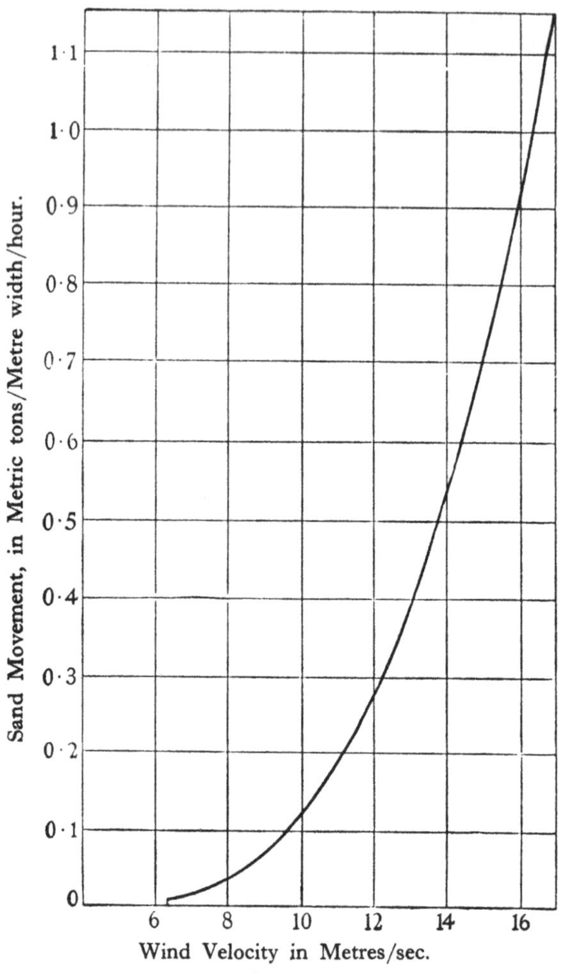

FIG. 22.—RELATION BETWEEN THE FLOW OF AVERAGE DUNE SAND AND THE WIND VELOCITY AS MEASURED AT A STANDARD HEIGHT OF ONE METRE

In the units used $q = 5{\cdot}2 \times 10^{-4}(v - V_t)^3$. This is obtained from equation 10 by taking $C = 1{\cdot}8$, $d/D = 1$, $p/g = 1{\cdot}25 \times 10^{-6}$, $k' = 1$ cm., $z = 100$ cm., $V_t = 400$ cm./sec.

per second, or 35 miles an hour, will move as much sand in 24 hours as would be moved in 3 weeks by a wind blowing steadily at 8 metres per second, or $17\frac{1}{2}$ miles an hour.

From the foregoing it will be clear that *over a surface of loose sand under steady conditions a wind of a given strength will drive sand at one definite rate, and this rate depends only on the character of the sand.* If by some disturbance the flow of sand is locally increased, the extra resistance which its movement offers to the passage of the wind will reduce its velocity, and will result in deposition taking place until the rate of sand flow returns, some distance down-wind, to its original steady value.

5. INCREASED SAND MOVEMENT OVER SURFACES CONTAINING LARGE GRAINS

If we compare the movement, under the same wind, of sands of uniform, with those of mixed, grain sizes, it is found that though the average grain size is kept the same, the rate of the sand movement increases with increasing diversity of grain size. The reason appears at once from a consideration of the paths traced out by the saltating grains. An increasing proportion of these encounter, on impact with the surface, grains more massive than themselves, and tend to rebound off them into the air instead of splashing into the surface to form a crater. The average upward velocity of rise w_1 thereby becomes greater, the saltating grains rise higher and travel further down-wind during their flight. In a given distance down-wind there are fewer impacts with the ground, and consequently fewer occasions when the granular momentum requires to be renewed from the air stream. The drag on the air stream is therefore reduced. Mathematically, since the drag τ' is equal to $q_s \frac{u_2}{l}$ and since (Section 3)

$$\frac{u_2}{l} = \frac{g}{w_1}$$

we have

$$\tau' = q_s \frac{g}{w_1}$$

so that an increase in the initial velocity of rise gives a proportional decrease in the drag—the sand movement q_s remaining the same.

As the surface grains are made more and more massive compared with those in saltation over them, there comes a stage when the conditions are those of sand driving over a surface of immobile pebbles. The high velocity of the flying grains now makes photography difficult, but under bright illumination the granular motion over sand and over pebbles can be compared by visual observation. The difference in appearance is shown in Fig. 10, Chapter 3.

The sand movement over a rough immobile or partially immobile surface differs in this important respect from that over a surface of dune sand; over the latter the intensity of the movement adjusts itself to the strength of the wind, sand being picked up from the surface or deposited on it till the relative flow of sand and air are in equilibrium with one another, and the wind may be said to be sand-saturated; in the case of the surface which does not yield under grain impacts, the sand movement for any given wind may be large or small, since there may be no sand available on the surface to be picked up. Further, owing to the reduced drag consequent on the change in the motion of the grains from splashing to bouncing, *a given wind can drive sand over a hard immobile surface at a considerably greater rate than is allowed by the loose sand surface.* This fact, as we shall see later, is of great importance, and explains the fundamental property possessed by wind-blown sand of accumulating on areas already sand-covered in preference to the surrounding country.

The maximum possible sand flow q appears still to be proportional to V'^{3}_{*}, and the value of the coefficient C in equation (9) (Section 3) may be taken as approximately 3·5; but the size and spacing of the pebbles seem to be important. This point requires further investigation.

6. SAND MOVEMENT UNDER WATER COMPARED WITH THAT IN AIR

In spite of years of research undertaken by universities and by irrigation and river control authorities in many countries, the physics of the transport of sand by running water is still not understood. The reason appears to be twofold. In the first place the difficulties both of observation and of measurement are far greater in the case of water than in that of air, because air and not water is the medium in which man normally lives. We can stand in a sand storm and watch what happens, whereas it is impossible to observe the movement of material along the bottom of a river in flood. In the second place the density ratio between the fluid and the transported particles is so little different from unity in the case of sand in water that it is extremely difficult to separate the effect of the motion of the surrounding water from that of the motion of the grains in it. Taking buoyancy into account, the density ratio for air and quartz is 1/2,000, and for water and quartz it is only 1/1·65.

This disparity in the density ratios is responsible for very marked differences in the interaction between the grains and the surrounding fluid, and consequently in the mechanism of grain transport. The momentum of a sand grain moving at the same speed as the transporting fluid is 2,000 times as great as that of its own volume of air, but it is only 1·65 times that of its own volume of water. Therefore in order that a current of the fluid may impart to one stationary grain a velocity equal to its own, the fluid must lose momentum equivalent to 2,000 grain volumes in the case of air, but only 1·65 grain volumes in the case of water. Hence the reduction in the velocity of a stream of water by a given saltation of sand along the bottom is less than one thousandth of the reduction in velocity effected by an identical saltation on a stream of air moving with the same original speed.

In the case of air this reduction in velocity close to the surface is so great that the residual drag due to the stationary surface underneath can be neglected altogether, and it makes very little difference whether the surface is rippled or plane. The velocity of the air near the surface is therefore controlled entirely by the intensity of the saltation of sand above the surface; and an equilibrium is set up between the two, nearly independently of the form of the surface below. But in water the reverse is the case; the direct effect of the saltation being negligible, the velocity of the water is controlled largely by the unevenness—rippling, &c.—of the stationary surface. This introduces very serious complications, for the degree of unevenness itself depends upon the movement of the grains of which the surface is built; and the surface features change continually with time owing to the migration of grains from place to place.

But a still more serious difficulty arises when, even under the simplest condition of an initial flat bottom, attempts are made to find the factors controlling the intensity of the sand movement. In air these are simple, and consist in the interaction between the wind and the intensity of the saltation which it produces and which in turn controls the drag it experiences in its passage. But this does not hold good for water, for the drag is here negligible. What then prevents the sand movement in water from rising to a very high value immediately the stream is strong enough to move the first grains?

White [1] suggests that experimental evidence supports the theory that in the initial stages, when the bottom is still flat and when the water speed does not greatly exceed that at which the first grains begin to move, the number of grains dislodged from unit area per second is controlled entirely by the probability of the occurrence at the surface of eddy velocities large enough to move an exposed grain. Since in water the drag caused by the grains that have already been set in motion is negligible, the water speed close to the surface is not limited to a fixed value as it is in air. As the water velocity is increased, so is the probability of grain dislodgement; and consequently more grains rise from unit area per second.

This leads to the idea that *were the bed to remain flat* the flow of grains would indeed increase almost indefinitely as we go down-stream from the upper edge of the sand bed, for any water speed above the threshold. But experiment shows that within a wide range of speeds between the threshold of movement and a certain higher value the flat bed is an unstable condition. Hillocks and pockets are formed in it. More will be said about these in Chapter 11 when ripples are discussed. These unevennesses adjust their shape and size till the drag they occasion so checks the surface water speed that for any given rate of stream flow the sand movement is limited to a definite value.

When the stream flow rises above a certain strength the surface features begin to disappear. Here, on White's theory, we have a gradual transition from saltation to suspension. Suspension begins to occur, as was mentioned in Chapter 1, when the turbulence components of the stream velocity exceed the terminal velocity of fall of the grains. These turbulence components are found not to exceed 7 times the drag velocity V_*. So when the stream has such a flow that $7V_*$ is greater than the terminal velocity of the grains, suspension begins to set in. At higher speeds, when suspension is fully developed, the grains move along with the water, and form with it a composite fluid. The concentration of the grains increases towards the bottom, and depends on the whole depth of the stream, the terminal velocity of the grains, and the drag velocity of the fluid, according to a definite exponential law.

This theory, when it has been further developed to include

[1] White, C. M. (1939). *Report to the International Union of Geophysics and Geodesy* (Washington).

the important and apparently wide transitional range of water velocities between full saltation and full suspension, and when account is taken of the extension of the theory which deals with the formation of the surface features in the bed, should mark an important step forward in our understanding of sand movement in water. A further paper is understood to be forthcoming in the *Proceedings of the Royal Society*.

The theory assumes that no appreciable drag is transmitted to the bed by the collision of the sand grains with it; and hence it would seem to be invalid for the case of sand in air, where this drag is very large and swamps any small residual surface drag.

7. TRUE SUSPENSION OF SAND GRAINS IN AIR

Though the mechanism of grain movement in air and water differs fundamentally at fluid velocities for which V_* does not greatly exceed one-seventh of the terminal velocity of fall V_s of the grains, it seems certain that at higher values of V_* the upward currents of turbulence within the fluid must cause suspension to take the place of saltation, in both fluids, as the predominant mode of transportation.

For true suspension White [1] by a modification of Schmidt's work arrives at the equation

$$\log_{10}\frac{\eta}{\eta_1} = 5{\cdot}75\frac{V_s}{V_*}\log_{10}\left(\frac{H}{y} - 1\right) \quad . \quad . \quad (11)$$

for the concentration η of particles at any height y when η_1 is the concentration at the mid-stream depth $y = H/2$. In the case of air the stream depth is infinite, and if η_1 is taken as the concentration at the bed (mass of sand per unit volume of the stationary bed), the sand flow q emerges from the above equation as

$$q = \frac{V_*^{3} d}{2{\cdot}5V_s^{2}}\left(0{\cdot}076 + \frac{1}{6{\cdot}6N}\right) \quad . \quad . \quad (12)$$

where $N = \frac{2{\cdot}5V_s}{V_*}$ and the conditions are such that $V_s < 7V_*$.

The term in brackets does not vary greatly with either V_*

[1] Loq. cit. See also recent papers by Hunter Rouse, published by the U.S. Department of Agriculture, Soil Conservation Service, Washington.

or d, and since $V_s \propto d$ over a wide range of grain size, equation (12) can be written

$$q = \frac{aV_*^{3}}{d} \text{ to a fair approximation} \quad . \quad . \quad (13)$$

Thus the suspension sand flow should vary as V_*^{3} and inversely as the diameter. This may be compared with my own corresponding relation for true impact-saltation sand flow

$$q = a'V_*^{3}d$$

For sand grains of diameter 0·25 mm. the suspension flow by equation (12) at the highest experimental value $V_* = 88$ for the wind gradient is only one-twentieth of the actual measured flow, so suspension seems to be inappreciable. In the case of very fine sand of diameter 0·08 mm., however, the suspension flow by equation (12) is more than half the measured value. This figure is very suggestive in view of the peculiar dual behaviour of this sand as regards ripple formation (Chapter 11 (12)). It may be that the transition from saltation to suspension coincides with the stage at which the grain-impact mechanism ceases to operate, and that in the behaviour of this fine sand in air we have some approach to the sand-in-water mechanism.

REFERENCES

BAGNOLD, R. A. (1936). *Proc. Roy. Soc. A.*, 157, p. 594

— — (1937). *Geogr. J.*, 89, p. 409

PLATE I

WIND TUNNEL SUITABLE FOR SAND EXPERIMENTS

PLATE 2

(*a*)

(*b*)

(*c*)

PHOTOGRAPHS OF GRAIN PATHS

Chapter 6

CONFIRMATORY MEASUREMENTS IN THE DESERT

1. THE APPARATUS USED

THE primary experiments on which the foregoing results are based were made in a small wind tunnel. It was obvious that subsequent verification, by field measurements of wind velocity distributions up to a much greater height and of the actual sand movement in the open, would not only confirm the correctness of the deductions but would allow of other tunnel experiments being applied to sand problems in general with far greater confidence.

Such field work was carried out in the early spring of 1938 in the Libyan Desert, with the aid of a grant of funds by the Royal Society. As this appears to be the first time that quantitative simultaneous measurements of sand movement and wind velocity have been made in the open, it may be of interest, before proceeding to the results, to describe briefly the apparatus used.

This consisted of a set of pitot tubes which could be mounted in various combinations on vertical masts, a multiple manometer for taking a number of pressure readings at the same time, and a set of sand collectors.

The pitot tubes were of the modified N.P.L. pattern described by Ower.[1] The bore of the pressure orifice was 1·6 mm. Each tube was 16 inches long and could be clipped at its leeward end to a vertical mast made of thin golf-club steel tubing. Rubber tubing $\frac{3}{16}$-inch bore led to the manometer situated sometimes as far as 100 feet away. Usually four pitots were clipped to one mast at heights of 1, 4, 16, and 64 inches above the ground. Surprisingly little trouble was experienced from the chokage of the small orifices of the pitots by sand grains.

The design of the manometer, which was home-made, had to embody several special features. It had to register both velocity and static pressures at at least six pitots simultaneously, to be

[1] Ower, E. (1933). *The Measurement of Air Flow.* (Chapman & Hall.)

capable of carriage by car across rough country without requiring readjustment, to be set up, levelled, and zero-ed rapidly, and to be read easily under the unfavourable conditions of an open dune during a violent sand storm.

The manometer is shown in Plate 3 and Fig. 23. The heights of the 12 inclined tubes A, each mounted in independent cradles, could be adjusted at each end by the screws B and C. Six tubes

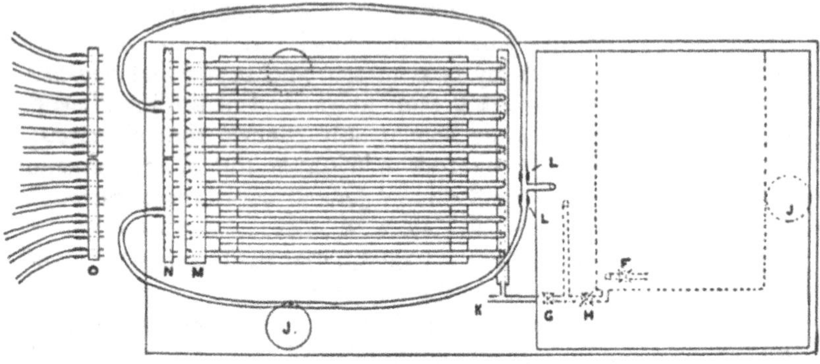

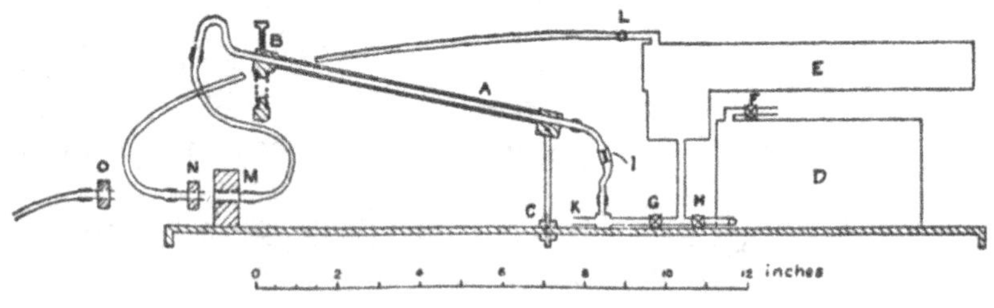

FIG. 23.—DETAILS OF THE MANOMETER

were given an inclination of 1/20 for the low pressures, and the remainder had an inclination of 1/5. Alcohol was stored for travelling in the tank D and thence could be driven up into the gauge tank E by blowing through the cock F, the cock G being closed. The cock H was then closed and G opened, allowing the liquid to rise into the gauge tubes A through the chokes I. The whole gauge could be levelled by the screws J and by theodolite bubbles (not shown) fixed to the base plate. When necessary the inclination of each and every gauge tube could be checked by means of a separate micro-manometer P embodied in the instrument. This was connected to the tube K and, when it was required, to one of the orifices L.

In order to zero all the gauges during a high wind it was necessary to short-circuit all the working connexions M of the gauges back to the air-space above the gauge-tank. This was done by providing special short-circuiting manifolds N which could be clipped rapidly into place. When the zero gauge readings had been recorded these manifolds and their connecting tubes to L were removed, and the manifolds O carrying all the working pitot connexions, both pressure and static, were substituted. One of the orifices L was then closed and the other connected to a breather of wire gauze lightly buried under the flat sand surface of the ground.

The instrument could be set up, levelled and zero-ed in six minutes even in bad conditions. The period of measurement varied from 15 to 45 minutes, and the readings of wind velocity were taken at intervals of from 1 to 3 minutes. The degree of damping provided by the chokes was such that no technical difficulty was found in taking the readings, and no trouble arose from the great lengths of connecting tube used.

2. MEASUREMENT OF THE RATE OF SAND MOVEMENT

The measurement of the total sand flow over an open surface can only be approximate, because the presence of any collecting instrument must interfere with the air stream. But if the collector is nearly streamline and offers but a narrow front to the wind, the flying grains (saltation) are unable to follow the deflected wind and pass straight into the mouth of the collector. This, however, is not the case at the ground surface; for the increased wind velocity along the sides of the vertical collector causes removal of the surface sand, with the consequent formation of a hollow. Thus the slow-moving grains in surface creep are carried round the sides of the collector and lost. It was therefore necessary to provide two collectors as shown in Fig. 24; a tall thin one for the saltation $\frac{1}{2}$ inch wide and 30 inches high, and a buried ground trap for the surface creep. The weight of sand collected in each, corrected for the differing widths of the orifices exposed, were assumed to give approximately the flow of sand in saltation q_s and that in surface creep q_c. The sum of these would give the total sand flow q. The ratio of q_c to q was found to agree well with that in the wind-tunnel experiments.

As neither the direction nor the time of occurrence of a sand storm could be foretold, both collectors had to be planted on the dune surface and to be removed during the storm. One

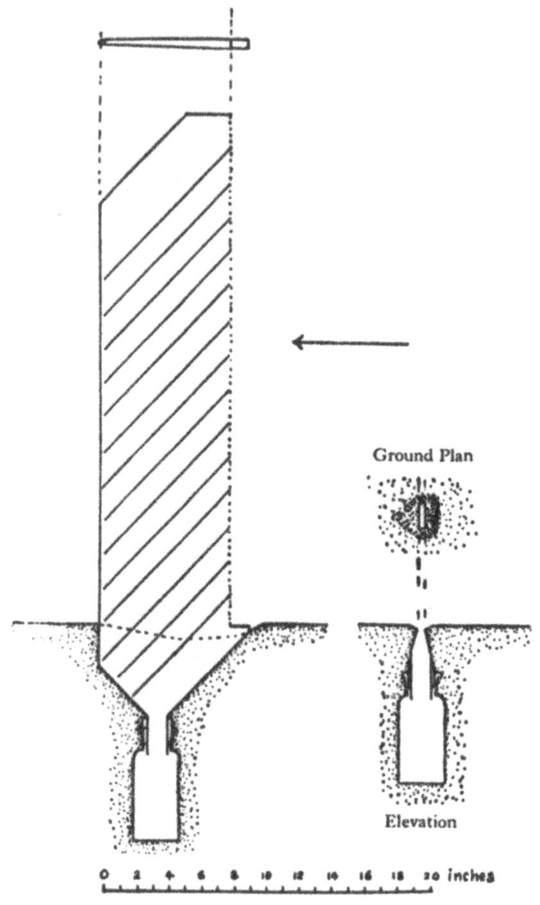

FIG. 24.—SAND COLLECTORS

Left, saltation collector. *Right*, ground trap for surface creep.

complete set of observations took an hour. It was found that during a heavy storm this was about the longest period that it was possible for an observer to work efficiently without better protection against the sand blast than was available.

3. RESULTS

In comparing the field results with those obtained in the laboratory it must be remembered that (*a*) the sand used in the wind-tunnel experiments was of uniform grain size, whereas the grains of the real dunes, though approximating closely to this in mean size, were not uniform; (*b*) the observations were made on different days with wind from different directions, so that the grain grading was not quite constant.

A further difficulty which it was feared might seriously affect the expected linear distribution of wind velocity with log-height lay in the fact that the surfaces of dunes are always curved; surfaces of any extent composed only of fine sand free of a covering of grit never being found on the flat sand plains. Measurements had therefore to be made on the surfaces of the flattest barchan dunes available: the radius of curvature of these was of the order of 1,000 feet. In every case, however, the manometer readings gave wind velocities which, when plotted against the log-height of the four pitots above the ground, led to reasonably linear distributions. Specimens of these are given in Fig. 25.

In this figure the wind velocities converge to an approximate focus in just the same way as they were found to do in the laboratory. The focus appears at a height k' of 1 cm. above the surface, whereas the corresponding height for uniform sand was 0·3 cm. If k' is interpreted as the height of the surface ripple, this change appears to tally with the observed increase of ripple amplitude as we pass from uniform to mixed natural sand.

The lateral position of the focus gives a threshold velocity V_t which is also somewhat greater than that found for a uniform sand of the same grain size. It would correspond with a diameter of 0·32 mm. instead of 0·25 mm. This might be expected since, as will be explained in Chapter 9, the grains of a surface layer of a mixed sand are larger than the average both of those in saltation and those constituting the main bulk of the ground material. Considering the collected grains of the surface creep as a fair sample of the surface layer controlling the threshold velocity, I found that the average size of these did in fact approximate closely to 0·32 mm.

In order to check the validity of the cubic relation dealt with in the preceding chapter, between the wind gradient V'_* and the rate of sand flow q, values of V'_* were found from the inclination of the velocity rays of Fig. 25. The cubes of these values were plotted against the measured values of the sand flow. If the cubic relation were true all the plotted points should lie on a straight line passing through the origin.

The result is shown in Fig. 26. The coefficient C, which is proportional to the slopes of the plotted lines, had been found from the wind-tunnel experiments to lie between 1·5 and 2·8,

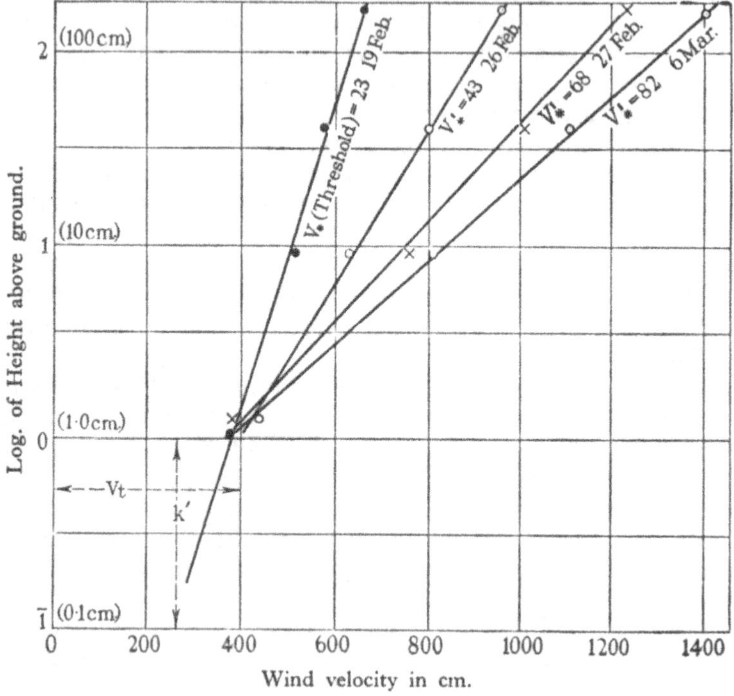

FIG. 25.—OBSERVED WIND VELOCITY DISTRIBUTION OVER A DUNE WHEN SAND IS DRIVING

depending on the width of the range of grain size in the sand. The value of 1·8 as given by the measurements in the open is just what was to be expected from the degree of uniformity of the sand on the dune tops.

Similar measurements of the wind gradient and the sand movement were made above the grit-covered surfaces of the flat sand sheet over which the dunes are creeping. Since, as has already been pointed out, there is in this case no fixed relation between V'_* and q, but only a maximum value of q for a given value of V'_*, there must be some uncertainty as to whether the wind was sand-saturated or not at the time of measurement. The sand was however driving heavily over the plain at the

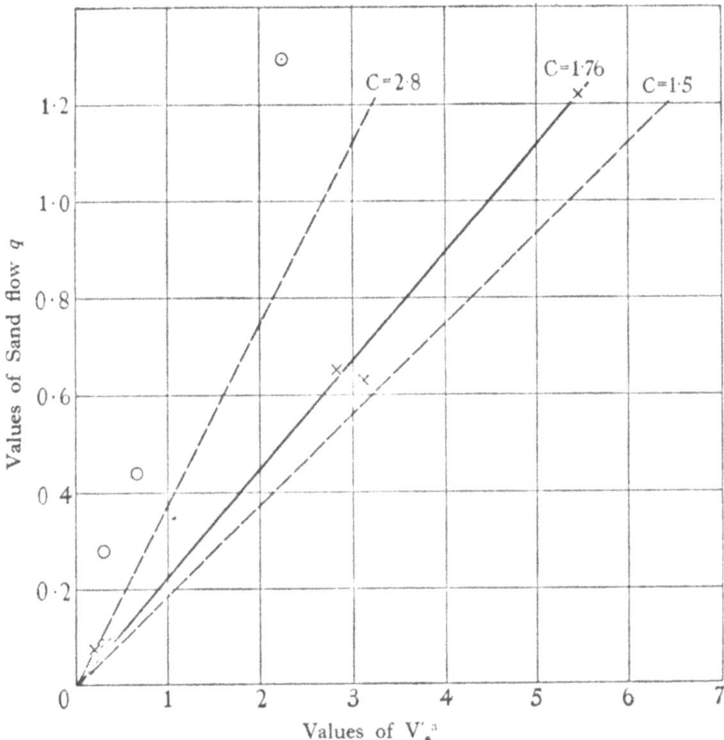

FIG. 26.—COMPARISON OF WIND-TUNNEL AND OPEN-AIR VALUES OF THE OBSERVED RATE OF MASS FLOW q OF SAND, AND THEIR PROPORTIONALITY TO V'^3_*

Results in open country

× Sand over sand surface (fairly uniform dune sand)
⊙ Sand over grit surface (sand-sheet)

Previous wind-tunnel results

Dotted line C = 1·5 indicates sand flow for uniform sand of same grain size as ×
Dotted line C = 2·8 indicates sand flow for sand of same mean size but very wide range of size

time, and was being temporarily deposited on the grit floor nearby in long narrow strips, so that the air was probably very near saturation. These values of q are plotted in Fig. 26 as dotted circles. Their positions confirm that the presence on the ground of the almost immobile grit grains greatly increases the rate of movement of the sand passing over them.

Although the season was so unusually calm that the number of real sand storms available for measurement was not as great as I could have wished, the figures obtained do corroborate very satisfactorily the predictions based on the wind-tunnel experiments. The latter may therefore be accepted with some confidence as providing a foundation on which further work can be built.

REFERENCE

BAGNOLD, R. A. (1938). *Proc. Roy. Soc. A.*, 167, p. 282

Chapter 7

THRESHOLD SPEED AND GRAIN SIZE

1. THE FLUID THRESHOLD FOR UNIFORM SAND

WHEN the flow of air or of water over a flat bed of loose grains is gradually increased, there comes an instant when a few grains here and there begin to be dislodged and moved downstream by the force of the fluid upon them. At the instant of dislodgement any individual grain so moved is being turned about its leeward points of contact with the underlying grains, as indicated in Fig. 27. The force of the grain's immersed weight, acting through the centre of gravity, is pulling the grain backwards and downwards; and this is just overbalanced by a drag force due to the

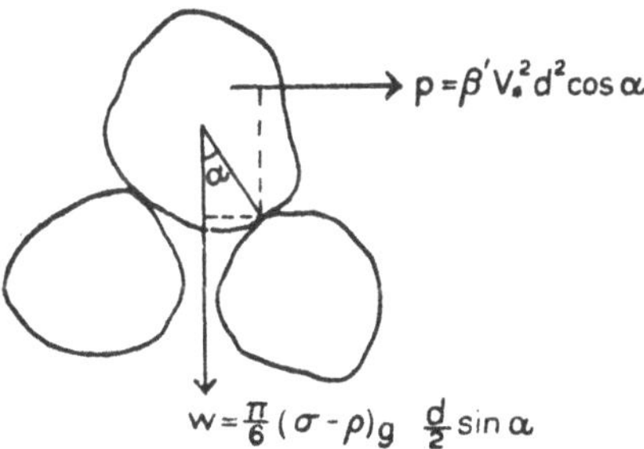

FIG. 27.—FORCES ACTING ON A GRAIN AT THE THRESHOLD OF MOVEMENT

fluid acting parallel to the general surface but at some rather indefinite height above the points of support.

The backward moment of the grain's weight would be easily calculated if we knew the value of the angle α, that is, if we knew how the grain is poised on its fellows; but actually, of course, the piling is haphazard and very variable. A good idea of the angle α can, however, be obtained by tilting a heap of sand until slipping occurs. In other words the angle α cannot be very different from the angle of repose. The immersed weight of the grain, considered as a sphere, is $\frac{\pi}{6}d^3(\sigma - \rho)g$, and its moment about the axis of support is therefore

$$\frac{\pi}{6}d^3(\sigma - \rho)g \times \frac{d}{2} \sin \alpha$$

where σ and ρ are the densities of the grain and the fluid respectively.

To calculate the balancing moment due to the fluid we must know the magnitude of the drag force on an individual grain and the level at which it acts; and moreover, since we are examining the conditions under which the first movement occurs, it is necessary to estimate not the mean value of the drag but the maximum momentary value which the turbulence of the fluid may exert on the grain.

The mean drag τ per unit area of the general surface is equal to ρV_*^2; and since some proportion of this acts on the projected area of the grain, the force on the grain is proportional to the square of its diameter, and can be written

$$p = \beta\rho V_*^2 d^2.$$

Hence the moment about the axis of support is given by

$$\beta'\rho V_*^2 d^2 \cos \alpha$$

where β' is some coefficient depending partly on the ratio of the maximum momentary velocities of turbulence to the mean velocity, partly on the proportion of the drag per unit area which is taken by the individual grain by virtue of its relative position in the piling, and partly on the height at which the drag force acts.

By equating these two opposing moments we get an expression for the threshold value of V_* in the form

$$V_{*t} = A\sqrt{\frac{\sigma - \rho}{\rho}gd} \quad . \quad . \quad . \quad . \quad (1)$$

That is, provided the general coefficient A is constant, the threshold value of V_* should vary as the square root of the grain diameter. From this the threshold fluid velocity v_t obtaining at any height z can be found from equation (4) of Chapter 4, by substituting for V_* the above expression for V_{*t}

$$v_t = 5{\cdot}75A\sqrt{\frac{\sigma - \rho}{\rho}gd} \log \frac{z}{k}$$

It is, however, very common in fluid dynamics to find that

numerical coefficients are only constant over limited ranges of the state of flow as defined by the Reynolds' Number

$$\frac{\text{velocity} \times \text{size dimension}}{\text{kinematic viscosity } \nu}$$

(Under atmospheric conditions ν can be taken as 0·14 for air, and as 0·01 for water.) As long as the Reynolds' Number remains of the same order of size, the coefficient is fairly constant.

Now in the case we are dealing with there are two states of flow to be considered, and therefore two rather different Reynolds' Numbers. In the first place we have the large-scale flow, whose state of large-scale turbulence depends upon the dimensions of the walls past which the flow is taking place. The cases of wind in the open, and of air flow in a wind tunnel some way down from the mouth, have already been dealt with in Chapter 4 (4), and we saw that for the Reynolds' Number there obtaining the flow can be taken as fully turbulent. This need not be so in many cases of water flow, and is certainly not so at the mouth of a wind tunnel where atmospheric air is entering and where no turbulence has had time to develop. For non-turbulent flow it has been found that the cofficient A in equation (1), for a given sand, may be more than double the value when turbulence is fully developed. This accounts for the fact that sand movement in a wind tunnel does not start at the mouth, but several tunnel diameters further down.

Confining ourselves to fully developed turbulent flow throughout the fluid, there remains the question of the small-scale flow over and round the individual grains on the surface. This depends on a Reynolds' Number of the form V_*d/ν, where d is the mean surface roughness which is of the order of the grain diameter. It has been found that when

$$\frac{V_* d}{\nu} > 3{\cdot}5$$

the grain behaves as an isolated obstacle in the path of the fluid, and throws off a chain of tiny eddies from its lee face. Moreover, under these conditions an exposed grain lying by itself above its fellows can carry the whole of the drag on the area it occupies, together with most of that on the surrounding shielded area, even when this is twenty times the projected area of the grain.[1]

[1] Colebrook, C. F., and White, C. M. (1937). *Proc. Roy. Soc. A.*, 161, p. 367.

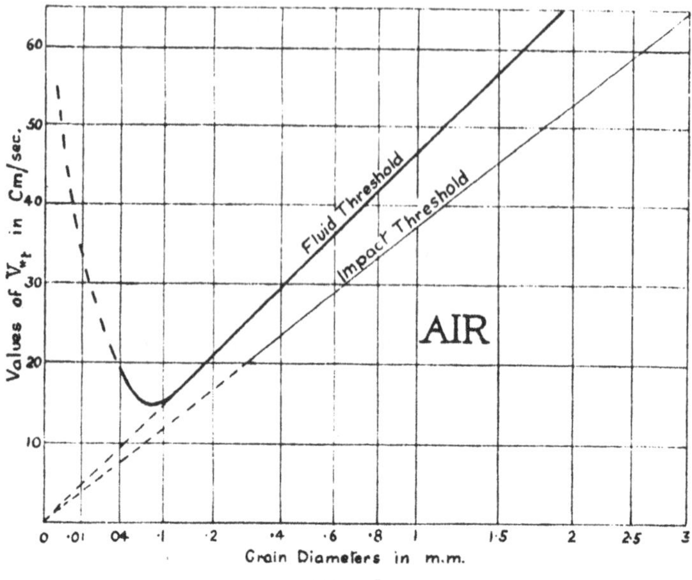

FIG. 28

VARIATION OF THE THRESHOLD VELOCITY

(Grain size drawn on a square-root scale to exhibit

The threshold value of V_* for a fine dune sand of diameter 0·025 cm. is about 20 cm./sec., and the corresponding value of $V_* d/\nu$ is very near the limiting value of 3·5. For this and for all sands of larger grain size it is found that the coefficient A in equation (1) is nearly constant. In air A = 0·1. For some reason which is not yet quite clear the corresponding value for water is rather larger, being nearer 0·2.[1] The discrepancy is probably due to a difference in the surface texture; for in air the surface is pitted with little impact craters, and individual grains on the crater lips are more exposed, whereas in water the surface is much smoother since grain impacts do not appreciably disturb it.

The critical Reynolds' Number

$$\frac{V_* d}{\nu} = 3{\cdot}5$$

[1] Casey, H. S. (1935). *Mitt. der Preuss. Versuchs fur Wasserbau und Schiffbau.* (Berlin.) Heft 19.
Shields, A. (1936). Op. cit. Heft 26.

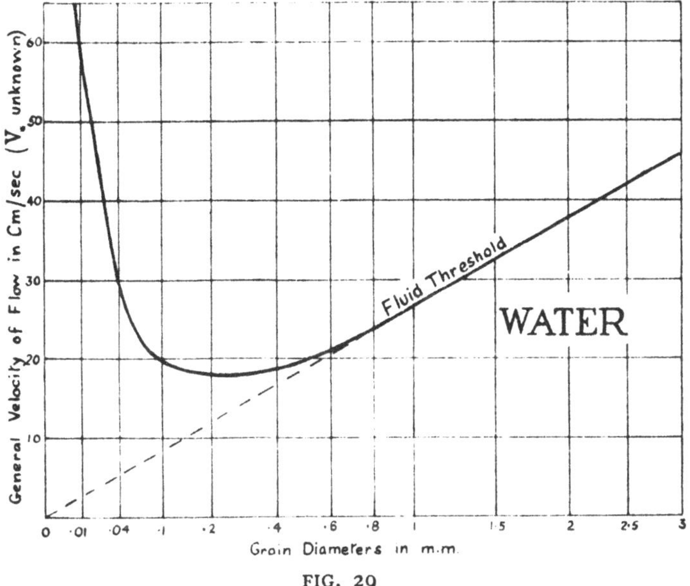

FIG. 29

WITH GRAIN SIZE FOR AIR AND WATER

the relation $v \propto \sqrt{d}$ for the larger grains)

distinguishes the condition under which a surface may technically be either 'rough' or 'smooth' (see footnote, Chapter 4 (6)).

2. THE FLUID THRESHOLD FOR VERY SMALL GRAINS

When the Reynolds' Number $V_{*}d/\nu$ is less than 3·5, that is, when either the grain diameter or the threshold velocity or both are smaller than for fine dune sand, the surface becomes 'smooth', and important changes take place in the flow close to the surface grains. Individual grains cease to shed little eddies of their own, and a semi-viscous non-turbulent layer of the fluid clings around them. The drag, instead of being carried by the few more exposed grains, is distributed more or less evenly over the whole surface. Consequently a relatively greater drag is required to set the first grains in motion.

As a result of these changes in the state of the flow, the value of the coefficient A for air begins to rise when the grain size falls below about 0·2 mm., so that the square root law no longer holds (see Fig. 28). For water the change begins at a diameter of about 0·6 mm. As the grains are made smaller and smaller a critical diameter is reached at which the threshold velocity needed to move them becomes a minimum. For air the critical diameter for quartz grains is in the neighbourhood of 0·08 mm., and for water 0·2 mm.

For still smaller grains the threshold velocity of the fluid has to be made actually larger before movement takes place.

Precise measurements in air with finer sands are difficult owing to (1) the trouble encountered in obtaining uniform grains in sufficient quantity,[1] and (2) the avidity with which the surfaces of such fine particles collect a sticky film of moisture from the atmosphere. But the somewhat startling experiment [2] of blowing a steady stream of air over a loosely scattered layer of fine Portland cement powder proves that no particle movement occurs in such material even when V_* exceeds 100—i.e. when the wind is strong enough to move pebbles of 4·6 mm. in diameter.

That the refusal of fine surface particles to be moved by a wind is not entirely due to cohesion caused by adsorbed moisture but is a true phenomenon of fluid dynamics is proved by the corresponding behaviour of sand in water. Sound experimental data for the case of water are difficult to obtain owing to the rather vague way in which the velocities are usually defined, but Hjulstrom [3] has collected some available data into an interesting curve, which is reproduced schematically in Fig. 29, of the threshold velocity (a mean velocity of flow) in terms of the grain size.

3. IMMOBILITY OF SETTLED DUST AND LOESS

It is evident from the results of the preceding section that once fine solid particles smaller than about 0·03 mm. have settled on the ground after carriage in suspension by a wind, they cannot be swept up again individually, because they sink into a viscid surface layer of air and are out of reach of the disturbing influence of the eddies of turbulence. The surface of the ground acts as a sort of dust trap. But the wind can still exert its local pressure

[1] It is essential when measuring the velocity gradient at which the fluid begins to cause grain movement that sufficient length of sand surface should be allowed up-wind of the point of measurement, so that the fluid may have an opportunity of taking up the velocity distribution appropriate to the texture of the sand bed. Otherwise, except at levels immeasurably close to the surface, the velocity distribution will be that of the unsanded floor further up-wind.

[2] Bagnold, R. A. (1937). *Geogr. J.*, 89, p. 436.

[3] Hjulstrom, F. (1936). *Bull. Geol. Inst. of Upsala*, 25.

on small aggregations of particles—little projecting heaps, the sharp edges around the impresses of feet or wheels—which the wind can treat as though they are sand grains. So that when a wind begins to blow, its first action is to tear off such projections and re-disintegrate them into dust. Once these projections have gone, however, the wind has no further effect on the surface until it is disturbed again by some third party.

This explains a common soil phenomenon. In arid pastoral plains of alluvial or wind-deposited material, dust lies thick and loose over the many converging cattle tracks which surround villages. Though a strong wind may be blowing it is often noticed that the air is only slightly hazy and no dust is picked up. It is not until a flock of sheep or a caravan passes that the familiar dense local cloud of dust appears. This moves along with the disturbance, leaving the ground dust immobile again immediately in rear of the last animal.

The disturbing influence is not confined to animals. Driving sand grains can also break up a powdery surface which would otherwise be too smooth to be affected by the wind alone. This can be demonstrated in the wind tunnel by covering the up-wind half of the floor with sand and the rest with powder such as cement. When the sand surface is fixed by wetting, no movement of the powder occurs, but if the sand is allowed to drive over the powder, a cloud of dust immediately appears. But only for a time. For the softness of the powder surface allows the sand grains to sink into it. The sand surface eventually creeps over the powder and covers the up-wind portion of it. The extent of the covering depends of course on the depth of the powder, for the layer may be eroded away down to the floor before the advancing sand covering can reach the down-wind portion. On the other hand the supply of sand from up-wind may run short, in which case the sand covering is itself removed and the powder may again be uncovered.

In this connexion should be noticed (*a*) the almost entire absence of recent deposits of fine material in erosion deserts, even though the production of loose fine material must here far exceed that of sand; (*b*) the absence of sand grains in the vast deposits of loess often found sufficiently far down-wind of such deserts to be out of range of the slowly advancing sand, e.g. in China; (*c*) the mean diameter of loess grains is about 0·05 mm.,[1] which

[1] Wentworth, C. (1932). *Univ. Ia. Stud. Phys.*, 14.
Barbour, G. B. (1936). *Geogr. J.*, 86, p. 54.

is just smaller than the critical diameter in the curve of Fig. 28; (*d*) the great depth attained by sunken roads and tracks in the loess country in China exemplifies the differential erosion of disturbed and undisturbed surfaces of fine material.

In the case of air the change of type of fluid flow is not the only cause of the relative immobility of small particles, though, as is shown by the parallel phenomenon in water, its effect is very real and probably predominates, at any rate for particles as large as those of loess. The adsorption of moisture also plays an important part, by holding the grains together. Evidence for this can be obtained from the changes in the angle of repose which take place when the humidity of the air is varied. Carefully dried clean quartz sand of average diameter 0·08 mm. begins to slip when the surface is tipped at an angle very little different from that for large grains. But when exposed to air of normal humidity it tends to stand in vertical walls like a powder.

By a curious coincidence there is also a change in the feel of the grain between the fingers when its size falls below about 0·07 mm. The material suddenly begins to feel smooth instead of gritty. Thus, as the size is reduced through the narrow range from 0·15 to 0·07 mm. four distinct changes occur in the properties of grains of the same material and the same shape. (*a*) When raised into the air they become so susceptible to the wind that they begin to be maintained aloft as dust by the wind's internal eddies. (*b*) They pass the critical diameter for which the threshold wind is a minimum and so are picked up from the ground with greater difficulty. (*c*) They begin to collect moisture to such an extent that they are noticeably bound together and become sticky. And (*d*) they cease even to feel like sand.

4. THE FLUID THRESHOLD FOR NATURAL SAND OF MIXED GRAIN SIZE

Returning from the above borderline material to grains of true sand—diameter bigger than 0·1 mm.—we can now consider the more natural case of a mixture in which one size of grain predominates, and in which the proportions by weight of grains of greater and smaller diameter fall off as the size departs from that of the predominant grains.

If the material is well mixed, and is spread out over the ground mechanically, the surface may be assumed to contain exposed grains in the proportions in which they exist in the body of the material. Most of the fine grains lie in crevices between the larger ones, and are screened by these from the drag of the wind.

PLATE 3

THE PORTABLE MANOMETER

PLATE 4

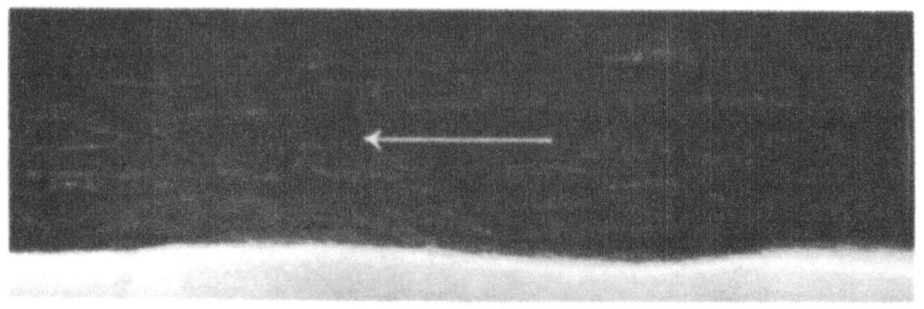

a. PHOTOGRAPH OF RIPPLE FORMATION

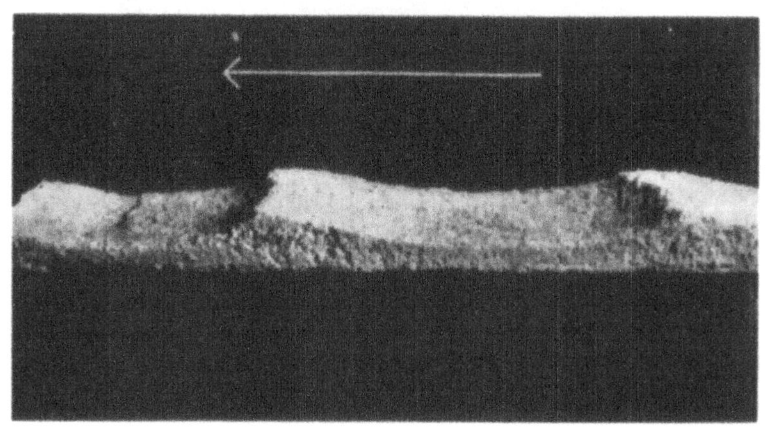

b. RIDGES PRODUCED IN THE WIND TUNNEL

Apart from a very temporary movement on the part of the few most exposed fine grains for which the threshold velocity is a minimum (Section 2), the *initial threshold wind* is that corresponding to the predominant diameter.

Here we must be careful to stipulate that the bed considered is limited in length, and that no sand is coming down from above the up-wind extremity of it; for only thus can we examine the true fluid threshold as distinct from the impact threshold, which will be dealt with in the next section.

If the wind is not increased above the initial fluid threshold strength, sand movement goes on until the grains of the predominant and smaller sizes have all been carried away from the exposed surface, leaving only those of larger diameter. Then the motion ceases. By raising the wind strength a further temporary movement is produced, and so on. Finally we are left with a much-lowered sand bed covered by a surface layer containing all the largest grains which were present in the removed layers.

If the wind strength is still further raised till the largest grains begin to move, the motion is no longer temporary, but goes on indefinitely till all the sand in the bed has gone. This *ultimate threshold* is that corresponding to the largest grains present in the bed.

Since the wind may drop before the ultimate threshold is reached, the sand may be left in any state of surface arrangement, and the wind strength required to move it again may be anything from the initial to the ultimate threshold. Nor is the surface isotropic, for, as we shall see in Chapters 10 and 11, the removal process collects the large protecting grains into ridges lying transversely to the wind direction, leaving the finer material in the hollows between them out of reach of either the wind or the saltation. So the threshold strength of the next wind that blows depends not only on the strength and duration of the previous wind but also on its relative direction. If the two are at right angles to one another the second wind can sweep along the hollows and disturb the now unprotected fine material in them.

With the sand of which dunes are composed things are simpler, for the biggest grains present are usually not more than twice the predominant diameter. Hence the ultimate threshold is commonly exceeded, and the transient stages occupy but a short range of wind strength.

5. THE IMPACT THRESHOLD WIND

This can be defined by the value of the wind gradient V_* at which the saltation produced by some artificial disturbance of the surface can just maintain itself indefinitely down-wind of the disturbance. Physically it marks the critical stage at which the energy supplied to the saltating grains by the wind begins to balance the energy losses due to friction when the grains strike the ground. There appears therefore to be little direct connexion between the impact threshold and the conditions at the surface which determine the fluid threshold.

Nevertheless the impact threshold gradient, for uniform sand of diameters between 0·25 mm. and 1 mm., seems from wind-tunnel experiments to follow the same square-root law as the fluid threshold but with a lower coefficient A of 0·08 instead of 0·1. The wind velocities measured at any height are therefore 20 per cent. slower than those for the fluid threshold. Measurements for sands above 1·0 mm. in diameter have not been made. For sands below 0·1 mm. the two thresholds appear to coincide.

For sands of mixed grain size the impact threshold is approximately that corresponding to the predominant diameter of the grains in surface creep.

In air the importance of the impact threshold wind condition lies in the fact that, as described in Chapter 5, the steady wind velocity at the critical height k' above a loose sand surface can never exceed the value reached at the impact threshold, no matter how strongly the wind may blow. The wind velocity does indeed rise momentarily to the higher, fluid, threshold before grain movement starts, but once the movement is started the drag immediately reduces the wind velocity at the level k' to the lower limiting value of the impact threshold. Thereafter fresh grains are raised into saltation, and the movement is maintained by the impact of the descending grains against the surface, and not by the direct force of the wind on the surface.

In water no corresponding action occurs, for the velocities are in this case relatively so much slower that the descending grains are incapable of ejecting other grains by impact. In water, therefore, there is but one threshold condition, the fluid threshold. And since, owing to the very small difference in density between water and sand, no appreciable extra drag is experienced by the water when the grain movement is started, the water velocity is not, as in the case of air, thereafter reduced to a lower value. The saltation continues to be maintained, as it was started, by the direct action of the water on the surface, and not by the impact of saltating grains.

As a corollary to the absence of an impact threshold condition in water, there is also no fixed focus of constant velocity near the surface when the flow is stronger, as is the case in air.

Chapter 8

SUMMARY OF THE PHYSICS OF GRAIN MOVEMENT IN AIR

1. THE FORCES ACTING ON SINGLE PARTICLES

THE movement of sand by wind is but one aspect of the wider subject of the carriage of solid particles of whatever kind by fluids in general. Great progress has been made in recent years both in our knowledge of the nature of the internal turbulent eddies within the fluid, caused by the presence of solid boundary walls, and in the effect of these eddies on the fluid flow as a whole. Much careful experimental work has also been devoted to the resistance offered by a fluid at rest to the motion through it of single particles of various shapes, sizes, and densities. But no general principles have so far been formulated whereby the precise effects which the presence of large numbers of such particles have upon the internal flow structure of the fluid surrounding them can be calculated.

The particles are acted upon by two forces; that of gravity downwards, and that of the fluid resistance in a direction opposite to the relative motion of the particle through the fluid. For particles of similar shape and of the same density moving through the fluid with equal velocities, the force of gravity is proportional to the cube of the linear size; and that of the fluid resistance is proportional to the square of the size. Hence the larger the particle, the more pronounced is the effect of gravity compared with that of the fluid resistance, and conversely for very small particles the fluid forces may be so great that the effect of gravity is negligible.

For identical particles moving through the fluid with different velocities the resistance is proportional to the square of the velocity, and to the density of the fluid. This relation, however, only holds good within limited ranges of the quantities involved. The factor of proportionality is only constant for a given value of a certain relation between velocity, particle size and fluid state known as the Reynolds' Number. In the case of spheres the factor has been found by experiment for all useful ranges of the Reynolds' Number.

The ratio of the force of fluid resistance to that of gravity acting on the particle, for any given relative velocity, is a useful concept which has been called the Susceptibility. When the two forces are equal the susceptibility is unity and the particle moves with uniform velocity. This equality occurs when a particle falls vertically through a fluid at rest, and the ultimate steady velocity attained is known as the Terminal Velocity.

The susceptibility of spheres can readily be found from established data, for all practical values of the relative velocity through the fluid, whether air or water; and from this it is possible to calculate with considerable accuracy the path which a spherical grain of any size will follow through a fluid, either at rest or in steady non-turbulent motion.

2. THE SIZE OF NATURAL PARTICLES IN TERMS OF THE EQUIVALENT SPHERICAL DIAMETER

Natural particles are not spheres; but in any natural collection of them one mean shape usually characterizes them all. If the collection is split up into a number of grades by sifting, the grains in each grade have a mean size which may, as a convenient approximation, be defined as that midway between the sizes of the apertures of the two sieves which isolated the grade. Experiment shows that natural grains, of any mean size as thus defined, after starting through a fluid with any initial velocity and direction, follow the same paths as those calculated for spheres of the same density and of a certain diameter. This diameter is equal to the mean diameter of the real grain multiplied by a suitable shape-factor. In the case of wind-blown desert sand this factor can be taken as 0·75.

3. THE TURBULENCE OF THE FLUID

The velocity of a fluid flowing between continuous boundary walls is zero very close to a wall, and increases with the distance from it. There are two types of flow, depending on the value of a Reynolds' Number in which the size dimension is in this case the separation of the walls from one another. When the fluid speed is relatively slow or the walls are close together the flow is streamline or laminar; that is, all elements of the fluid move steadily forward, and successive layers of faster-moving fluid situated at increasing distances from the wall slip smoothly past each other. But in nature streamline flow is rare. For the Reynolds' Number is usually too large, and when either the velocity or the spacing of the walls is increased beyond a certain limit, internal eddies are set up within the fluid. This means that portions of the fluid now have velocity components at right angles to the main direction of flow ; and in the case of horizontal flow over an open bed there are always portions of the fluid which are temporarily moving upwards as well as in other directions.

4. SUSPENSION, AND TRANSPORT ALONG THE FLOOR. DISTINCTION BETWEEN DUST (OR SILT) AND SAND

If the velocity of these upward currents is greater than the terminal velocity of fall of particles in them, the particles are carried up and travel in suspension, moving forward at the same mean speed as the fluid. The maximum velocity which the upward turbulence currents can attain increases with the height above the bed, but at low heights and over even ground it rarely exceeds one-fifth of the mean forward velocity at the height of measurement. Hence, since the terminal velocity of a grain increases with the grain's size, there exists for any given forward velocity of the fluid a critical grain diameter. Grains smaller than this diameter can be carried in suspension, to a greater extent as the size decreases. Such small grains constitute the dust of the atmosphere, and the fine silt of rivers. Grains larger than the critical diameter are not carried in suspension, but move along close to the bed, with which they collide repeatedly. These grains constitute sand.

In air, for the normal wind speeds prevailing on the earth's surface, the critical diameter is about 0·2 mm. ; and grains of this size are found to predominate in the finest sand—that which collects at the tops of dunes. In water, the speed of the current on which the critical diameter depends varies over a much wider range.

The upper limit to the size of sand grains is reached when the grains cease to be moved either by the strongest current or by the impact of other grains set in motion by it.

5. TURBULENT FLOW NEAR THE BED

If the fluid velocity is measured at a series of heights above the bed, and the results are plotted against a logarithmic scale of height, it is found that provided the flow is unaccelerated the plotted points always lie in a straight line. This straight line, when prolonged downwards, meets the ordinate of zero velocity at a point O (Fig. 15*b*, Chapter 4), which is at a certain small but definite height k above the level of the bed. If the surface is 'rough' (Chapter 7 (1)), the height k is equal to $\frac{1}{30}$ of the size of the surface irregularities, i.e. of the grain diameter d. Over any rough surface the velocity distribution according to the log-height is given for all strengths of the flow by a series of straight lines or velocity rays, all of which pass through the same point O on the axis. The stronger the flow the more is the velocity ray inclined away from the vertical.

The ratio $$\frac{\text{velocity difference}}{5{\cdot}75 \times \text{difference in log-height}}$$

between any two points on a velocity ray gives a quantity V_*, which is a measure of the velocity gradient of the flow. (The 'difference in log-height' in the above expression may also be written 'logarithm of the height ratio'.) The fluid velocity v, as measured at any height z, the gradient V_*, and the roughness of the bed k, are all related by the equation

$$v_z = 5{\cdot}75 V_* \log \frac{z}{k} \quad . \quad . \quad . \quad (1)$$

6. THE DRAG τ, AND THE DRAG VELOCITY V_*

V_* is also a measure of the drag τ dynes per sq. cm., which the fluid exerts on the bed, according to the equation

$$V_* = \sqrt{\frac{\tau}{\rho}} \quad . \quad . \quad . \quad . \quad (2)$$

where ρ is the density of the fluid ($1{\cdot}22 \times 10^{-3}$ gm./cm.^{3} for atmospheric air, and 1 for fresh water). As thus defined V_* is called the Drag Velocity. Its value is equal to that obtained from the velocity distribution in the case when the flow is steady and the bed reasonably flat. When the flow is made to converge, so that the fluid is accelerated, the drag velocity is greater close to the surface than the value given by the velocity gradient higher up. This condition occurs on the up-stream side of a raised mound in the bed. Conversely, on the lee side of the mound, where the flow is diverging and the fluid is retarded, the drag on the surface is less than that given by the velocity gradient.

7. FLOW OVER A FLAT SURFACE WHOSE TEXTURE CHANGES ACROSS A TRANSVERSE BORDER. THE BOUNDARY LAYER

If the mean size of the surface irregularities suddenly changes across a transverse border from d_1 on the up-stream side to d_2 on the down-stream side, the level of zero fluid velocity which was at a height $k_1 = d_1/30$ above the bed level, falls abruptly to a lower height $k_2 = d_2/30$. Hence the fluid in the layer just above k_1 is accelerated till it reaches a new and faster velocity, as shown in Fig. 16 of Chapter 4. As the fluid continues its course this change of speed is gradually communicated upwards to the higher layers, and eventually the whole fluid takes up a new velocity distribution such that the gradient is the same as before, but the fluid has increased its speed by the same amount at all heights. The new velocity distribution can be represented graphically by a velocity ray parallel to the previous one, but displaced in the direction of greater velocity.

Similarly, when the fluid encounters a change of surface texture in the opposite sense, from a smaller grain to a larger, the bottom layer of fluid is checked, and the checking slowly spreads upwards as the flow continues down-stream.

Therefore, as we go down-stream from the border, the space next to the surface is occupied by a layer of fluid of increasing thickness in which the change of speed initiated at the border has been completed: and above this layer the fluid has not yet had news of the existence of the border. At a great distance down-stream the boundary layer comprises the whole fluid.

At any distance down-stream the thickness of the layer is proportional to the change in the size of the surface irregularity, and is independent of the velocity.

8. THE FLUID THRESHOLD OF FLOW REQUIRED TO MOVE GRAINS ON THE BED

The Reynolds' Number characterizing the flow close to the surface is $\frac{V_* d}{\nu}$, where d is the mean size of the surface roughness, which is of the same order as the grain diameter, and ν the kinematic viscosity of the fluid has a value of 0·14 for air and of 0·01 for water, both under atmospheric conditions, and in C.G.S. units.

If $\frac{V_* d}{\nu} > 3{\cdot}5$ the surface is 'rough', and the threshold velocity gradient V_{*t} which must be attained by the fluid before it can move any surface grains varies as the square root of the grain diameter according to the equation

$$V_{*t} = A\sqrt{\frac{\sigma - \rho}{\rho} gd} \quad . \quad . \quad . \quad (3)$$

From this the threshold velocity v_t at any height z above the surface is given by

$$v_t = 5{\cdot}75\, A\sqrt{\frac{\sigma - \rho}{\rho} gd} \log \frac{z}{k} \quad . \quad . \quad (4)$$

where σ is the density of the grain material (2·65 for quartz). For air the coefficient A is equal to 0·1, and for water it is nearly 0·2. The above holds in air for grains exceeding 0·2 mm. diameter, and in water for grains exceeding 0·6 mm.

For smaller grains, when $\frac{V_* d}{\nu} < 3{\cdot}5$, the surface approaches the 'smooth' condition, and the flow very close to it begins to obey different laws. The coefficient A is no longer constant, but increases as the grains become smaller and smaller. The threshold value of V_* reaches a minimum, and thereafter grows bigger, till for very fine grains the initial movement of individual grains is not easily effected by the fluid.

In the case of beds of mixed grain size, the grains which are first moved by a fluid whose velocity is slowly increased are those which are most exposed. The threshold velocity therefore depends on the past history of the surface as well as on the size grading of the bed. If the bed material has been spread out mechanically so that grains of all sizes are exposed on the surface, the grains first moved are those for which V_{*t} is a minimum. These are generally few in number and are soon carried away. For practical purposes, therefore, the initial threshold velocity is that required to move the grains of the predominant diameter. As these are carried away, the diameter of the remaining surface grains increases, and the threshold velocity rises progressively as the removal continues. The ultimate threshold velocity is that corresponding to the diameter of the largest grains present in the bed mixture. The above presupposes that no fine grains are coming down from up-stream to replace those removed from the surface.

9. SAND MOVEMENT IN AIR AND WATER. THE SALTATION DRAG

Up to this point the physics applies equally to a sand bed in air or in water. But once the grain movement has started, the conditions are very different in the two media. This is due to the great difference in the ratio of the density of the grain to that of the fluid. In air quartz grains are 2,000 times as dense as the fluid, but in water they are only 2·65 times as dense (1·65 if buoyancy is taken into account).

This difference in the density ratio is manifest in two ways:

(1) *The impact mechanism.* In air, the grains, when once set in motion along the surface, strike other stationary grains, and either themselves bounce high (a distance measured in hundreds if not thousands of grain diameters) into the relatively tenuous fluid, or eject other grains upwards to a similar height. The bouncing grains therefore attain forward speeds of the same order as that of the fluid at this high level. On descending (at an angle whose tangent is approximately the ratio of the forward velocity to the terminal velocity of fall, and varies between 10° and 16°), they strike the surface with sufficient momentum to eject other grains to as great a height. The subsequent grain motion further downstream is maintained, in the case of air, by this ejection of grains by the impacts of preceding ones, and not by the picking-up of new grains by the fluid itself, since, for reasons given below, the surface velocity of the air during sand movement is limited to a smaller value than the initial fluid threshold.

If the physics of this impact-ejection mechanism is applied to sand in water, it is found that the impact momentum of the descending grains is insufficient to raise surface grains to a height greater than a small fraction of one grain diameter. And observation confirms that at fluid velocities correspondingly near the threshold of movement, the grains, though they do follow much the same downwardly curved paths (saltation) as in air, are raised by the direct force of the water upon them, and only rise to heights of a few grain diameters. The saltation in water cannot therefore be maintained by grain impact.

(2) *The drag due to the saltation.* The ejected grain starts with little or no forward velocity, but before ending its path through the fluid by an impact with the surface, it has attained a velocity very nearly equal to that of the fluid in the layer at the top of its path. The momentum gained, which is all destroyed on impact, has been extracted from the fluid. When a large number of grains are in saltation, the rate at which momentum is continually being

extracted in this way is equivalent to a steady force or drag resisting the flow of the fluid. This saltation drag is a maximum at a level above the surface approximately equal to the height of the top of the mean path traced out by the grains.

In the case of sand in air the momentum extracted by each grain during one bound is equal to that given up in completely stopping a volume of air 2,000 times the volume of the grain. The saltation drag in air is therefore very large, and renders negligible the residual surface drag due to fluid friction against the stationary surface below. As a result the velocity of the air in the layer below the top of the mean grain path is entirely controlled by the intensity of the saltation of sand grains below. The greater the number of grains in saltation the greater is the drag; and experiment shows that under steady conditions a balance is maintained, such that, however large may be the velocity gradient of the wind, the velocity V_t at a certain fixed height k' above the surface remains constant. The velocity closer to the surface is actually reduced as the wind above is made stronger. Hence, at the level of the top of the stationary surface grains, the wind velocity is less than the fluid threshold, and the wind is prevented from picking up any more grains from the surface by its own direct action.

The sand flow q (the mass of sand moving along a lane of unit width past a fixed transverse line in unit time) is found in air to depend only on the velocity gradient of the wind above the mean level of the saltation, and on the size-grading of the grains. It appears to be independent of the existence or otherwise of small-scale surface features—ripples, &c.—caused by the flow.

A fluid of the density of water, on the other hand, has a momentum so much greater per unit volume, that the amount extracted in imparting the same motion to a grain of the same size is equal to that given up by stopping a volume of the fluid only twice the volume of the grain. The amount by which the flow of water is checked by the same number of grains in saltation is therefore but a thousandth as great as in the case of air. So the saltation drag is negligible. The water experiences only the frictional drag due to the stationary bed plus the 'form drag' of the hillocks and pockets which the sand movement builds in the bed surface. Since the former is likely to remain constant for any given value of the velocity gradient V_* the sand flow q must depend on the shape assumed by the bed as a whole and by the surface features formed in its bottom by the sand flow itself.

Research has so far been unsuccessful in correlating this shape with the value of V_* for the flow causing it.

10. SAND MOVEMENT IN AIR. WIND VELOCITY DISTRIBUTION

The velocity of the air above the surface during sand movement varies with the log-height according to a straight-line relation, as in Section 5. But the straight velocity rays for different strengths of wind pass through a new fixed focus. This focus, instead of lying on the ordinate of zero velocity at a height k equal to $\frac{1}{30}$ of the surface roughness size (Fig. 18, Chapter 5) now lies at a fixed height k' of the same order of magnitude as the height of the surface ripple formed by the sand flow, and on an ordinate corresponding to a fixed velocity V_t determined by the diameter of the surface grains. The wind velocity v_z at any height z conforms approximately to the following modification of equation (1)

$$v_z = 5{\cdot}75V_* \log\frac{z}{k'} + V_t \quad . \quad . \quad . \quad (5)$$

The height k' is of the order of 0·3 cm. for a fine uniform sand and 1 cm. for normal dune sand. V_t is the impact threshold velocity (see below) for the sand in question, as measured at the height k' above the surface.

11. THE IMPACT THRESHOLD

A continuous saltation of grains can be maintained for an indefinite distance down-stream by a wind of feebler strength than the fluid threshold, provided that the sand surface further up is kept disturbed by the impact of oncoming grains upon it. The threshold wind strength at which this is possible marks the critical stage at which the energy supplied to the saltating grains by the wind just balances the energy losses due to friction when the grains strike the ground.

In water there appears to be no lower threshold of this nature, for the saltation is not maintained by grain impact, but by the direct drag of the fluid on the surface grains.

For sand grains of diameter 0·25 mm. and over, the impact threshold wind has been found by experiment, both as a gradient V_{*t} and as a velocity to be measured at any given height, to be given by equations (3) and (4) if the coefficient A is made equal to 0·08 instead of 0·1. For grains of smaller diameter, the impact threshold appears to approach closer to the fluid threshold, and it probably ceases to exist as a separate threshold at the critical grain size for which V_{*_t} is a minimum.

Once sand movement has started, either by the direct action of a stronger wind at or above the fluid threshold, or by the artificial stimulation of the surface under a wind at or above the impact threshold, the extra drag due to the movement prevents the velocity of the surface wind at the height k' from rising above the impact threshold, no matter how strongly the wind above is subsequently made to blow.

The value of V_t in equation (5) is given by equation (4) if A is made equal to 0·08, and z to k'. So

$$V_t = 5{\cdot}75\, A \sqrt{\frac{\sigma - \rho}{\rho} g d} \log \frac{k'}{k} \qquad (6)$$

and for air and quartz grains

$$V_t = 680 \sqrt{d} \log \frac{30}{d} \text{ in C.G.S. units} \qquad (6a)$$

For sands of mixed grain size, d must be taken as the diameter of the mean surface grain. This is generally larger than the mean diameter of the underlying bed.

12. SALTATION AND SURFACE CREEP. SAND FLOW IN TERMS OF WIND STRENGTH

Of the total sand in motion in air about three-quarters moves in saltation and a quarter in surface creep. The surface creep consists of the slow jerky advance of the surface grains which are knocked along the surface by the impact of the descending saltation rather than ejected upwards into the air stream. An impact by a grain from the saltation can move a surface grain in this manner, even though the latter is six times its own diameter. Hence a saltation of fine grains can maintain a surface creep over a bed composed of grains far too large to be moved by the direct action of the wind.

The whole sand movement q depends upon the mean grain diameter, on the degree of uniformity of grain size, and on the velocity gradient V'_* of the wind above the sand cloud, according to the equation

$$q = C \sqrt{\frac{d}{D}} \frac{\rho}{g} {V'_*}^3 \qquad (7)$$

where D is a standard grain diameter of 0·025 cm. and C is a coefficient having the following values:

1·5 for nearly uniform sand,
1·8 for naturally graded sand such as is found on dunes,
2·8 for a sand of a very wide range of grain size.

In the extreme case where the surface grains are so large as to be immobile (pebble and rock surfaces) the value of C is considerably greater and may exceed 3·5.

It follows from the above that (1) the sand movement increases very rapidly with the wind strength, and (2) there is a tendency to deposition of sand on to the surface whenever a sand stream which has been picked up from and transported over a surface containing large grains reaches an area where the surface grains are finer and more uniform.

In terms of the wind velocity v as measured at a standard height of 1 metre above the bed, the flow q of average dune sand is given by

$$q = 1{\cdot}5 \times 10^{-9}\,(v - V_t)^3 \text{ in C.G.S. units} \qquad (8)$$

The relation between v and q is given in the form of a curve in Fig. 22, Chapter 5.

13. THE MEAN GRAIN PATH OF THE SALTATION AND THE WAVELENGTH OF THE SURFACE RIPPLE IN AIR

From evidence supplied by the velocity distribution of the wind within the layer occupied by the sand cloud, it is possible to measure the level at which the saltation drag is a maximum, for any given value of V'_*. This level is assumed to indicate the height of the top of the mean path followed by the grains during their bounds from impact to impact. Calculation of the path of an ideal grain which would rise to this measured height in the same wind distribution, yields a value for the horizontal range of the path which agrees well with the measured wavelength of the ripples formed on the sand surface. There is evidence, therefore, that the ripple wavelength of blown sand in air is a manifestation of the length of the mean path followed by the grains in saltation. The ripple wavelength is a minimum at the impact threshold wind strength, and increases with V'_*. When V'_* reaches a value between $3V_{*t}$ and $4V_{*t}$, the ripples flatten out and disappear.

PART II

SMALL-SCALE EFFECTS. GRAIN SIZE DISTRIBUTION. SURFACE RIPPLES AND RIDGES

Chapter 9

GRADING DIAGRAMS

1. MECHANICAL ANALYSIS

THE technique of sampling fine particulate materials, of measuring the particle size, and of defining the proportionate size make-up of the material has of recent years been studied very carefully in the U.S.A. by Wentworth, Krumbein, and others, and a wealth of useful detail will be found in a book by Krumbein and Pettijohn.[1] An excellent bibliography on the subject of the measurement of small particles by sifting, elutriation, and other methods is given in a paper by Heywood.[2]

The collection of the sample in the first instance requires some care, because if the piling of a naturally deposited sand bed is disturbed in any way an immediate change in the distribution of the grains takes place ; the fine material tends to filter downwards through the body of the sand, and the biggest grains roll down the outsides of all steep slopes formed during the disturbance. If a sample is wanted of the sand in a special place—in some particular layer, or at the top of a ripple, for example—it is best simply to push a straight-sided thin-walled sample tube steadily into the undisturbed material till the tube is nearly full. A number of such samples can be taken, mixed together, and the total quantity reduced, if necessary, by quartering. If, on the other hand, a sample is wanted of the average sand of a larger mass, or if an unavoidably large quantity has been

[1] Krumbein and Pettijohn. *Manual of Sedimentary Petrology.* (Appleton-Century.)

[2] Heywood, H. (1939). *Proc. Inst. Mech. Eng.*, 140.

obtained artificially—say, in the collecting box of the wind tunnel—the whole mass must be reduced to a weight sufficiently small for analysis. This is done by the well-known method of quartering.

The usual and most practical method of analysing a sample of sand in order to find the proportions in which the grains of each size are present, is by sifting through a series of sieves, beginning with the one having the largest aperture.

The sample is passed successively through the sieves, and the separated material is weighed. Finally each weight is divided by the total weight of the sample in order to turn it into a percentage.

The problem now is how to display the resulting figures so that the composition of the sand by grain size can be most conveniently studied. The particular method used depends largely on the purpose for which the information is wanted, and on the outlook of the user. Most methods are diagrammatic. The essential need is to plot some measure of the *frequency of occurrence* of grains of a certain size against some measure of that *size*.

If the user is a practical engineer, or a sand merchant, interested in the grading of the sand only in so far as it affects the quality of structural concrete, if he is not concerned either with the mutual relations between grains of one size and those of another, or with the manner in which the original deposit at the sand pit was laid down by nature, and, further, if he is only interested in a narrow range of grain size, then the simplest measure of the grain size is the actual mean diameter as obtained from the size of the sieve aperture. An ordinary linear scale of grain diameter is therefore all that is wanted as abscissa on the diagram. But, as has already been emphasized in Chapter 1 and elsewhere, the linear scale, which exhibits the *differences* between the measures (in this case the grain diameters), is not necessarily the most useful or convenient scale to use when natural processes are to be examined. It is more often far better to use a log-scale which exhibits the *ratios* between the measures.

Krumbein [1] has advocated the use of a quantity ϕ which is the logarithm to the base 2 of the grain diameter, because of the prevalence of standard sets of sieves having a ratio of 2 or $\sqrt{2}$ between successive sieve sizes. I prefer to keep the method of representation independent of the sieve sizes, and to use the

[1] Krumbein, W. C. (1938). *J. of Sedimentary Petrology*, 8, p. 84.

common logarithm to the base 10, for which tables are in every-day use.

2. THE ‘ PERCENTAGE-SMALLER ’ DIAGRAM

In this the vertical scale is marked off in percentages, with zero at the bottom and 100 at the top. As each sieve is used, the percentage weight of all that has passed through it is plotted against the size of the sieve aperture as read off the horizontal diameter scale. Starting at the top a series of points is thus obtained, until the weight passing through the finest sieve is negligible (zero). The ordinate of the diagram therefore gives the percentage of all the sand of grain diameter smaller than that of the corresponding abscissa. Fig. 30 is such a diagram; the data from which it was constructed is given in Columns 2 and 3 below:

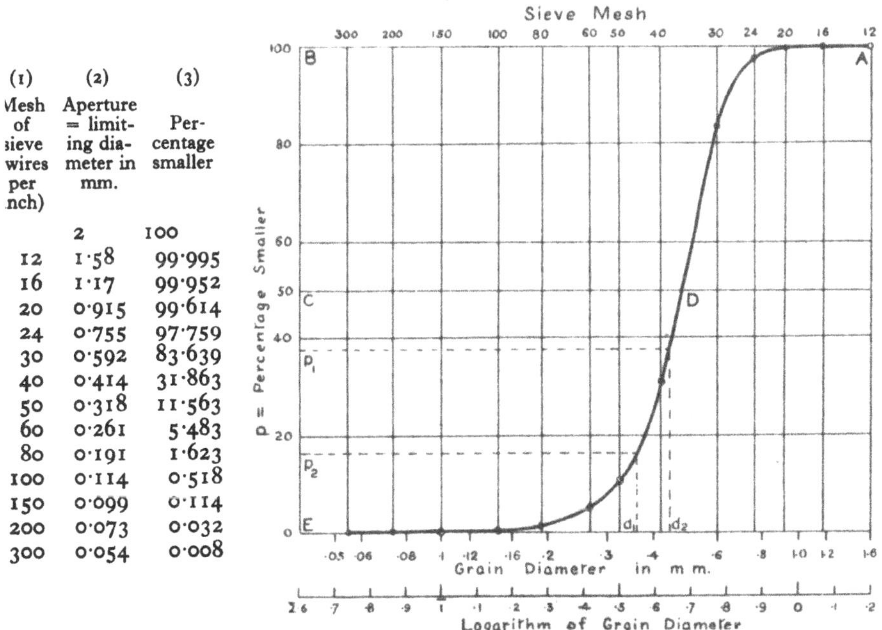

(1) Mesh of sieve wires per inch)	(2) Aperture = limiting diameter in mm.	(3) Percentage smaller
	2	100
12	1·58	99·995
16	1·17	99·952
20	0·915	99·614
24	0·755	97·759
30	0·592	83·639
40	0·414	31·863
50	0·318	11·563
60	0·261	5·483
80	0·191	1·623
100	0·114	0·518
150	0·099	0·114
200	0·073	0·032
300	0·054	0·008

FIG. 30.—PERCENTAGE-SMALLER DIAGRAM

If we want to know the percentage of sand present whose grain size lies between any two given limits, say d_1 and d_2, the answer is given by the difference $p_1 - p_2$ between the corresponding ordinates. To find the predominant diameter we can, theoretically, take a set of diameters separated by equal intervals, say by the ratio $\sqrt{2}$, and note the percentage differences. The predominant diameter clearly occurs at the steepest part of the curve, at the point where the greatest interval is to be found between the ordinates. Unfortunately, owing to the shape of the curves met with in practice, the steepest part cannot be found by inspection, and various approximations are used to define in some arbitrary manner the mean diameter of the sample. The most common definition is that diameter through which a vertical line can be drawn which will cut off equal areas above on the right and below on the left. Only if the curve is symmetrical (skew symmetry) about the 50 per cent. line will this mean diameter coincide with either the 50 per cent. mean or with the predominant diameter as defined by the steepest part of the curve.

Some idea can be got of the degree of uniformity of the sample from the slope of the curve at its steepest part (for an entirely uniform sand the curve becomes a vertical straight line); but the usual method of defining the rates at which the proportions of the side-grades of greater and smaller diameter fall off is by Kramer's Uniformity Modulus M. This is the ratio of the area CDE to the area ABCD. But since the position of the vertical line BE on the log-diameter scale must be arbitrary (a log-scale having no zero), Kramer[1] used a linear diameter scale. The position of his line BE was then made that of zero grain diameter.

The percentage-smaller curve has the advantage that it can be plotted directly from the sifting data, and is independent of the sizes of the sieves used in the analysis. On the other hand, as a means of displaying for subsequent use the true size composition of a sand sample, it has little to recommend it.

3. THE BLOCK DIAGRAM

This has been used to some extent by geomorphologists and others. Here the actual percentage weight of any grade, as defined by the diameter interval between the sieves, is given as the height of a rectangle, as shown in Fig. 31. The total length of all the rectangles added together end to end is therefore equal to 100. The diagram as it stands has the outstanding

[1] Krumbein and Pettijohn. *Manual of Sedimentary Petrology.* (Appleton-Century.)

defect that the heights of the ordinates depend on the interval between the sieves. This is partially overcome by using special sets of sieves whose apertures are very carefully chosen to give grain diameters bearing exactly the same ratio to one another—usually 2 or $\sqrt{2}$; so that the heights represent percentage weights per (some arbitrary common) multiple of diameter. But

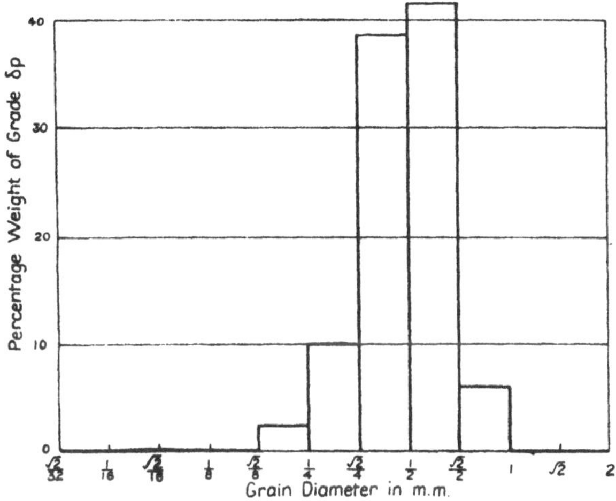

FIG. 31.—THE BLOCK DIAGRAM

even so, the diagram is a function of the diameter interval used, and cannot represent an inherent property of the sand. For instance, if the interval is halved, say from 2 to $\sqrt{2}$, the heights of all the rectangles are also halved, for there is now less sand in each grade. In the extreme case of an infinite number of sieves, the ordinates would all be infinitely short, and we should be left with no diagram at all.

4. THE DIFFERENTIAL DIAGRAM

This difficulty is overcome very simply by dividing each percentage weight p by the interval between its diameter limits d_1 and d_2. When the logarithm, R, of the diameter is used as a measure of grain size and is plotted as abscissa on the diagram, this diameter interval is given by $R_1 - R_2 = (\log d_1 - \log d_2)$ or $\log \frac{d_1}{d_2}$.

The new ordinate N[1] now represents $\frac{\text{percentage weight}}{\text{diameter interval}}$, and the area of each rectangular block represents the percentage weight of the sand of that particular grade. The area of the whole diagram is the weight of the whole sample, which we have made equal to 100 units at the beginning.

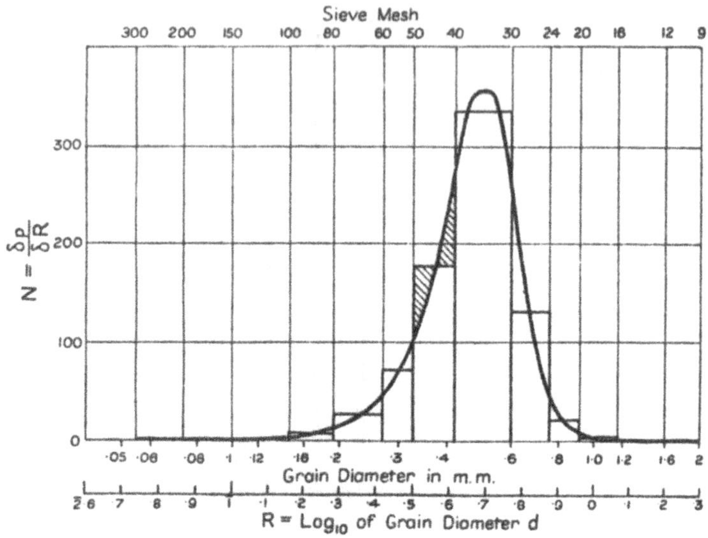

FIG. 32.—THE DIFFERENTIAL DIAGRAM

Finally, by drawing a continuous line as shown in Fig. 32, so that the pairs of little shaded areas cut off and added to each rectangle are equal to one another, we get a curve which is entirely independent of the sieve sizes used in the analysis. We are, therefore, no longer under the necessity of using any special set of sieves. Fig. 32 has been constructed from the same data as Fig. 30, so the two curves can be compared.

The numerical value of N—over 300 in some cases—is due to the fact that N is the percentage weight of sand *per unit of*

[1] In my original paper I used the symbol ø for this quantity. Since I now find that Krumbein (loq. cit.) has used it in the same type of diagram for another quantity $\log_2$ (diameter of grain), I have substituted the letter N. In any case the symbol ø should perhaps be avoided, as it is often used to signify ' diameter '.

the log-diameter scale. If preferred N can be divided by 100 so as to give the percentage per *log-cent.* change of diameter. Since, however, it is often very useful to use the logarithm of N, it is best to retain the high values in order to avoid negative values of the logarithm.

To the mathematically minded it will be apparent that if δR is the logarithm of the small interval d_1/d_2 between two consecutive sieve sizes, and δp is the corresponding weight of sand isolated by them, the ordinate N is equal to $\frac{\delta p}{\delta R}$; and if an infinite number of sieves were used $N = \frac{dp}{dR}$. Hence the ordinates of the curve in Fig. 32 are the first differential coefficients of the curve of Fig. 30. The height of the peak in Fig. 32 is numerically equal to the steepest slope of the curve of Fig. 30, and its position is that of the predominant diameter.

The advantage of Fig. 32 is that the predominant diameter, which is for many purposes the most important quality of the sand, can be seen at a glance, whereas in Fig. 30 it is not at all easily found.

5. THE LOG DIAGRAM

The methods of representation in both Figs. 30 and 32 suffer from the same serious disadvantage. The proportions in which the extremely fine and extremely big grains are present in the sample are too small to be plotted at all. For this reason they have in the past invariably been neglected. Consequently, since it is difficult to use sieves separated by a narrower diameter ratio than $\sqrt{2}$, there are insufficient points on the curves to attempt any generalization as to the laws governing the rates at which the grades fall off on either side of the predominant or peak diameter.

It occurred to the writer to remedy this by plotting N on a log-scale, by which, as we have seen, all values, however small, are given equal prominence.

The results [1] soon suggested the interesting likelihood that the grading of all naturally deposited sands tends towards one simple law. Experimental corroboration will be described in the next chapter, but as its implications cannot be readily grasped without some familiarity with the quantities involved and the special

[1] Bagnold, R. A. (1937). *Proc. Roy. Soc. A.*, 163, p. 250.

method of representation which is needed, the remainder of this chapter will be devoted to their examination.

In Fig. 33 the same data as before have been used, and the curve is that of Fig. 32 with its ordinates converted into their logarithms. The complete operation involved in arriving at the numerical figures will be made sufficiently clear by the following table.

Sieve	Diameter in mm.	$\delta R = \log \frac{d_1}{d_2}$	δp = per cent. weight	$N = \frac{\delta p}{\delta R}$	$y = \log N$
	2·000	·102	0·005	0·049	$\bar{2}$·69
12	1·58	·130	0·043	0·331	$\bar{1}$·52
16	1·17	·107	0·338	3·16	0·50
20	0·915	·0828	1·855	22·4	1·35
24	0·755	·107	14·12	132	2·12
30	0·592	·155	51·776	334	2·52
40	0·414	·114	20·3	178	2·25
50	0·318	·084	6·08	72·4	1·86
60	0·261	·137	3·86	28·2	1·45
80	0·191	·124	1·105	8·91	0·95
100	0·144	·1614	0·404	2·51	0·40
150	0·099	·133	0·082	0·617	$\bar{1}$·79
200	0·073	·133	0·024	0·182	$\bar{1}$·26
300	0·054		0·008		

The operation is not lengthy, since the first three columns refer only to the set of sieves used, and remain the same for every analysis done with it.

It is now for the first time apparent that outside a definite central zone the grades to right and left of the peak fall off each at its own constant rate ; this means that we are again confronted with the same logarithmic law of distribution which runs through the whole subject.

It should be noted here that if log N had been plotted against a linear scale of grain diameter instead of a log-scale, this important relation between the frequency of occurrence and the diameter would not have been detected. This fact provides yet another indication that the ratio scale of grain diameter is a more natural one than the linear scale. In addition, as Krumbein has pointed out,[1] the average grading diagram for natural sand deposits is

[1] Loq. cit.

nearly symmetrical when plotted on a ratio scale of diameter, but is very far from symmetrical on a linear scale.

The two straight arms of the curve, if continued upwards, meet in a point O which we will call the *Peak*. Its coordinates will be

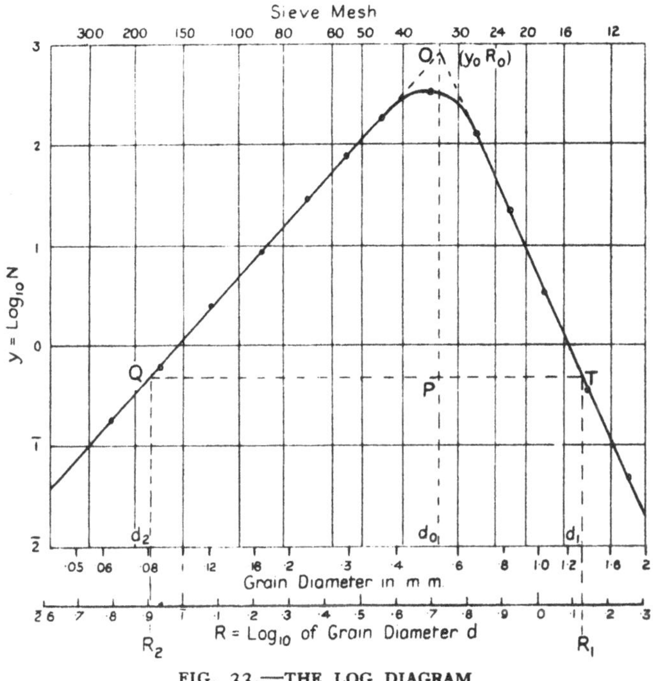

FIG. 33.—THE LOG DIAGRAM

called y_0 and R_0, where $y_0 = \log N_0$, and $R_0 = \log d_0$, d_0 being defined as the *Peak Diameter*.

Taking any two points y_1, R_1, and y_2, R_2, on the right and left arms of the curve, the slope of each arm is given by

$$c = \frac{y_0 - y_1}{R_0 - R_1} \text{ for the coarse grades on the right;}$$

$$s = \frac{y_0 - y_2}{R_0 - R_2} \text{ for the small grades on the left.}$$

Now $y_0 - y_1 = \log N_0 - \log N_1$, or $\log \dfrac{N_0}{N_1}$

and $R_0 - R_1 = \log d_0 - \log d_1$, or $\log \dfrac{d_0}{d_1}$

hence $\log \frac{N_0}{N_1} = c \log \frac{d_0}{d_1}$ for the coarse grades

or $$\frac{N_0}{N_1} = \left(\frac{d_0}{d_1}\right)^c$$

Similarly, for the small grades—

$$\frac{N_0}{N_2} = \left(\frac{d_0}{d_2}\right)^s$$

I have called c and s the *coarse-grade coefficient* and *small-grade coefficient*, respectively. It will be noted that c must always be negative because N decreases on the right as d increases. The grading coefficients c and s define the rates at which the side-grades fall off in proportional weight as the grain diameter departs from the peak size. Their values can readily be measured off the diagram by dividing the vertical interval between any two points on the straight arms by the horizontal interval between them, using in each case the logarithm scale for measurement. Alternatively c and s can be found directly from the curve of Fig. 32 by dividing the log of the ratio of the N values, at any two points sufficiently far away from the peak, by the log of the diameter ratio between them.

Experiment appears to show that the gradients c and s of the two arms of the log curve are to a large extent independent of one another, and that during a cycle of sand movement changes in the inclination of one arm have little or no effect on the other. Hence if we define the lack of uniformity of the sand by a single quantity W, it is clear that this quantity must be expressed as a function of both c and s. The simplest definition of the *Width W* of the size distribution seems to be the ratio of the length of the base QT of any such triangle as OQT in the figure to its height OP. We then have

$$\frac{1}{W} = \frac{1}{s} - \frac{1}{c} \text{ (remembering that } c \text{ is negative).}$$

6. SYMMETRICAL GRADED SANDS. COMPARISON WITH THE 'NORMAL PROBABILITY CURVE'

In the case of a symmetrical sand the angles QOP and TOP are equal, and $s = -c$. A practical example is given by the continuous curve of Fig. 34*a*. The data for this came from the analysis of a sand at the base of a desert dune. The curve is

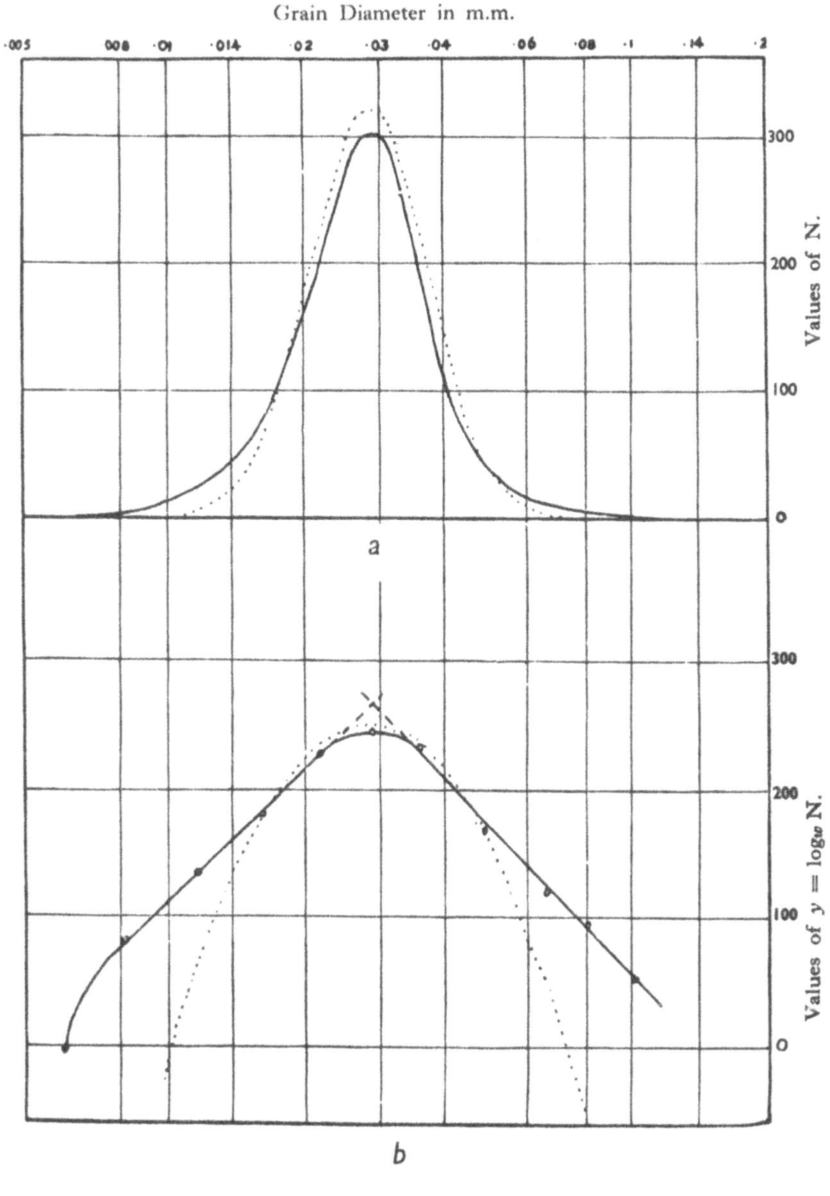

FIG. 34.—COMPARISON OF SAND-GRADING CURVE (HEAVY LINE) WITH PROBABILITY CURVE (DOTTED)

a, ordinates on usual linear scale; *b*, ordinates on log scale

almost but not quite symmetrical about the peak ordinate. The shape of such a curve so much resembles that of the 'normal probability curve' that it has been held by some that the grading of sands is a random phenomenon. If this is true the frequency of occurrence N′ of those grains which depart from the most frequent log-diameter R_0 by an interval $R - R_0$ should be given by the probability equation

$$N' = \frac{a}{\sqrt{\pi}} e^{-a^2(R-R_0)^2}$$

where a is a modulus defining the degree of probability. The dotted curve gives the grain distribution according to this equation, with a chosen so as to make the curve approximate as closely as possible to that of the actual sample.

In Fig. 34*b* N has been replaced by $y = \log N$, as in Fig. 33. The normal probability curve now becomes a parabola $y' = -a^2(R - R_0)^2 + \log B$, whereas that of the actual sand sample is seen to depart very considerably from it and to resemble a hyperbola. From the results of many analyses of sand samples it seems clear that if sand grading is a random phenomenon, from which conclusion it is difficult to escape, then some special probability function must be looked for.

7. REGULAR AND MIXED SANDS

I have called *Regular Sands* those whose grading conforms to the simple arrangement we have been considering, whether symmetrical or not. The results of both wind-tunnel experiments and observations in the open desert go to show that all homogeneous sand deposits (eolian) laid down under steady conditions of wind and of up-wind sand supply are regular; and their grading can be completely defined by the three quantities R_0, c, and s.

When, however, the conditions change—the wind's strength alters or it changes its direction—and deposition happens to continue, the new superimposed deposit may have a different grading. In this case, if a sample is dug out of the deposit, it may contain portions of both the lower and the upper layers, and these portions may be present in it in any ratio. Subsequent analysis will give a *Mixed Sand* whose grading is no longer regular.

For examples of grading differences between various layers of deposited sand one has but to look at the cut faces of sand pits or at weathered sandstone cliffs. Numerous analyses which I have made of samples of dune sand show quite appreciable differences in the grading at the same spot between sand at the surface and 6 inches down. In general the stratification of eolian deposits indicate that really steady conditions rarely last long enough to build up homogeneous layers more than a few millimetres thick; but within the body of a dune the differences between such layers are usually of a very minor nature—a slight shifting of the peak diameter, for example—which have only the effect of flattening out the rounded part of the curve in its neighbourhood. But more considerable grading differences may occur—for instance, when a dune moves over an existing sand bed and the coarse sand at its foot becomes mixed with the finer sand of the bed. The dune may subsequently move on elsewhere, leaving an otherwise unaccountable zone of irregular grading.

Let us consider the diagrammatical representation of a mixture of two regular sands A and B added together in the proportions 2 parts of A to 3 parts of B, A being the coarser sand of the two. Their compositions are given by the two curves of Fig. 35. Since we are dealing throughout with percentages, the areas under each are equal and represent 100 units. Therefore, in order that the area under the curve representing the mixture shall also be 100 units, we must first reduce all the ordinates of the curve A to two-fifths of their original height, and those of B to three-fifths. The reduced curves are shown by the broken lines of Fig. 36. We can now add the heights of the two sets of ordinates together and arrive at the curve of the resulting mixture, which is given by the heavy line.

The mixture, with its two components, is shown on the log-diagram in Fig. 37. It should be noted particularly that in this case the reduction of all the ordinates in any constant ratio merely consists of subtracting the log of that ratio from each of them, so that the curves are lowered bodily without altering their gradients or their shapes.

The log-diagram is clearly preferable for the more practical reverse process of finding the regular components of a sand sample whose grading data are known. Taking the example of Fig. 37, we can proceed as follows:

(i) The straightness of the right-hand arm is evidence that over this range of diameters the coarser component A predominates, and the slope gives the value of c_A at once.

(ii) At any point of intersection of the component arms y must be the same for each, so that N for the mixture is doubled,

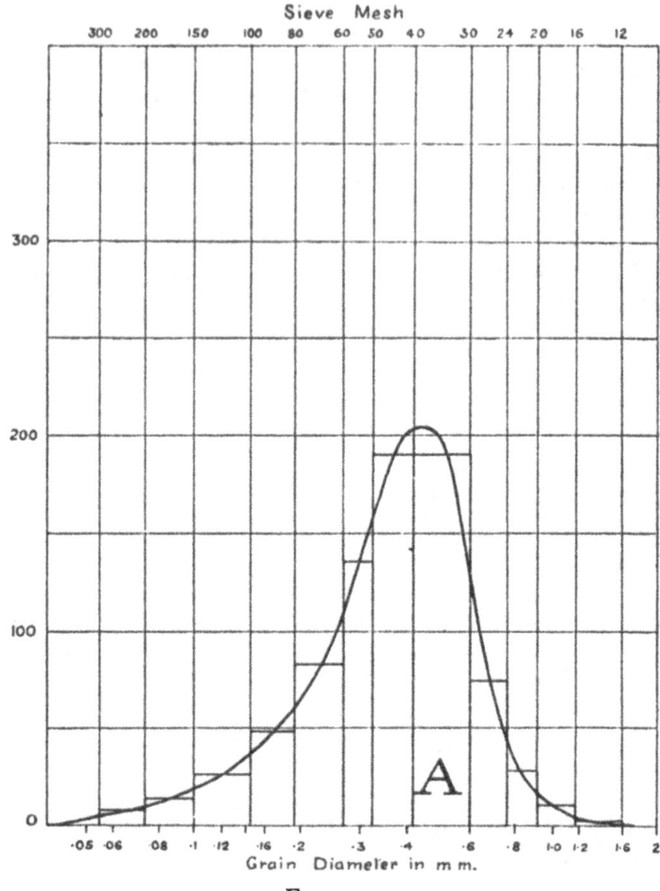

FIG. 35*a*

FIG. 35.—GRADING OF TWO

and the height of the combined curve must be a distance of log 2 = 0·3 above the intersection. Taking an ordinate midway between the peaks and measuring down a distance of 0·3 gives us the approximate point of intersection of the *s*-arm of A and the *c*-arm of B.

(iii) That the *s* (left-hand) arm of the combined curve is not straight is evidence that the A component reappears in predominance towards the extreme left; and since here

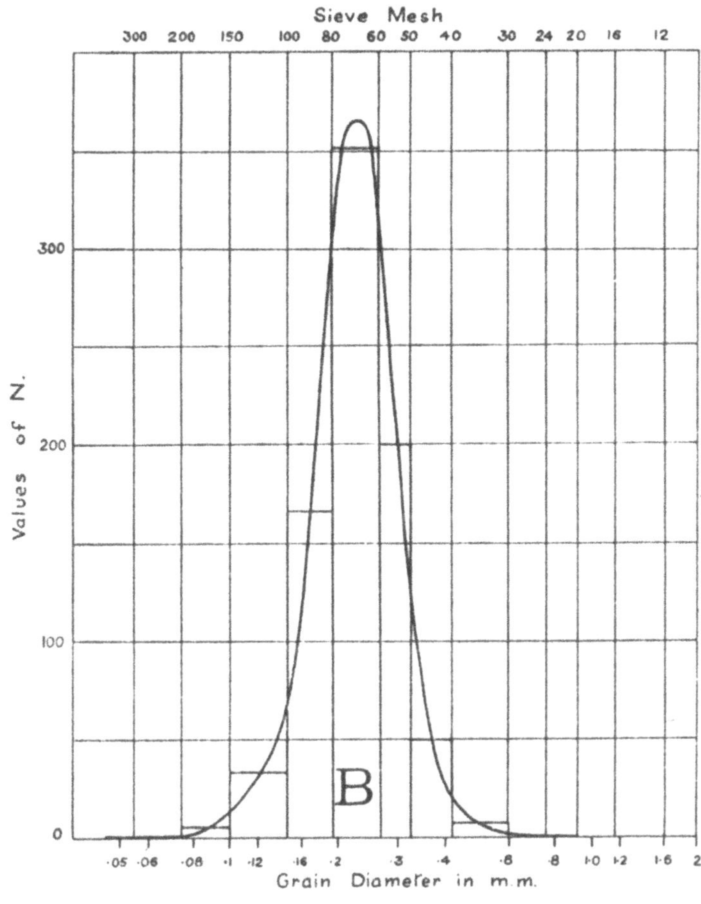

FIG. 35*b*

TYPICAL REGULAR DESERT SANDS

its direction is seen to approach that of a straight line coming to join it from the above point of intersection, this line must be the *s*-arm of A. So we have a complete and fairly accurate knowledge of the grading of component A.

(iv) The slope of the upper part of the left-hand arm gives some idea of the *s*-grading of B. It is steeper than that of A, and there must therefore be another point of intersection. This must also lie at a distance 0·3 below the combined

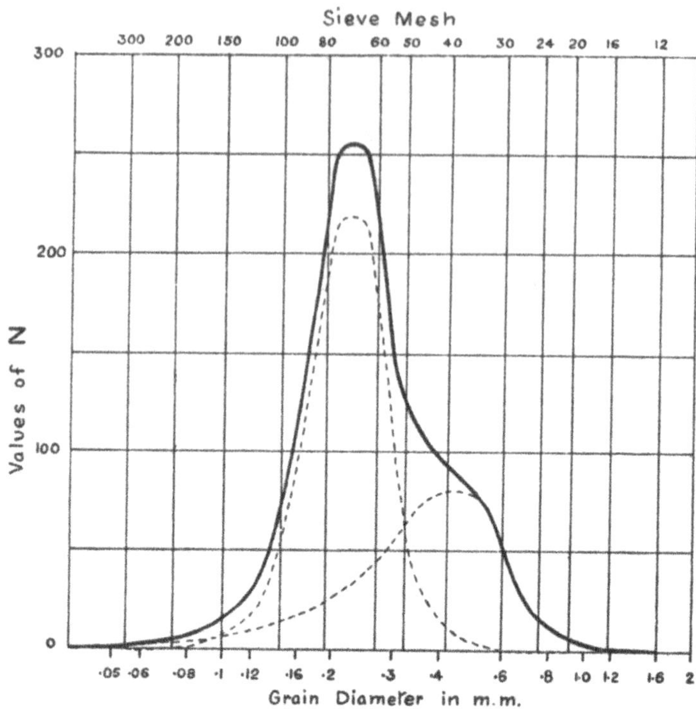

FIG. 36

GRADING OF THE MIXTURE OF THE TWO SANDS OF FIG.

curve, so there is only one possible position for it, and therefore for the line s_B.

(v) The line c_B is not so clearly defined. The position of the first point of intersection gives us some idea of the direction, and we know it cannot be less steep than c_A or it would cross it and cause a bend in c_A, which does not exist. Also, for reasons which will appear later, its slope $-c$ is unlikely to exceed 9 numerically.

(vi) At the peak diameter of B the values of N_A and N_{0B} can be found, and log $(N_{0B} - N_A)$ gives us the peak height of the B component.

(vii) Finally both components can be plotted as in Fig. 36, and their relative areas will give the proportions in which each is present.

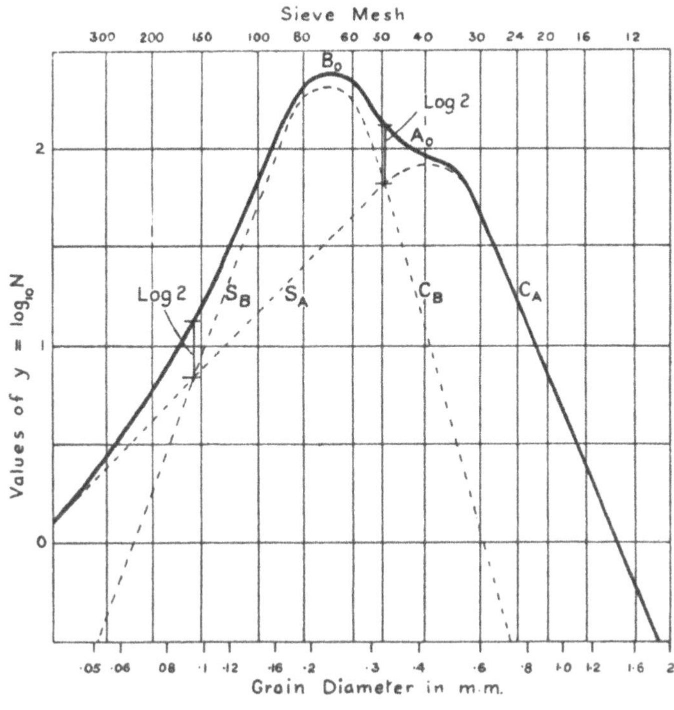

FIG. 37

34 IN THE PROPORTIONS 2 PARTS OF A TO 3 PARTS OF B

8. GRAIN DIAMETER DEFINED BY SIEVE APERTURE. A METHOD OF ADJUSTMENT

The closeness with which the values of N derived from the sifting operation can be expected to conform consistently with any assumed grading law connecting N with the grain diameter depends not only on the validity of the law but on the accuracy of the measurements. The main source of error lies in the estimation of ratio of the diameter limits defining each grade isolated.

In examining the evidence on which the existence of any grading law may rest, we are concerned not with the absolute magnitudes of the grain sizes but only with the ratios between them. The particular method of estimating the mean diameter is therefore of minor importance so long as it is applied consistently. The method used by the writer was the simplest possible—that of measuring, with a microscope, the mean dimensions of the square apertures in the mesh of the sieves.

Unfortunately the weaving of the sieves cannot be perfect, and the apertures are not always square, nor are they of exactly uniform size. Furthermore, it is well known that the same analysis results are not obtained with sieves which, though they have the same apparent apertures, are made with slightly different combinations of mesh and wire gauge. It was found necessary therefore to devise some means of making final small adjustments to the measured aperture sizes where found necessary.

This adjustment was made as follows: A number of sand samples were obtained which, when analysed by the set of sieves to be used, gave grading curves of more or less regular shape, but for which the position of the peak varied considerably along the scale of size. Now since the ordinate of the N – R diagram is the quotient of the percentage weight divided by the log ratio of the limiting apertures, an error in estimating one of these apertures will cause a corresponding error in N. It would also cause an error in the opposite sense in the N of the next grade. The result would be a kink in the final grading curve.

Such a kink might, however, arise from a real irregularity in the sand grading. But if the kink occurs in a series of samples at the same grain size but in relatively different positions on the curves—e.g. on the left-hand side of one and the right-hand side of another—it is clearly due to an error in the estimated size of the sieve. And if a slight adjustment can be made which causes the kink to disappear simultaneously in all positions on the curves, that adjustment is legitimate.

Chapter 10

GRADING CHANGES IN NON-UNIFORM SAND

1. THE CYCLE OF SAND MOVEMENT. REMOVAL, TRANSPORTATION, AND DEPOSITION

IN this chapter the changes will be described which take place in the size-grading when non-uniform sands are removed by the wind from a sand bed, transported over the surface, and re-deposited. These three processes constitute a cycle of operations which all sand must go through when it is set in motion either by air or water. But since no detailed work appears to have been done for the case of water, the results can only be taken as applying to air. It will be as well to begin with a short examination of the conditions under which each part of the cycle of operations occurs.

Sand Removal. The conditions of wind speed and gradient, under which a non-uniform sand starts to move, have already been discussed in Chapter 7. In that chapter the case was limited to the consideration of initial movement by wind only, and we postulated an up-wind limit to the sand surface, at which no oncoming sand was arriving to cause a disturbance of the surface by impact. This limitation will be continued in the present chapter; and the case of the continued disturbance of a surface of coarse sand by an oncoming stream of fine grains in saltation will be left till the following chapter.

We saw in Chapter 7 (4) that sand removal must cause a progressive coarsening of the bed surface as the finer grains are carried away, and that when the wind is above the ultimate threshold speed corresponding to the largest grains present in the bed material the sand movement goes on indefinitely. But when the wind strength is below the ultimate threshold, movement must cease after a certain interval of time, because the surface becomes stabilized by the formation of a protective layer of grains sufficiently large to be immovable.

If, while the movement is going on, the point of observation is shifted down-wind from the starting place of the movement, the intensity of the sand flow, q, is found to increase with the distance until it reaches an equilibrium state (Chapter 5). The wind is now saturated, so that no more removal of the surface can occur further down-wind. At any instant, therefore, we have removal taking place over a limited length only, the length depending on the rate at which the sand flow builds up to saturation point. But as time goes on and the removal surface coarsens, the whole removal area moves down-wind, leaving a longer and longer length of quiescent stabilized surface behind.

Since the coarsening is a purely surface effect, the bed beneath remaining untouched, it is impossible to measure the grading of the surface sand directly, because that would involve collecting a sample from a layer of undefined thickness. But we will make the somewhat arbitrary assumption that the sand in surface creep is a fair sample of the surface material. The surface creep can be readily collected for analysis by means of the trap mentioned in Chapter 3 (7).

Transportation. The sand movement consists, as we have seen, of three modes of travel: (*a*) a small proportion of fine grains in partial or complete suspension; (*b*) the saltation; and (*c*) the surface creep of grains rolled or impelled along the surface by the impact of the grains descending from the saltation. Where removal of the bed is taking place, the intensity of the total movement increases as we go down-wind; it then remains constant for as long a distance as the dual conditions of wind strength and surface texture do not alter, and decreases wherever deposition occurs. But over the whole length of the movement the grains travel by all three modes simultaneously.

The surface creep consists of a large mass of sand (per unit area of surface) moving very slowly; whereas the saltation, carrying the bulk of the flow, consists of a relatively small mass moving at a speed of the order of half that of the wind. Hence in their journey down-wind the grains in surface creep lag far behind those in saltation.

The grading of the sand which is moving past any point can be measured in two ways. We can either collect the saltation and the surface creep independently as the movement goes on, or in the case of a wind tunnel we can stop the movement and analyse a sample of the total amount of sand which has passed the point and has been afterwards deposited.

Deposition. There appear to be three ways by which grains reach their final resting-places in a sand deposit. (*a*) True *sedimentation*, in which the grains falling through slowly moving air strike the surface with insufficient forward velocity either to be carried on again or to jerk other surface grains forward. In the case of very fine grains carried in true suspension this is probably the only method of deposition possible. A familiar example of sedimentation is the fall of snow flakes through still air. (*b*) *Accretion.* The intensity q of the sand movement over a continuous sand surface is reduced if either (i) the surface wind becomes more feeble, through external causes, or (ii) the surface changes its texture in such a way that the constant C of Chapter 5 (3) is smaller. A reduction in q must mean a deposition of the surplus sand carried. In accretion the grains in saltation may strike the surface with sufficient velocity to jerk other grains forward, and so contribute to a diminished surface creep, but more grains find a final resting-place than are disturbed. The resulting deposit is built up from the saltation and the surface creep simultaneously. The essential difference between sedimentation and accretion is that in the former the grains do not move after reaching the ground, but in the latter case they are knocked along the surface till they find the securest hollow in which to lie. This will be found to be of importance later on when we come to consider, in Chapter 16, the physical properties of the different kinds of sand deposit. (*c*) *Encroachment.* If the surface is not continuous, but contains an obstruction of any sort, e.g. an abrupt step up or down, the surface creep is held up while the saltation may pass on. The resulting deposit, which need not require any diminution of the wind for its occurrence, consists only of the surface creep. In the case of a steep slope down, such as the slip-face of a dune, the surface grains roll over the crest of it and come to rest because they become sheltered from the impelling bombardment of the saltation. The slope encroaches down-wind, forming a relatively coarse deposit.

2. GRADING EXPERIMENTS, AND REPRESENTATION OF THE RESULTS

Changes in the grading may take place during any part of the cycle of movement, and it was the object of the following experiments to find out what these changes are and in what part of the cycle they occur; and whether or not, when log N is plotted against the log-diameter, the result shows under all circumstances a general tendency towards the simple grading law discussed in the preceding chapter.

For this purpose the down-wind end of the parallel tunnel was exchanged for an expanding section as shown in Fig. 38. The working sand bed was spread out in the parallel portion AB, and a very thin layer of the same sand was also laid over the floor of the expansion section from B to F in order to make the whole surface texture uniform at the commencement of each experiment.

Removal of sand took place in AB, beginning near A and moving slowly down as the removal surface coarsened. Deposition from

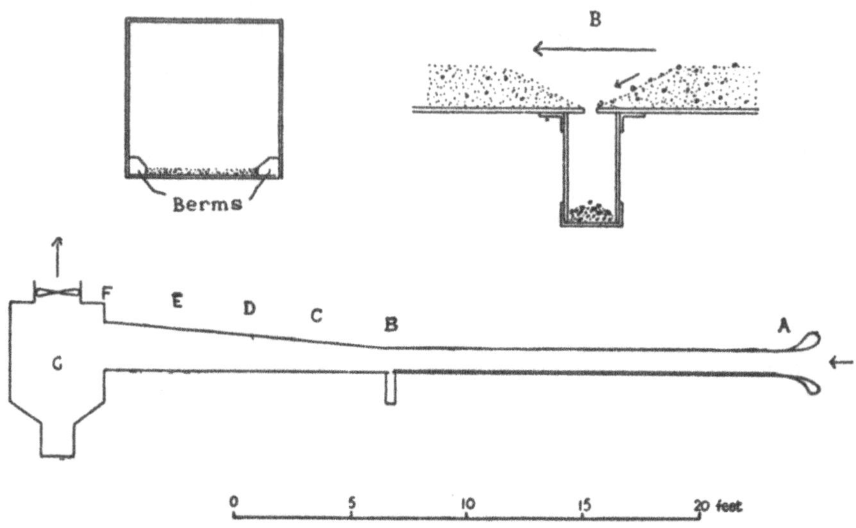

FIG. 38.—WIND TUNNEL FOR GRADING EXPERIMENTS

B onwards was ensured by the slowing-up of the wind due to the widening of the cross-section through which it passed.

A difficulty was encountered at the outset which brought out in an interesting way both a difference and a similarity between the movements of sand in wind and water. In the case of water the effect of gravity constrains a stream to follow the channel which it has formed by the removal of material from the land surface. A stream of water is therefore essentially bounded by its banks. And because of the banks the water at the sides of the stream flows less fast than that in the middle. If the stream is carrying silt, the result is a tendency for the finer particles to be deposited at the sides, leaving the coarse grains to move down the middle of the bed.

In the case of wind the fluid is ubiquitous, and there is no tendency to form stream beds. Consequently there are no side boundaries and we have a more or less uniform movement of sand over a desert plain perhaps 200 miles wide. But when we try to isolate a narrow longitudinal strip of the plain, and to imitate the sand movement between the walls of a tunnel, the conditions are no longer uniform across the section; the water stream conditions now reappear, and the finer grades of sand tend, as they do in water, to separate sideways, and to collect in the zones of slow-moving air along the tunnel walls.

This trouble was overcome by speeding up the flow of air at the sides. To do this smooth wood berms were placed along the sides, as shown inset in Fig. 38. The surface of the berms, being free from the drag of the sand movement, allowed the air over them to move at a greater speed. By suitably adjusting the relative width of the berms and the sand bed between them, it was found possible to make the wind velocity very nearly uniform across the section of the sand surface.

Starting with a bed composed of sand graded in various known ways, and in each case using several winds of different strengths continued for a set of different periods of time, the following measurements were made:

(*a*) A small sample of the surface creep was trapped at B and analysed.

(*b*) The whole of each of the portions of the deposit in the sections BC, CD, DE, EF, and in the box G were removed separately, weighed, and analysed.

(*c*) All these elements of the complete carry-over were then thoroughly mixed together, sampled and analysed.

As was explained in Chapter 9 (7), the relative percentage in which two or more sands are present in a mixture can be represented on the $N - R$ diagram by reducing the ordinates of each component in the ratio of the percentage in which it is present, thus making the area of the resulting mixture diagram equal to 100 units. On the $\log N - R$ diagram the reduction consists of lowering the whole curve, unchanged in shape, through a distance equal to the log of the appropriate ratio. Treating the total carry-over as a mixture, we can in this way represent on one diagram not only the grading of each of the component deposits at various points along the deposition area, but also the relative percentage by weight in which each component has been laid down.

A reference to Fig. 39 will make this clear. The original bed grading, as a weight of 100 units, is shown by the heavy continuous curve. The whole carry-over of the removed sand is also shown as a 100 per cent. weight, by the dotted curve. But the grading curve for each of the component deposits making up the total weight of sand carried over has been lowered because

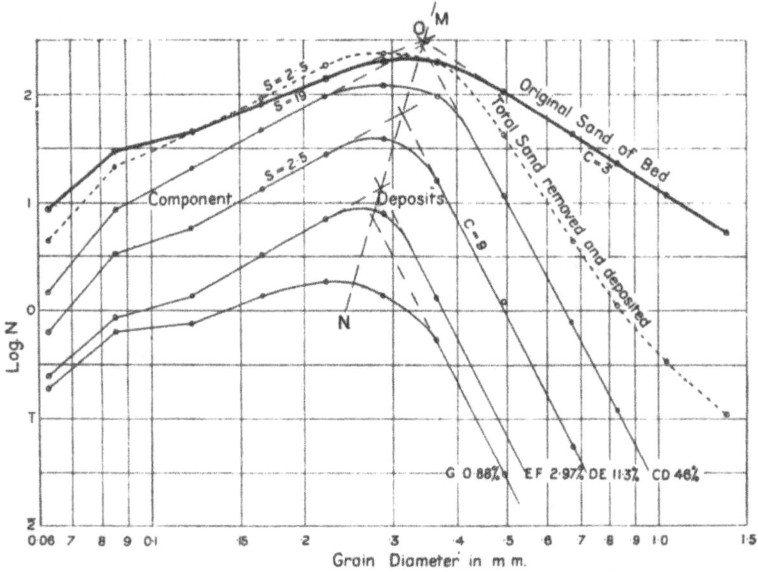

FIG. 39.—GRADING OF ACCRETION DEPOSITS. MODERATE WIND—EARLY STAGES

it represents a relative weight less than 100 units. These (thin continuous) curves are marked CD, EF, &c., according to the relative position of the deposit on the floor, and the percentage weights are marked against each. For instance, for the curve marked EF all the values of log N got from the analysis of the deposit in the part EF of the tunnel floor have been lowered from their full 100 per cent. values through a distance equal to log 0·0297 because the weight of the deposit in EF was only 2·97 per cent. of the total.

In all the curves the little circles represent the actual values of the ordinates, reduced or otherwise, obtained from the various siftings. Horizontally they are placed midway between the ordinates defining the diameter limits of the grades to which they refer.

The above method of representing the fractional deposits takes no account of the actual distance along the deposition section at which they were laid down. This would be of little interest because of the artificial and arbitrary conditions we have imposed on the rate of slowing-up of the wind by the shape of the expanding tunnel. More important are the shapes of each grading curve and the shift of its peak towards smaller grain diameter in relation to the proportion by weight in which the particular element of the deposit is present.

3. GRADING CHANGES DUE TO WIND ACTION DURING THE CYCLE OF SAND MOVEMENT

(*a*) *Moderate wind. Early stages.* The sand of the bed was made up artificially by adding together quantities of stock sands each composed of a single grade. The grading was that of a regular sand, except that by an accident an excess of the penultimate grade on the fine side was added during the mixing. This excess was purposely allowed to remain, in order to see what would happen to it. The width of the sand was made abnormally large, as can be seen from the flatness of the two arms of the curve.

This sand was spread over the bed AB, and a wind turned on whose strength was just enough to move a uniform sand of the same diameter as that of the peak of the graded bed material. After a short run of 3 minutes the wind was stopped, and all the deposits were removed and analysed.

Omitting for a moment the extreme up-wind part BC of the deposit, an examination of Fig. 39 will yield several points of interest.

(i) *Separation.* By continuing the straight parts of the arms of the deposit curves CD, DE, EF, to meet at their respective peaks, it will be noticed that these peaks lie in a straight line MN. This means that the peak height N_0, which is a measure of the proportion by weight in which each component deposit is present, falls off logarithmically with the diminution of the peak grain diameter as the tunnel expands and the wind slackens. The smallness of the shift of peak diameter, as the deposits get finer and dwindle in weight, is surprising. It will be seen that even the finest sand, constituting only 0·88 per cent. of the total, which did not settle on the floor at all, but was carried over into the box G, has a peak diameter as large as 0·28 mm., which is but 12·5 per cent. smaller than the peak diameter of the original bed.

Just as the slopes of the straight arms of the curves themselves give us the indices *c* and *s* which define the rate of falling off of the grades by weight, so the slope of the line MN gives a similar index defining the rate of falling off of the weight of sand deposited at any place, in terms of its peak diameter. Thus just as we found that

$$\frac{N_0}{N} = \left(\frac{d_0}{d}\right)^c$$

where N_0 and N referred to the ordinates of the grading curves of any one regular deposit, so

$$\frac{\mathbf{N}_0}{\mathbf{N}} = \left(\frac{D_0}{D}\right)^t$$

where $\mathbf{N}$ and D refer to the peak ordinates and peak diameters of each component of an accretion deposit caused by a slackening wind. I have called $1/t$ the *separation*. Its value in the example is 0·061, as can be verified by measurement from the diagram.

(ii) The slopes *c* and *s*. It will be seen that the right-hand slopes *c* of all the deposits are the same—the value of *c* being in each case 9. They are considerably steeper than that of the parent sand of the original bed. The left-hand slope *s* for all the components except the last 0·88 per cent. are also the same, and again they are steeper than that of the parent sand. The constancy of the slopes is somewhat remarkable since not only are the deposits formed each under different wind conditions, but each grade, as defined by its absolute grain diameter, occurs in each curve in a relatively different position.

(iii) The accidental irregularity in the parent sand has re-appeared almost unchanged in each of the deposits.

(iv) The surface creep. The grading of this, obtained by trapping a small sample of it at position B in the tunnel, is shown in Fig. 40. The peak diameter, 0·49 mm., is considerably coarser than that of the parent sand, 0·34 mm. The grading conforms to the usual linear law ; i.e. the surface creep is also a regular sand. The slope *c* on the right is steeper than that of the bed sand, but less steep than those of the deposits. The slope *s* on the left is on the contrary slightly steeper. The irregularity on the left has in this case almost gone.

(v) The first deposit BC. This is also shown in Fig. 40. Here, owing to the advance of the surface creep into the deposition area, we have a mixture of a coarse sand with a finer sand, with the consequent bending of the lower part of the right-hand arm of the curve. On the extreme right the two coarsest grades, belonging only to the surface creep and not to any appreciable extent to the accretion, are present in the relative proportions of

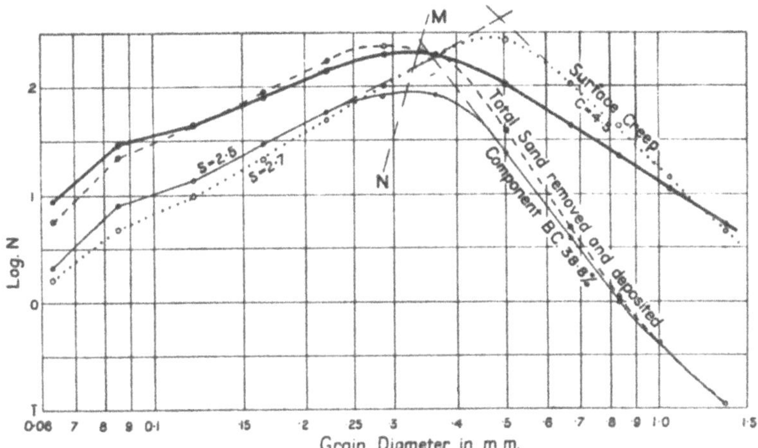

FIG. 40.—GRADING OF THE SURFACE CREEP, AND OF THE MIXTURE FORMED BY ITS ADVANCE OVER THE ACCRETION DEPOSIT

Same conditions as Fig. 39

the former, so that the end of the curve runs parallel to that of the surface creep. Higher up the arm, too, the influence of the advancing surface creep is shown by the flatter angle of the slope, and by the shift of the peak to the right of the line MN on which the peaks of the pure accretion curves lie.

(vi) Position of the line MN. At this early stage in the removal of sand from the parent bed, the surface of the latter has had little time to become coarser. We should therefore expect, intuitively, by virtue of the strange geometrical simplicity of the whole phenomenon, to find some diagrammatical link between the peak diameters of the accretion deposits and that of the parent sand. It will be seen that such a link exists, for the line MN passes through the peak O of the original bed material.

(vii) The last deposit. The left-hand slope of component G is much flatter than the others. It is probable that the excess of the finest grades represents the material carried in suspension, most of which would in the open be removed altogether or would settle later by sedimentation. Its relative proportion, even with

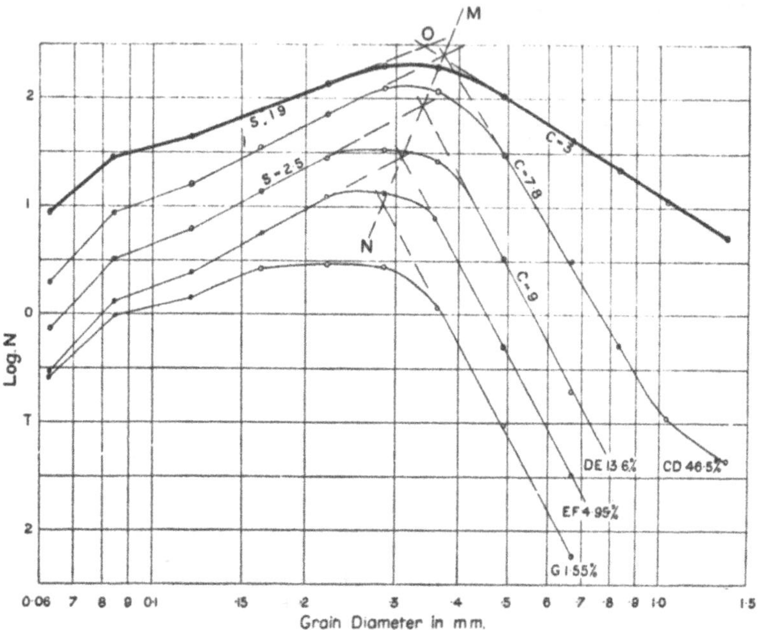

FIG. 41.—GRADING OF ACCRETION DEPOSITS. LATER STAGE. DOWN-WIND DEPOSITS

this exceptionally wide sand rich in fine material, is remarkably small.

(*b*) *Moderate wind. Later stages when removal bed has become coarse.* Figs. 41 and 42 show the state of affairs when, with the same sand and the same wind strength, the run was continued until the bed was stabilized and all sand movement ceased.

The left-hand slopes of all the deposit curves have remained entirely unchanged, as have the right-hand slopes of the accretion curves DE, EF, and G. The curve of the surface creep has become slightly flatter on both sides. But the surface creep has also advanced further ; there is a greater proportion of it mixed with the first deposit BC, and it has also begun to affect the grading of the deposit in the second section CD.

The coarsening of the removal bed has caused a corresponding coarsening of the up-wind deposits, so that their peaks have shifted over to the right. The line MN now no longer passes through the original peak of the parent sand surface.

(*c*) *Strong wind.* The same sand was exposed to a wind capable of moving grains considerably larger than the peak diameter of the parent sand on the bed. Fig. 43 shows the results after a short run of 2 minutes. The sand movement was of course very

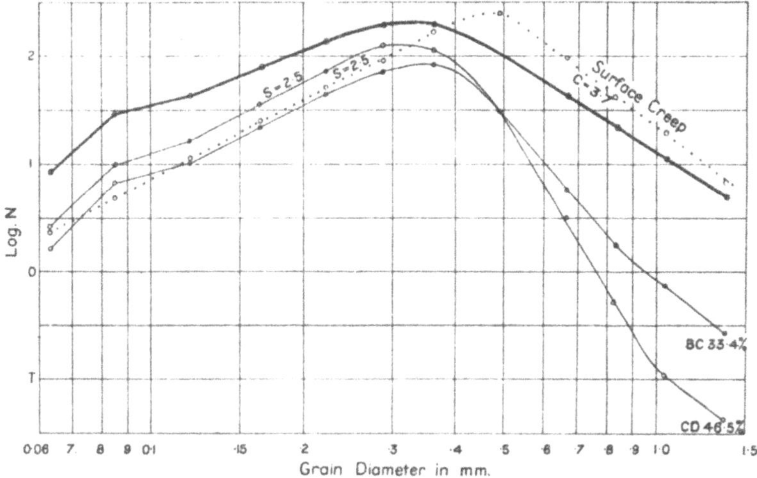

FIG. 42.—GRADING OF ACCRETION DEPOSITS. LATER STAGE. UP-WIND DEPOSITS

much more intense, so that removal even in this short period had proceeded far. Hence the line MN has already shifted over to the right of the peak O.

On the left the increased wind has had the effect of making the slopes of the deposit curves approach very closely to that of the parent sand; but the slope of the surface creep has remained almost the same as for the gentler wind. On the right the deposit slopes are also the same as for the gentler wind, and *c* is again equal to 9.

The peak of the surface creep has shifted much further to the right, and has a diameter of 0·56 mm. Since the irregularity on the left has again disappeared, we have a very long left-hand slope consisting of eight analysis points, and their straight-line relationship illustrates very well the reality of the law of regular grading. The right-hand slope of the surface creep curve has become steeper than before. Presumably in the final stage, when the wind is above the ultimate threshold, the peak of the surface creep shifts so far to the right that the slope of the right-hand arm approaches the common value of 9, as suggested by the thin dotted line in the figure.

(*d*) *Narrow sands.* Fig. 44 shows the behaviour of a natural

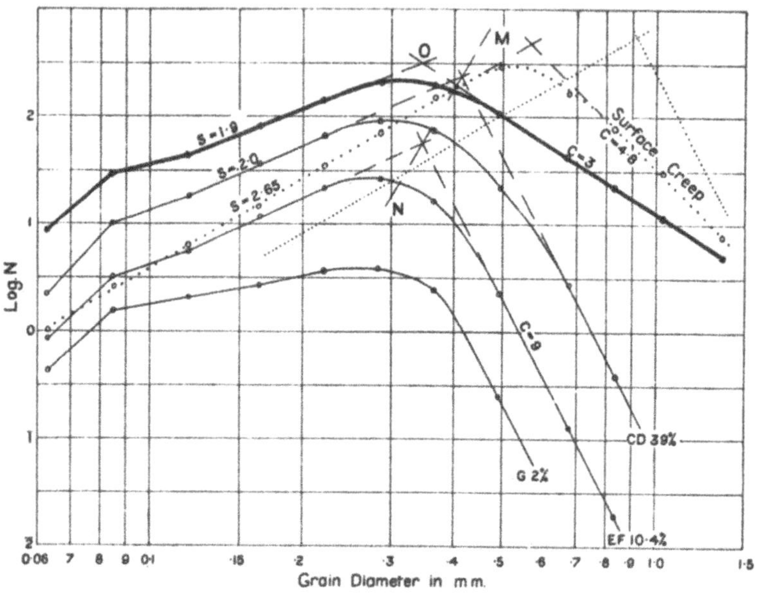

FIG. 43.—GRADING EFFECTS OF A STRONG WIND

'fine silver sand' as obtained from a builder's merchant. The peak size is finer than that of the artificial sand previously discussed, and both this and the slopes of the two arms of its curve are typical of dune sand.

The wind in this case was again higher than the threshold strength for the peak grain diameter, and therefore, as we should expect from the corresponding behaviour of the wider sand, the left-hand slopes of the deposits are almost parallel to that of the original sand. On the right, notwithstanding the difference between the slopes of the new and the previous sand, the common slope of the deposits is again just the same as before, and c is again equal to 9. Owing to the relative lack of coarse grains in this sand the coarsening of the removal bed, as indicated by the

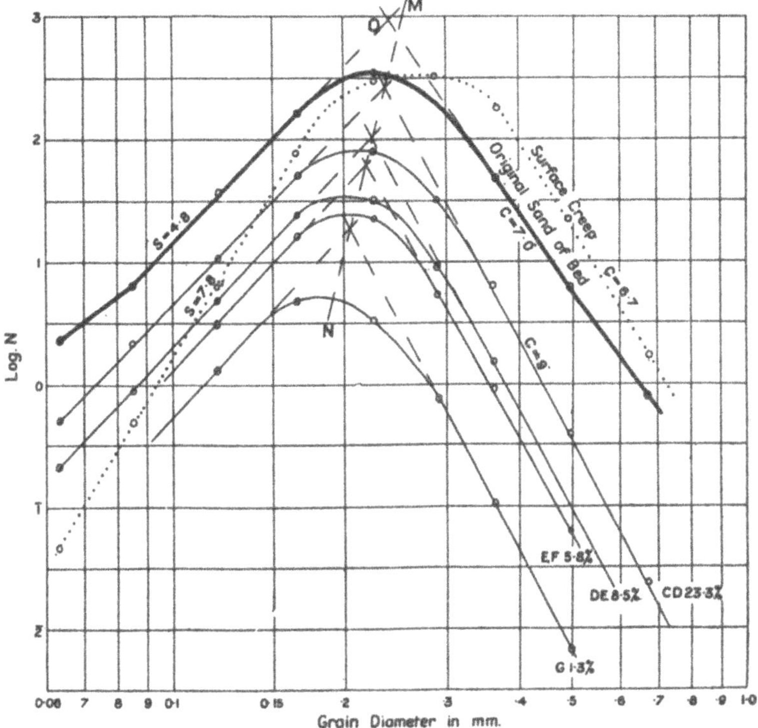

FIG. 44.—ACCRETION DEPOSITS FROM A 'NARROW' SAND

shift in the line MN, is considerably less than in the corresponding case of the wide sand.

The slope of the left-hand arm of the surface creep curve is again steeper than either that of the deposits or of the parent sand, and on the right its angle again lies between the two.

4. SUMMARY OF GRADING CHANGES DUE TO WIND ACTION. REGULAR SANDS

The conclusions to be drawn from the foregoing results can be summarized as follows:

(*a*) *Removal.* The grading of the total sand removed from a bed of regular sand and set in motion by a wind is not itself regular, but it can be treated as a mixture of three regular constituents which appear to correspond to the three modes of transportation—saltation, surface creep, and suspension.

A moment's reflection will show that if the slope of either arm of the grading curve of the removed sand is steeper than that of the parent material on the bed, the extreme grades towards the lower end of the arm must tend to be left behind, and to be concentrated on the bed ; the relative rate of concentration depending on the angle between the slopes of the parent and removed sands. On the right side (coarse grains) experiment shows that unless the grading coefficient c of the bed is already as great as the apparent limiting value of 9, removal must be synonymous with a progressive concentration of the coarser grades, whatever the strength of the wind.

On the side of the finer grades the angle between the slopes of the parent and removed sands depends on the wind strength ; and for gentle winds this angle is quite appreciable, so that in this case there must also be a concentration of fine material left behind on the removal bed. For high winds, however, the grading of the removed sand approaches conformity with that of the bed. The effect on the bed surface of these two concentrations will be dealt with in the following chapter. They play a large part in the formation of ripples and ridges.

(*b*) *Deposition on a flat sand surface.* The three constituent sands which make up the total sand in motion tend to separate out by virtue of their different speeds and modes of travel into three kinds of deposits.

(i) The surface creep. This being the slowest, is deposited in the largest proportion at the beginning of the deposition area where, having a different grading coefficient, it forms a non-regular mixture with the earliest accretion deposit. The grading curve of the surface creep on the coarse side is always steeper than that of the parent sand but less steep than that of the saltation and its accretion deposits. On the fine side it is in general steeper than both.

(ii) The saltation. Its coarse-grade coefficient appears always to be the same, no matter what is the grading of the parent sand or the strength of the wind. Its fine-grade coefficient is always less than that of the parent sand but approaches the latter as the wind strength increases. The saltation separates out in a diminished wind into a series of accretion deposits each retaining the same grading coefficients but having a smaller and smaller peak diameter as the wind slackens down-stream. (A mixture of a number of regular sands all having the same grading coefficients is itself a regular sand.) The quantities of each component deposit fall off logarithmically, and very rapidly, with the decrease in peak diameter.

As time goes on, the wind conditions remaining the same, two progressive changes occur. The surface creep advances further and further over the existing accretion deposits, causing the grading of the upper and later layers of each in time to become non-regular. At the same time the sand from the source, and with it the saltation, becomes coarser, so that the peak diameter of the accretions at any fixed spot also increases even where unaffected by the surface creep. Hence it seems that all deposits laid down over a flat surface of sand must get progressively coarser as long as the sand movement lasts. This no doubt explains the close layers of stratification found in the structure of accretion deposits; each layer corresponding to one period of wind (see Chapter 16). (The only case in which a coarsening of the deposits would not occur would be when the source consists of a nearly uniform sand and when the wind is above its ultimate threshold, e.g. when a strong wind blows parallel to a line of dunes.)

(iii) Suspension. There is a small residue of very fine material which probably represents sand in suspension. Its grading appears to be regular on the coarse side but not on the fine side. In the open air this material is presumably dispersed and settles evenly over the country when the wind drops, forming a very small sedimentation deposit. If enough of it settles after each wind it may upset the regularity of the extreme fine grades of a sample of an otherwise regular sand deposit. There is some evidence that this does happen. For instance, the grading of the natural sand of Fig. 44 shows not only a probable admixture with an oncoming surface creep on the right but also a distinct widening on the extreme left.

(*c*) *Deposition of the surface creep by encroachment.* If the surface is not continuous the surface creep can become wholly or partially separated from the saltation, and may form a deposit of its own. The example of the deposit formed in the shelter of the slip-face of a dune has already been given. But it should be noted that the separation is here only partial since the face is usually long enough to receive in addition to the surface creep a good proportion of the saltation which settles on it through the relatively still air. We have a better example in the case of the smaller transverse ridges to be described in the next chapter: here the separation is almost complete.

A partial separation also takes place when a sand-driving wind arrives at the foot of a dune. The sudden upward angle of the surface has little retarding effect on the saltation, but may completely hold up the large grains which are driven along by impact. As a result we commonly find the material at the foot of a dune to be relatively coarse, and to become finer as the surface angle steepens.

(*d*) *Changes in the grading of an encroachment due to an up-current of air.* Experiment seems to show that grading curves with the steepest left-hand slopes are obtained in deposits formed by the trapping of the surface creep as it falls over a brink. And yet the analysis of samples of natural dune sands have shown that in many cases the left-hand slopes are steeper than any which it had been possible to produce by trapping the surface creep through the floor of the wind tunnel. Some further grading process was therefore to be looked for. Such was found in the elutriating or winnowing action of the upward air current due to the permanent wind eddy in the lee of a dune crest. For in imitation of this upward current an indraught of air was made to rise through the collecting slot; and as a result, though there was no change in the right-hand side of the grading curve, or in the position of the peak, the left-hand side became considerably steeper. It was noteworthy that in this process, too, the altered left-hand side still retained its linear form.

5. GRADING CHANGES DUE TO MECHANICAL MOVEMENT OF THE GRAINS DOWN THE SLIP-FACE OF A DUNE

It has been found similarly that the slope c of the right-hand side of many analysis curves of natural dune sand are greater than the apparent limiting value of 9 which wind action can yield unaided. The explanation is probably to be obtained in the sorting process that occurs when a steep sand slope collapses owing to accumulation at the top. No exact measurements appear to have been done on this, but it is common knowledge that when sand or gravel is tipped out into a heap the larger and rounder grains tend to roll down the slope and to collect at the bottom.

PLATE 5

Photo *R. F. Peel*

GIANT SAND RIDGES (LIBYAN DESERT)

PLATE 6

a. UNRIPPLED SAND-SHEET, SAND RIPPLES AND PEBBLE RIDGES

b. SAND RIPPLES IN AIR

6. HOW DO IRREGULAR SANDS BECOME REGULAR ?

The experiments described in the foregoing sections show that regular sands tend to retain their logarithmic grading no matter how their coefficients may change. Further experiments were made to ascertain whether, and if so, in what part of the cycle, a non-regular sand is transformed into a regular one. The natural

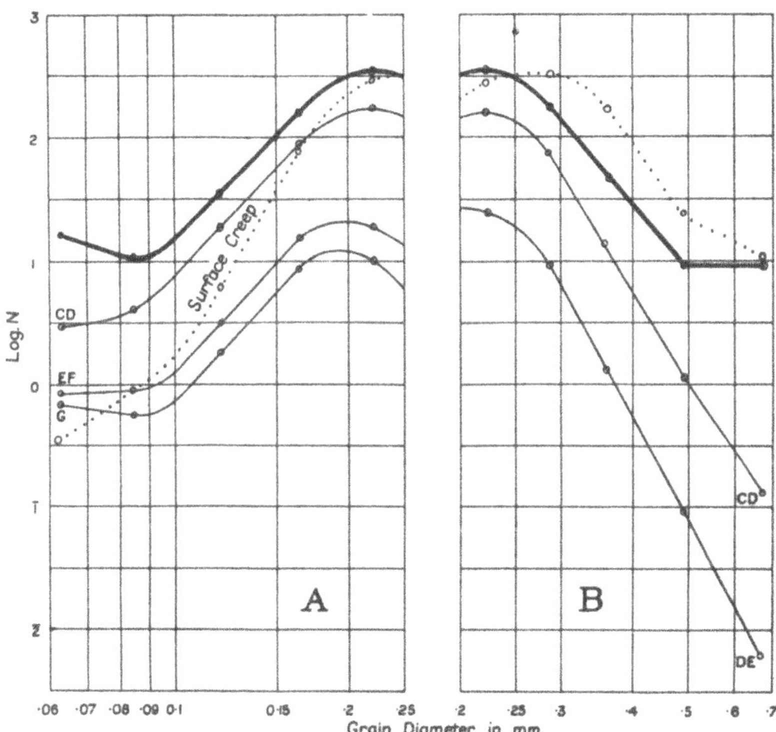

FIG. 45.—RESTORATION OF A DISTORTED SAND TO THE REGULAR GRADING PATTERN

sand of Fig. 44 was used; and by the addition of more sand (*a*) the extreme fine grade, and (*b*) the extreme coarse grade, were separately increased to many times their proper proportions for a regular grading. Since changes in the grading of one side of a curve seem to have no appreciable effect on the other side, the irrelevant halves of the curves are omitted from Fig. 45.

If the *distortion n* is defined as the ratio of the content of a grade actually present in a sand to that of the same grade if it conformed to the general pattern of the regular grading curve, then the difference in the height y of the ordinate in the figure between the straight line and the actual curve is log n.

In Fig. 45*a*, the distortion artificially caused was about sevenfold for the extreme fine grade. It will be seen that, as we have already noticed in the case of the wide artificially constructed sand, the distortion is very much reduced in the surface creep, and

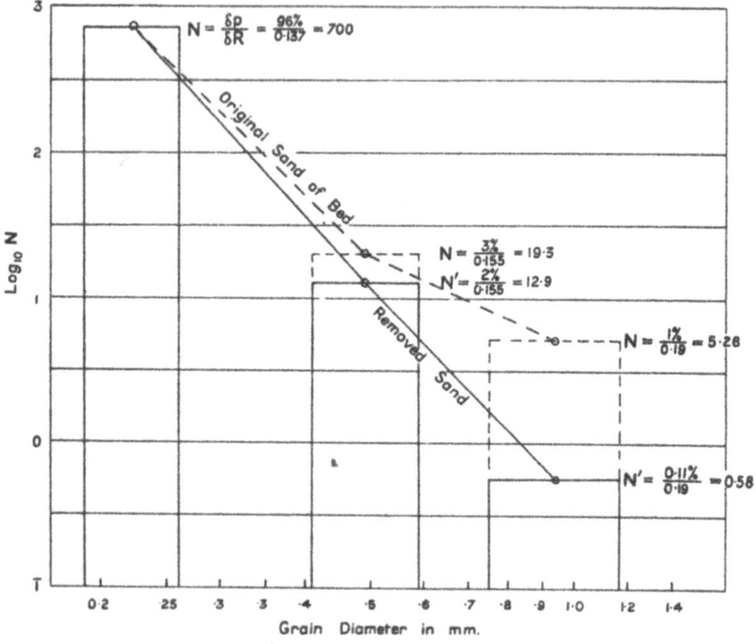

FIG. 46.—DISCONTINUOUS GRADING

Tendency towards logarithmic relation between N and *d*

hardly at all in the accretion deposits. (The apparent reduction in the distortion for the deposit CD is to be accounted for by the mixture of the surface creep with it.) Most of the excess of this finest grade was left behind on the removal bed, where it formed smooth sheets over which the wind passed without causing any movement on them (see Chapter 7 (3)).

Fig. 45*b* shows the changes which took place in the distortion on the right of the curve. In this case n was made equal to 10 in the original sand of the bed, i.e. there was ten times too much of the extreme coarse grade present. For this distortion by a coarse grade we find just the opposite effect. The reduction in n is least in the surface creep, and gets progressively more pronounced in the down-wind deposits till near the end of the tunnel the distortion has disappeared entirely. Again most of the excess of the distorted grade was left behind on the bed.

We can conclude therefore that the processes, still entirely unexplained, which tend to produce the logarithmic relation between the proportion by weight and the grain diameter, are different on the fine and coarse sides of the grading, though both must occur in the early part of the cycle of movement.

7. INCOMPLETE SANDS

The tendency of the grains to grade themselves according to the logarithmic law is not confined to natural sands composed of a complete continuity of grain size. Fig. 46 shows the result of an experiment with a mixture of three nearly uniform grades with an entire absence of grains of intermediate diameters. As before, the grading tends to become logarithmic, and c increases towards the apparent limiting value of 9.

REFERENCES

BAGNOLD, R. A. (1937). *Proc. Roy. Soc. A.*, 163, p. 250

TWENHOFEL, W. H. (1926). *Treatise on Sedimentation.* (Baillière, Tindall & Cox, London.)

Chapter 11

SMALL-SCALE SAND FORMS. TRANSVERSE RIPPLES AND RIDGES

1. SAND WAVES AND WATER WAVES NOT ANALOGOUS

THOUGH the cross-section of a rippled sand surface often assumes an outline which closely resembles both the actual cross-section of a disturbed water-air surface, and also the graph on a time basis of any kind of simple vibration, the resemblance is in appearance only. For the essence of a true wave is in the propagation of energy, either through the body of a material as in the case of sound, or along its surface as with a surface water wave. In a sand ripple or wave there is no such propagation of energy. A sand ripple is merely a crumpling or heaping up of the surface, brought about by wind action, and cannot be regarded as a true wave in a strict dynamical sense. The similarity lies only in the regular repetition of surface form.

2. CLASSIFICATION OF SAND RIPPLES AND RIDGES

We will examine in this chapter how it is that a flat sand surface is generally unstable when grains are in motion over it, why the form of the crumpling tends to be regularly repeated, and the factors that control its height, shape, and repetition distance.

In the classification of these phenomena a difficulty arises from the fact that no one main factor underlies the whole subject, and different combinations of a number of factors are responsible for the different, though visually similar, effects. The phenomena result from the mutual interaction of five factors:

(*a*) The wind, which imparts the primary motive power to the grains in saltation, and which is in turn controlled by the intensity of the saltation:

(*b*) The saltation, which in its turn causes movement among the surface grains (surface creep) by impact:

(*c*) The surface grains, which are moved to a greater or less extent according to their individual size, and which by their relative movement are sorted out and heaped up into ripples and ridges:

(*d*) The resulting surface relief, which by virtue of the local changes it implies in the angle between the surface exposed to the bombardment and the direction of descent of the bombarding grains, causes place-to-place variations in the rate of ejection of new grains into the saltation:

(*e*) The state of the sand movement—whether deposition or removal is taking place, or whether the sand flow is steady in the area considered.

This last factor controls the size and the grading of the surface grains, and so has such a pronounced effect upon the resulting surface form that it will be used here as the primary basis of classification. What follows may be made clearer if a summary is given here of the various surface forms to be dealt with, and the conditions under which they occur.

I. Rapid Deposition	Flat surface, no small-scale surface relief
II. Slow Deposition, or Equilibrium Sand Flow	Ripples, whose wavelength depends on the wind strength, and whose height/wavelength ratio depends on the 'width' of the surface grading For nearly uniform sand this ratio is very small. It increases with greater variation of grain size
III. Removal	
(*a*) Wind above the ultimate threshold strength for the largest grains	Ripples. As for II
(*b*) Wind below ultimate threshold	Ridges. Size and wavelength increase indefinitely with time, rate of growth depending on quantity of coarse material available, and on intensity of the oncoming saltation

In all cases the coarsest material collects at the crests, and the finest in the troughs. This characteristic distinguishes without exception the small-scale surface sand forms from the large-scale forms of the dunes, wherein the reverse is invariably the case.

3. INSTABILITY OF A FLAT SAND SURFACE. EFFECT OF CHANGES IN THE ANGLE OF INCIDENCE OF THE DESCENDING SALTATION

In examining the stability of the position of any solid object, or of the shape of a deformable structure under the influence of a force or other deforming agency, it is useful to adopt the following reasoning: If by chance a very small deformation occurs, it must, in general, give rise to a change in the incidence of the deforming agency. If this change is such as to accentuate the deformation, then the arrangement is inherently unstable. But if the change is in the opposite sense, and tends to neutralize the deformation, then the arrangement is stable.

Let us apply this to the case of a smooth flat sand surface over which a saltation is taking place. Since the grains are of finite and varying size, the surface cannot be perfectly even, and we can

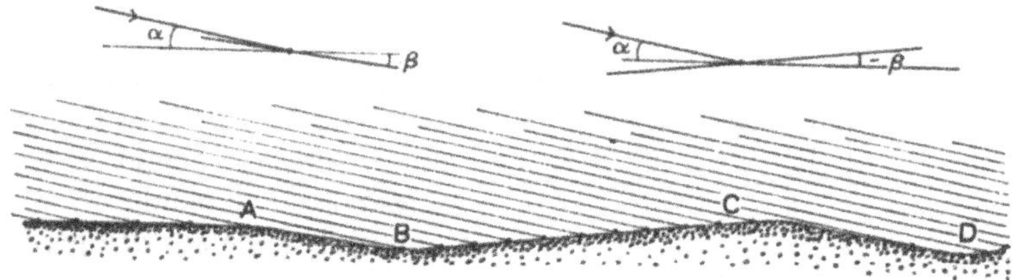

FIG. 47.—DIFFERENTIAL INTENSITY OF BOMBARDMENT ON WINDWARD AND LEE SLOPES

imagine the existence of a number of tiny chance unevennesses. These may be caused, for instance, by more grains happening temporarily to be moved out of a certain small area than are moved into it. A tiny hollow is formed, such as that shown, much magnified, in Fig. 47.

Now it has been shown already that the propelling saltation descends at a flat and nearly uniform angle. If we assume for a moment that the distribution of the descending grains is uniform over the whole area, they can be represented diagrammatically, as in Fig. 47, by a series of parallel and equidistant straight lines. If we assume further that the mass flow q_c of the grains in surface creep at any point is proportional to the number of forward impulses which each unit area of the surface at that point receives per second, it follows that q_c at that point is proportional to the closeness to one another of the points of impact in the diagram.

On the lee side AB of the hollow these points are far apart, indicating relatively few impacts, but on the windward side where they are much closer together the bombardment is more intense; hence many more grains are driven up the slope BC than down the reverse slope AB. This means that the original hollow will get bigger. And since the bombardment is more intense on the slope BC than it is on the level surface down-wind, the grains that have been excavated from the hollow will accumulate at C, because they are not being removed down-wind as quickly as they are arriving. As the accumulation at C rises, it forms a second lee slope CD, and here the grain movement is again feeble. This in turn causes the surface at D to be depleted of grains, because they are being removed from D by a more intense bombardment faster than they can now move down the slope CD. A second hollow is therefore formed, and so on.

From the above it appears that a flat sand surface must be unstable, because any small chance deformation tends to become accentuated by the local sand-removing action of the saltation. This differential effect of the saltation is due to its sensitivity to changes in the angle of incidence between it and the surface. The differential intensity of the bombardment on the windward and lee slopes of a ripple is shown in action very clearly in the photograph, Plate 4*a*.

Before proceeding to the subsequent history of the incipient deformation of the surface, it may be interesting to examine more closely the effect of changes in the surface angle upon the grain-propelling power of a uniform saltation.

4. SURFACE CREEP DEPENDENT ON THE ANGLE OF INCIDENCE OF THE SALTATION

The surface intensity of the propelling bombardment is very sensitive to changes in the relative angle between the descending saltation and the surface of impact. If α (Fig. 47) is the angle of descent, and β that of the local surface of impact, both with regard to the general plane of the surface, and if the effect I of the propelling impulses is unity when β is zero, i.e. when the surface is flat, it can be shown that the component of the effect along the inclined surface is given by the expression

$$I_\beta = \frac{\tan\alpha - \tan\beta}{\tan\alpha} \cdot \frac{\cos(\alpha - \beta)}{\sec\beta}$$

the angle β being taken as positive for a lee slope and negative for a windward slope. In practice, for the small angles found in nature, the factor on the right is so nearly unity that it can be disregarded, and we have

$$I_\beta = 1 - \frac{\tan \beta}{\tan \alpha}$$

For lee slopes where β is equal to or greater than α, the saltation never strikes the surface at all, so the impelling effect is zero.

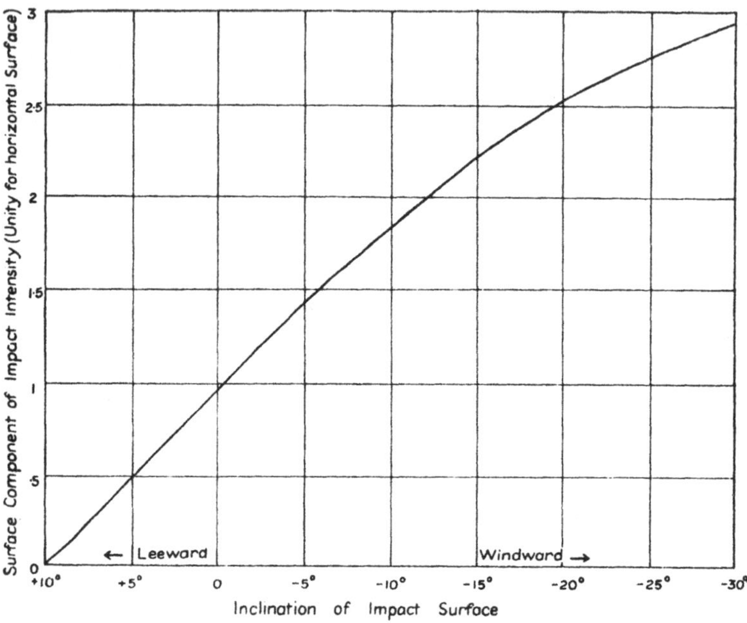

FIG. 48.—LOCAL INTENSITY OF THE SURFACE CREEP IN TERMS OF THE INCLINATION OF THE IMPACT SURFACE TO THE ANGLE OF DESCENT OF THE SALTATION

(Constant angle of descent of 10°)

Fig. 48 shows the relative impelling effect of the saltation on the surface creep for a standard angle of descent of 10° for various inclinations of the impact surface. It will be seen that even for a very flat ripple such as that shown in the photograph, Plate 4*a*, where the lee slope is 7° and the windward slope 3°, the forward urge on the grains up the windward slope is more than four times what it is down the lee slope.

5. RIPPLES FORMED UNDER EQUILIBRIUM CONDITIONS

(*a*) *Factors controlling the repetition distance* (*wavelength*). It was shown in Section 3 that a flat sand surface is unstable, and tends to the formation of alternate crests and troughs when sand drives over it. We have now to trace the subsequent history of these incipient ripples under the various conditions given in the table in Section 2, and to examine the factors which control the wavelength, height, and general character which the ripples ultimately acquire.

It will be seen in the table that the term '*ripple*' has been applied to those surface forms whose wavelength depends on the wind strength, and remains constant as time goes on; and that those other forms whose wavelength may increase indefinitely with time are called *ridges*. The latter occur whenever the surface grading grows steadily coarser owing to sand removal. They will be dealt with in a later section. Ripples tend to form whenever the surface grading, whatever it may be, remains constant, or nearly constant, with time, but their amplitude decreases if deposition is taking place, and they may become undetectable when the deposition is heavy.

The dependence of the ripple wavelength on the strength of the wind can be readily explained in terms of the 'characteristic path' discussed in Chapter 5. Now in Fig. 47 the grains descending from the saltation were assumed for simplicity to be uniformly distributed along the general plane of the surface. Though this is very probably true at the onset of the sand movement while the surface is still flat, it cannot remain true once the surface is deformed in the manner described in Section 3. The reason is clear if we remember that each grain in saltation, from the place of its ejection from the surface to the point where it strikes the surface and ejects another grain, describes a certain path through the air. Though the ranges of these grain paths are very various in length, yet for any given strength of wind there exists a definite average or characteristic path. In other words, of all the grains which are ejected from any given small area of the surface, a greater number will fall on a second small area, situated at a distance of one characteristic path down-wind, than on any other area.

If grains were ejected in equal numbers from all over the surface, the distribution of their impacts would still be uniform; but if, owing to a local tilting of the surface, a greater number of ejections occur at one point, then the effect must be felt most markedly at another point one characteristic path down-wind. At this second point the density of the impacts will be greater than elsewhere, and not only will more grains be ejected from here—to strike the surface at a third point the same distance further on—but the local increases in the rate of the surface creep at each place will lead to the formation of local hollows and mounds. The repetition distance will be the length of the characteristic grain path.

This distance may be much longer than the scale of the initial random irregularity up-wind. But, as we have seen, the little random irregularities in the surface themselves tend to grow bigger and to multiply; in a short time the two processes fall into step, and the ripple wavelength becomes equal to the length of the characteristic path. The final stage is sketched in Fig. 49. Cause and effect then mutually assist each other: the variation in the distribution of the descending saltation causes a correspond-

FIG. 49.—COINCIDENCE OF RIPPLE WAVELENGTH AND RANGE OF CHARACTERISTIC PATH OF GRAIN

ing variation in the rate of movement of the surface creep; this in turn leads to alternate hollows and mounds, with an accompanying alternation in the angle of incidence between the bombardment and the surface; as the slopes become steeper the variation in the distribution of the saltation is accentuated; and so on. Consequently, if no other factor operated, we should expect the height of the crests to go on increasing. The limits set to the actual height they attain will be discussed a little later.

(*b*) *Wind strength and characteristic grain path.* The experimental evidence for the identity of the characteristic path with the ripple wavelength was described in Chapter 5. The existence of the characteristic path was deduced from the appearance of kinks in the plotted curves of wind velocity measured at different heights above the surface. Assuming that the height at which these kinks occurred, for any given strength of wind, was a measure of the height of the top of the path of the average grain in saltation, the range of such a path was calculated theoretically. This range was found to agree well with the actual wavelength of the ripple formed in the sand bed during the wind measurements.

Experiments with a variety of different wind strengths showed that the ripple wavelength increases with the wind gradient V'_*, but that the ripples flatten out and disappear [1] when the wind rises above a certain strength. Figures for the particular sand used are given in Chapter 5 (2). For this sand it was possible, therefore, to use the ripple wavelength, which is easily determined, as a measure of the wind gradient. Unfortunately time has not permitted further work to be done on the exact relation between ripple length and wind gradient for natural non-uniform sands. There is little doubt, however, that provided the grading is approximately constant, the wavelength always increases as the wind strengthens.

A further inquiry into the dependence of ripple wavelength and wind gradient for a set of sands of different grading would seem to be well worth while. The knowledge so obtained would provide an extremely useful aid to the study of wind movement over the surfaces of dunes. A tape-measure is all that would then be necessary in order to ascertain the mean wind velocity and direction at any desired spot.

(*c*) *The ripple height and shape depend on the surface sand grading.* It was suggested at the end of Section 5*a* that the mutual interaction between the intensity variation of the saltation and the alternations of surface angle on either side of the ripple crest should of itself tend to make the crest ever higher and the troughs ever lower. But as the crests rise and become more pronounced, they must interfere, in the manner sketched in Fig. 50, with the flow of the wind. Over the crests the wind velocity increases with the height at a greater rate than it does over the troughs. These local changes in the wind gradient become more violent the higher the crests rise, the wavelength and the mean wind gradient remaining constant. Hence there must be an increasing tendency, as the crests rise, for the crest grains to be carried over and deposited in the hollows where the wind current near the surface is slacker.

When the sand grains are nearly uniform in size this very soon neutralizes the ripple-forming tendency, so that with such sand only very low ripples are possible. It was found experimentally

[1] For a nearly uniform sand of grain diameter 0·25 mm. the ripples disappeared when V'_* exceeded 65, or about three times its threshold value.

that with a single grade of sand whose grain size ranged between 0·19 and 0·27 mm. only, the ratio of height to wavelength was usually but 1 to 70, and never more than 1 to 30.

Sands of a greater range of grain size, on the other hand, form ripples whose height-wavelength ratio is 1 to 15 or even 1 to 10. This greater ripple height is no doubt due to the well-known fact that the coarsest grains always collect at the crest. For, as such grains are less easily moved, they protect the crest and allow it to rise into a region of stronger wind than would otherwise be possible.

The progressive increase in grain size from the trough to the crest of the ripple can be exhibited and studied by means of a very pretty experiment. A quantity of sand is separated into its constituent grades by passing it through a set of sieves. Each

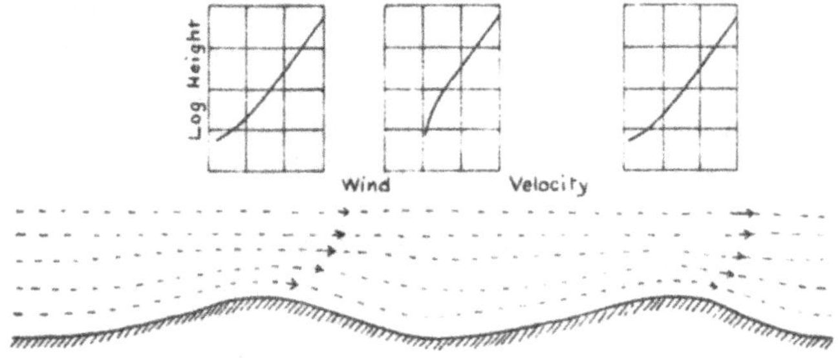

FIG. 50.—LOCAL DISTRIBUTION OF WIND VELOCITY OVER RIPPLES

grade is treated with a different aniline dye, and the grades are then remixed. With a little care the dyes can be chosen so as to give the mixture a neutral hue. On spreading the sand in the wind tunnel and blowing wind over it the colours reappear as bright bands running along the ripple slopes like layered contours on a map.

This sorting out of the grains appears to be due to the differential action of the saltation in propelling grains of different sizes up the windward slope at different speeds. The smaller grains tend to be knocked over the crest and to reach the bottom, or beyond it, before coming to rest; whereas the large grains tend to stop at the top immediately the change in the surface angle diminishes the intensity of the bombardment.

This action also explains the fact that tall ripples, formed in sand containing a good proportion of coarse grains, are markedly asymmetrical, the lee slopes being steeper than the windward ones. This asymmetry is far less pronounced in the case of the flat undulating ripple formed in nearly uniform sand.

Thus, in a sand having any given peak diameter, the cross-section of the ripple is controlled by the proportions in which the coarser grains are present in the surface layer.

6. RIPPLES DURING DEPOSITION

Here the sorting-out process, whereby the coarse grains are collected into raised ripple crests, is hindered by the continuous deposition of unsorted sand over the surface. This deposition is heavier in the troughs, where the wind gradient is feebler, than it is on the crests. The troughs therefore tend to fill up. But if the general rate of deposition is not too rapid a balance is reached between the relative flattening out of the crests and the consequent reduction of the differential rate of deposition on trough and crest. The result is a flatter, but still stable, ripple.

But as the general rate of deposition is increased, this balance is reached at a lower and lower ripple height, till under very rapid deposition the ripples disappear altogether.

The process of sand accumulation by accretion on a smooth wind-swept surface is therefore marked by a relative absence of rippling. Seligman [1] has noticed that snow deposits formed while the material is being driven over the surface (wind-packing) are also unrippled. There are, however, two other conditions under which the ripples disappear. We have already noticed that they do so when the wind exceeds a certain strength relative to the grain diameter (Section 5*b*). For snow this critical wind strength may well be lower owing to the smaller density of the grains. There are also certain sands of irregular grading which inhibit rippling. This point will be dealt with in Section 8. A lack of rippling therefore gives no positive evidence that deposition is taking place.

7. RIPPLES AND RIDGES DURING SAND REMOVAL

(*a*) *Limited removal. Coarse, steep-faced ripples.* When discussing in Chapter 7 (4) the threshold wind required to move the surface of a non-uniform sand, it was pointed out that under any wind of feebler strength than the ultimate threshold needed to set the largest grains in motion, the sand movement lasts for a

[1] Seligman, G. (1936). *Snow Structure and Ski Fields.* (Macmillan.) p. 221.

limited time only. As removal proceeds the surface becomes coarser, and the movement ceases when there remain on the surface no more exposed grains of diameter small enough to be set in motion by the wind. It was pointed out, however, that this only refers to motion initiated by the direct action of the wind, under conditions where there is no oncoming saltation from up-wind of the area considered. Motion then ceases because the direct force of the wind cannot raise any more grains into saltation.

It is prevented from doing so because the finer material which is still exposed in the troughs is sheltered by the now very coarse-grained and stable ripple crests. For towards the end of the removal period the ripples have become very pronounced, and their leeward faces are now so steep (Section 5*c*) that the wind is no longer able to sweep down them. Instead it flows over them, as over a little cliff, leaving pockets of comparatively stagnant air below.

The wavelength of these final ripples is somewhat greater than at first. This is to be expected, since the wind velocity near the surface is now unchecked by the drag offered to it by the heavy saltation which flowed initially. The saltation has been growing less and less in quantity; but the few remaining grains in it are now exposed to a greater wind velocity, and therefore have a longer characteristic path.

(*b*) *Removal maintained by an oncoming saltation. Unlimited growth of ridges.* Though a wind of a given strength cannot by itself move grains larger than a definite size, a saltation set up by that wind can by impact move grains exceeding six times the size of those composing the saltation. Hence, if a continuous supply of grains is driven down from up-wind, so that a saltation is maintained over the removal area even though that area has itself run short of suitably small grains, then those far bigger grains that have collected to form the ripple crests can still be kept in motion.

Moreover the descending grains can penetrate into the troughs, and can bombard the exposed bed material which is protected from the direct blast of the wind. This material, having the composition of the original bed, contains but a small proportion of coarse grains. But as the finer grains are driven off, to augment the saltation, more and more coarse grains are gradually excavated.

Fig. 51 illustrates the action. The bombardment, descending in the direction AC, strikes the exposed area CD of the bed. As new large grains are exposed they are driven by impact up the windward slope CDA and over the crest A, till they come to rest in the complete shelter of the lee slope. None are able to pass on across the stagnant zone ABC. In consequence, since new grains continue to arrive, and no corresponding grains leave the ripple, the previous wavelength limitation imposed by the length of the characteristic path is no longer effective. The ripple, which must now go on growing bigger and bigger, has become a *ridge*.

The essential difference between ripples and ridges lies in the relative magnitudes of the wind strength and the dimensions of the crest grains. In the ripple, the wind is strong enough to carry away the topmost crest grains whenever the crest rises above

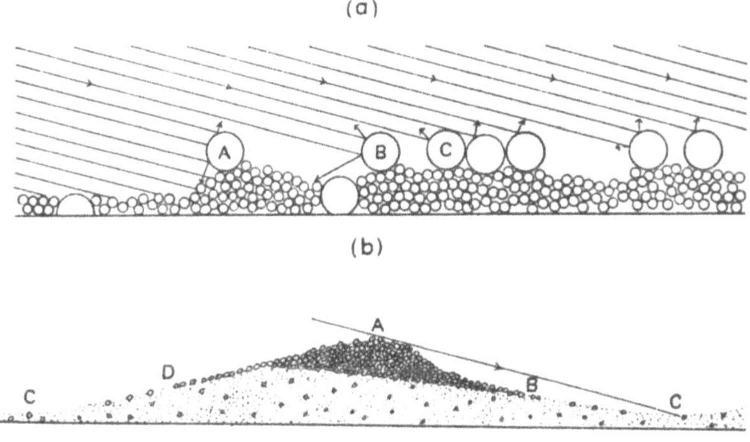

FIG. 51.—RIDGE FORMATION

a limiting height. In the case of the ridge the wind is too feeble, relatively to the size of the crest grains, to do this. The wind condition favourable to ridge formation may be looked upon as an extended range of strengths lying between the impact threshold and the fluid threshold.

Sand ridges may grow to a great size. Wavelengths exceeding 20 metres and heights of over 60 cm. are common in some parts of the Libyan Desert. Such ridges are illustrated in Plate 5.

The conditions necessary for their growth appear to be as follows:

(i) An adequate supply of large grains of suitable diameter. This diameter must be between 3 and 7 times the mean diameter of the prevailing saltation. The presence of larger and immobile pebbles tends to inhibit the growth of ridges by holding up the surface movement. The ridge-forming material is usually made available from below by excavation. But in wind-swept desert valleys, especially in sandstone country where the ridges are most common, the material may be brought direct to the site from the neighbouring hills by occasional rain storms.

(ii) There must be a constant supply of fine sand to provide the necessary motive power in the form of saltation.

(iii) This saltation must not be too intense; that is, removal conditions, real or potential, must prevail. If the saltation approaches saturation, its drag so checks the wind velocity that the fine material settles in the troughs and fills them up, beginning with the sharp hollow beneath the steep lee slope. When this happens, and when the lee slope becomes less steep than the angle of descent of the saltation, the big crest grains can no longer find shelter from the bombardment, and are 'floated off' over the new surface of fine sand.

(iv) The wind must never reach the threshold strength at which it can begin to dislodge the crest grains (see the next sub-section).

All these effects have been reproduced and studied in the wind tunnel. The growth of the ridges is very slow. Those in Plate 4*b* took two hours to attain a wavelength of 18 cm. It seems reasonable to suppose that the rate at which fresh grains are driven up the windward slope to swell the body of the ridge is independent of the dimensions of the ridge, and depends only on the impelling saltation. Hence, if the saltation is kept constant, the rate of growth should become slower and slower as time goes on. In fact, the dimension of the ridge should vary as the square root of its age. It seems probable, therefore, that we must estimate the age of such giant ridges as those shown in Plate 5 in decades or centuries.

Similar transverse ridges are formed in very cold weather when the erosion of an old snow surface produces a supply of coarse ice grains.[1]

(*c*) *Ridges in very strong winds.* When the wind attains a strength sufficient to move the crest grains by its own unaided force, the big grains go into saltation. The conditions therefore revert to those of ordinary sand movement. The massive crest grains removed from the ridges impinge violently on the windward slopes of other ridges down-wind. Removal of the finer

[1] Cornish, V. (1914). *Waves of Sand and Snow.* (T. Fisher Unwin, London.) p. 101.

PLATE 7

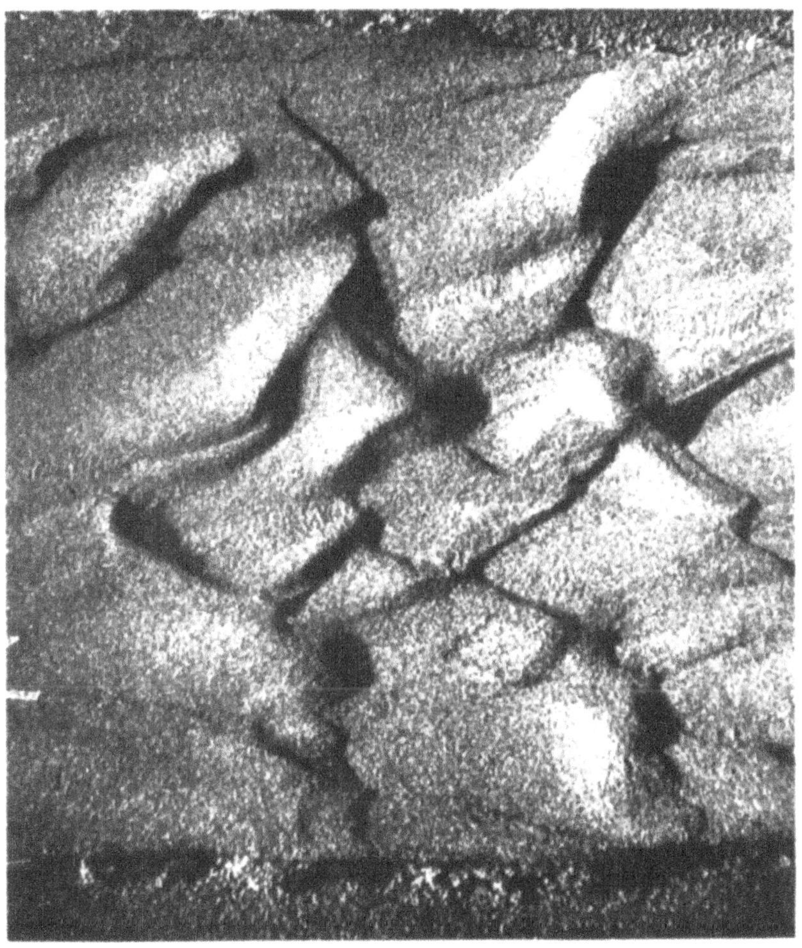

Photo : C. M. White

Direction of flow ⟶

SAND RIPPLES ON BED OF A STREAM OF WATER

(Mean ripple dimension approximately the same as on Plate 6*b*)

PLATE 8

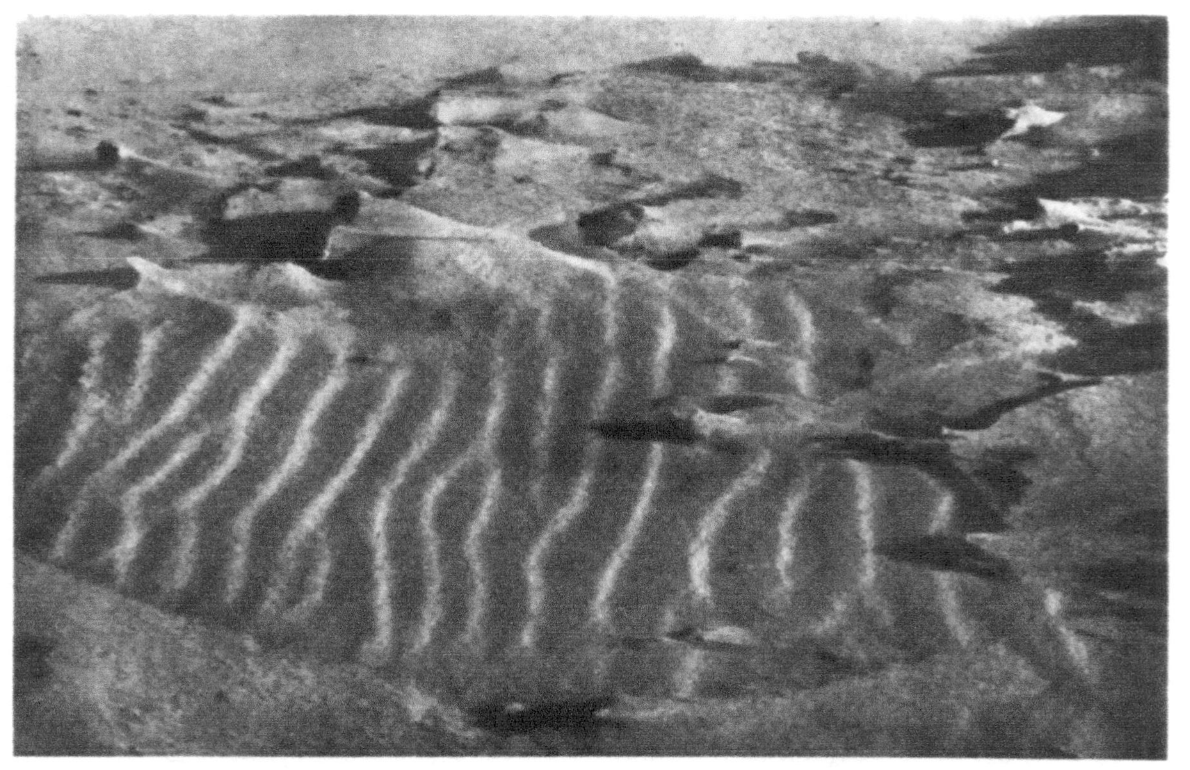

Photo : V. Cornish

RIPPLES IN OLD GRANULAR SNOW

material from their lower levels takes place in the early stages at such a rate that the windward slopes become steeper than the lee slopes, so the ridges appear to be reversed in aspect. Thereafter the hollows are soon filled up, the ridges break down, and the now flat surface becomes covered with small ripples whose wavelength once more depends on the wind strength.

8. RIPPLE-LESS SAND MIXTURES. THE SURFACES OR SAND SHEETS

The preceding sections have related to ripple and ridge formation in regular sands. In these the proportions in which the extreme grades, both coarse and fine, are present diminish progressively as the diameter departs from the mean or peak value (Chapters 9 and 10). Hence, though the crest of the ripple or ridge contains a few grains of the very biggest size, yet these few are always surrounded by many more grains of but slightly smaller size. No grains are conspicuously larger than their neighbours.

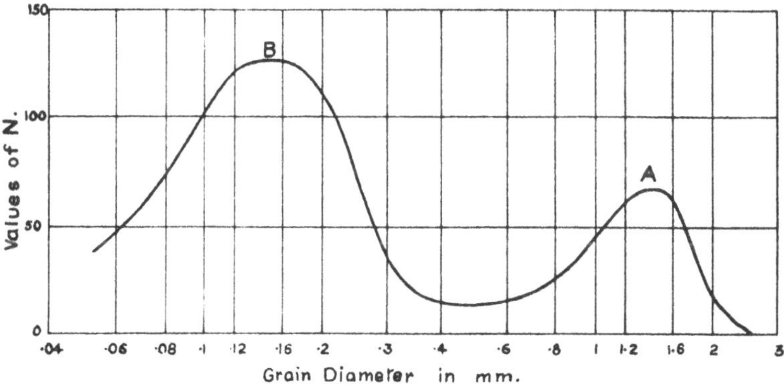

FIG. 52.—GRADING OF SAMPLE FROM THE SURFACE OF SAND SHEET

But in the case of a mixture of two sands A and B whose peak diameters are widely separated (Fig. 52) this is not true. For there are now some grains or pebbles belonging to component A, of very much larger diameter, scattered about among the much smaller grains of component B which comprises the bulk of the mixture. These pebbles have diameters more than six times those of the grains in the saltation (whose mean diameter is very nearly that of B). Being therefore almost immobile, they tend to break up the orderly advance of the ripples, just as scattered boulders would disorganize a company of soldiers advancing in line. The effect can be readily verified by sprinkling a handful of pebbles or coarse grit on a rippled sand surface in the open during a wind. The ripples are suppressed.

Under moderate winds the scattered pebbles are not moved forward by impact, so they have no tendency to collect, as do large sand grains, to form the crests of ripples. On the contrary, we find a new mechanism operating whereby they tend to disperse, especially under removal conditions, to the most uniform distribution possible.

This new mechanism can be demonstrated by the following experiment. A light even sprinkling of little pebbles 2 mm. or more in diameter is dropped over a surface of fine sand. Sand is removed from the surface by a wind until the pebbles, which have sunk in somewhat as a result of their fall, project sufficiently far above the surface to protect it from further sand removal. The surface becomes stable, even when a saltation from up-wind is passed over it. All the pebbles lying on any selected area are then picked up by hand and placed in a close group X (Fig. 53) in the centre of the area, leaving exposed sand around it.

The wind can now remove more sand from the exposed area, and a hollow is formed. The group X is left at the top of a little isolated hill. As this becomes undercut by the removal of sand from its exposed edges, each of the little pebbles, one by one, rolls away from its neighbours and down into the depression. The same thing happens to the pebbles on the outer edge of the depression, and gradually the bare area is once more covered by the pebbles.[1]

If the wind becomes very strong, however, the pebbles may begin to move forward in surface creep as coarse sand grains. When this happens, the surface behaves very much as described in the preceding sections, and under removal conditions the pebbles collect into transverse steep-fronted crests. When the

[1] This scattering of objects larger than sand grains, whenever surface removal takes place, is very noticeable in the case of desert archaeological sites. Implements, flakes, fragments of pottery or ostrich shell, originally in close contact, are often found scattered over the surface of a mound of natural undisturbed material. The fragments are closest together at the top, which presumably has remained at or near the original ground level. Round the sides of the mound they are regularly arranged so that the mean separation varies as the distance from the top. Since these large objects cannot roll owing to their shape, it is probable that their movement down the slopes has been assisted by a minute but long-continued caterpillar action due to diurnal expansion and contraction.

wind drops again these collections of pebbles once more become unstable and slowly disperse over the surface.

The surfaces of the almost ripple-less *sand sheets* which occupy vast areas of flat desert country are controlled in the above manner. Samples taken from the surface always give grading curves such as that of Fig. 52. The whole process of the gradual scattering of the overlying pebbles after a storm has been observed repeatedly by the writer; and it can be imitated in the wind tunnel. The ratio of the two peak diameters should exceed 10 to 1. If the ratio is less than 7 to 1 the big grains take part in the normal surface creep even in moderate winds.

The photograph in Plate 6*a* illustrates the behaviour of both sand and pebbles on a flat surface. Sand has previously been

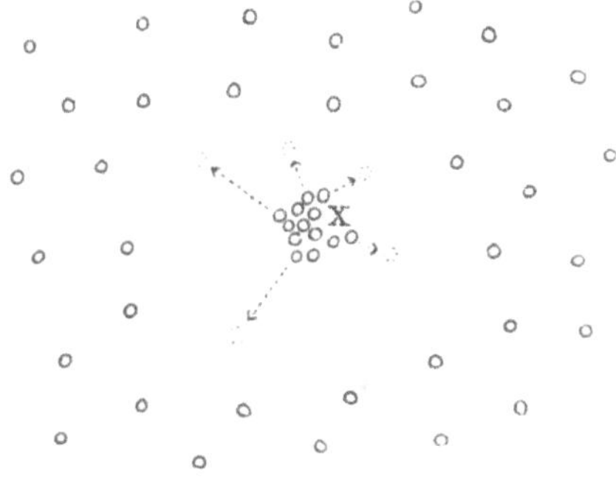

FIG. 53.—DISPERSION OF PEBBLES ON A SAND SURFACE

driving heavily under a strong wind from left to right across the pebble-covered sand sheet. As a result fresh sand has been deposited in long narrow strips, one of which is seen in the foreground and two more in the middle distance. (Further reference will be made to these large-scale phenomena in the next chapter.)

Owing to the impacts of the saltation along these strips, the smaller of the surface pebbles at the up-wind end of each strip were rolled along and driven a little way on to the new sand surface, as it rose by deposition. This happened in the immediate foreground. Further away, beyond the implement, the same thing happened away to the left out of sight. Later on, the oncoming saltation was no longer saturated and removal began at the up-wind end of each sand strip. This caused the pebbles which had encroached on to the sand deposit to be thrown up into ridges. Further away the new sand contained no pebbles, and as removal had not yet set in there, the surface still carries the ordinary ripple-mark.

A rarer instance of a ripple-less sand than that of a sand sheet occurs when the coarser component of the mixture predominates (Fig. 54) and when the finer component consists of a very fine sand below the critical diameter (Chapter 7 (2)). Here the fine

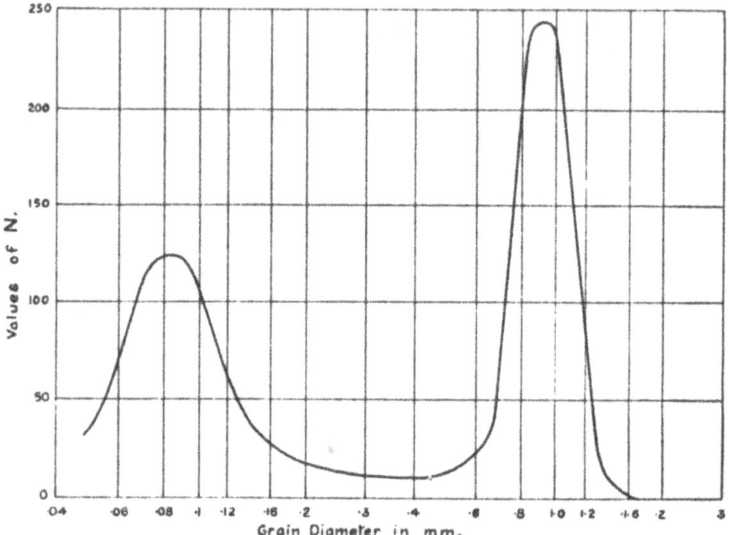

FIG. 54.—GRADING OF A SAMPLE OF A RARER TYPE OF RIPPLE-LESS SAND

material is concentrated by differential removal (Chapter 10 (4)) into smooth sheets whose individual grains the wind cannot disturb. The coarse grains roll over these without causing ripples. This phenomenon may occur over small areas on the rounded tops of low barchan dunes, in country where fine material is present in quantity. On one occasion the writer discovered in the Libyan Desert a plain several miles wide composed of such a sand. The surface was entirely smooth, with hardly less unevenness than a billiard table.

9. THE TRANSVERSE ALIGNMENT OF SAND RIPPLES IN AIR

In the explanation of the formation of ripples and ridges we have dealt only with the shape of a cross-section along a vertical plane parallel to the wind direction. But no consideration has yet been given to the ground plan, and to how and why the initial isolated irregularities in the surface join up into continuous crests at right angles to the wind.

This aspect of ripple formation can be treated as a question of the relative stability of small windward ripple faces inclined in azimuth at various angles to the wind. If it can be shown that the transverse direction is more stable than any other, then the rest follows at once.

The raised portion of the initial isolated ripple must be either transverse, or curved forward or back, as in Fig. 55 (*a*) and (*b*); and we can compare the result of the bombardment by the on-

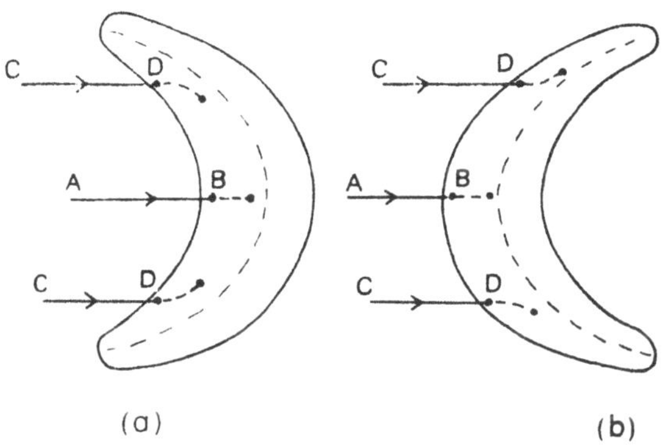

FIG. 55.—STABILITY OF IMAGINARY CURVED RIPPLES

coming saltation on the transverse and on the outer inclined portions of the windward face.

In all cases the impact, which is assumed constant everywhere in magnitude and direction, tends to knock the surface grains forward, and so to cause a general advance of the ripple by removing grains from the windward slope and leaving them on the lee slope.

Now in the case of the normal impact AB the surface grain has to travel straight up the hill; but in the inclined impact CD, the grain, though it started in the same direction, travels obliquely up the hill, and tends to roll sideways. This applies equally to both ripples (*a*) and (*b*). In ripple (*a*), however, the grains roll *inwards* towards the more transverse portion, and tend to accumulate there. This causes the rate of advance of the transverse portion to become slower than that of the more oblique portion. In ripple (*b*), on the other hand, the grains roll *outwards* away from the transverse portion and thereby increase the rate of removal, so that the transverse portion moves faster.

In both configurations, then, there is a tendency for curved ripples to straighten out till they lie at right angles to the wind direction. Moreover, this same tendency must encourage the joining up of two neighbouring ripples which are not in the same transverse line. For once they become connected by an inclined ridge, there should be a drift of sand along it from the leeward to the more windward ripple. This in turn should slow up the latter and hasten the former till the two are in line.

The above explanation, though simple, is at present merely tentative. It has not been verified experimentally owing to the difficulty of building artificial ripples whose grains are graded and arranged in the correct manner.

Further remarks on the stability of transverse ripples will be found in Chapter 13 (7), where ripples and dunes are compared.

10. SAND RIPPLES IN AIR AND WATER COMPARED

That too great a reliance on a similarity of effect as an indication of a similarity of cause may lead to a confusion of ideas, is well exemplified by the case of sand ripples. Everyone is familiar with the pattern of sand ripples on a sea beach—their uniformity of wavelength, their rounded, almost sinoidal profile, the great lengths over which they may run parallel to one another, and their typical 'finger-print' design. And it would be hard indeed to find a single point wherein they differ in appearance from the wind ripples seen on the surfaces of dunes.

Yet the mechanism of their formation cannot be the same in the two cases. The conditions are quite different. The beach ripple is due essentially to the *alternating* flow of water backwards and forwards under successive wavelets as they play over flat shallows. The continuity of the parallel crests and troughs, and the great constancy of the wavelength over wide areas, are both due to the fact that a large mass of water over them is rocked to and fro as one body by the passage of the surface waves above. Experiments carried out by the writer [1] at Imperial College, London, strongly suggest that the wavelength of the beach ripple is merely a function of the distance by which the water is displaced along

[1] To be published during 1940 in the *Journal of the Institution of Civil Engineers*.

the bottom. Beach ripples are the product of a violently accelerated water flow. With each movement of the water a long horizontal vortex is formed above and in the lee of each ripple crest, and some of the sand from the crest is carried up into the vortex. When the water sweeps back again this vortex is carried back with it and the reverse motion 'unwinds' it, so that the sand is re-deposited on the same crest from whence it arose. The same thing happens on the other side of the crest during the second half of the water oscillation. These long parallel vortices carrying sand round inside them are never formed on sand beds when either wind or water flows steadily over them in one direction only; and the beach ripple must be considered as the result of a very special kind of fluid motion.

When ripples are compared which have been formed under the same conditions of steady flow in one direction by air and water respectively, nearly all the similarity disappears. The wind ripple is long-crested, and runs transversely to the flow (Plate 6*b*), whereas the water ripple consists of isolated hillocks and pockets which show no tendency to straightness or to a transverse direction (Plate 7).

It seems reasonable to attribute this striking difference in the character of the ripples in air and water to the difference in the mechanism whereby the surface grains are moved. In air the ripple is the result of repeated impacts with the surface on the part of grains which have travelled through the fluid a certain average distance from an area whence they were ejected from the surface by previous impacts. The wavelength of the ripple in air appears to correspond with this average distance of travel between impacts.

In water the grains taking part in the saltation strike the bottom so feebly that they can neither eject other grains into saltation nor knock them along the surface in surface creep. Each moving grain is set in motion independently by the direct force of the water upon it, and the average distance through which the individual grains travel bears no direct relation to the scale of the hillocks formed by the general grain movement.

It seems almost certain that the scale of the sand ripple in water is somehow inherent in the flow of the fluid, whereas the wavelength of the ripple in air is inherent in the paths of the sand grains. A promising theory has been outlined by White [1]

[1] White, C. M. (1939). *International Union of Geophysics and Geodesy*. Washington.

in which the profile of the up-stream faces of the hillocks formed in water can be predicted mathematically by the application of the Karman-Pohlhausen boundary layer theory to the variation of surface drag with the distance down-stream from the base of the incipient hillock. A free layer of moving water is supposed to come into contact with the sand surface along some arbitrary transverse border. In the case of a new flat sand surface the border is the up-stream edge of the sand area. When hillocks have already started to form, the border is on the lower up-stream slope, and the water layer has moved across over stagnant water in the lee pocket from the crest of the previous ripple.

The conditions are those mentioned at the end of Chapter 4 (9). The water encounters at the border a surface of greater roughness, and its surface velocity is checked. This causes the drag at the border to have a high value. But if the surface immediately down-stream is flat, the drag falls again to a steady value as the distance from the border increases. Hence, if the drag at the border is sufficient to remove grains from the surface, they must tend to be redeposited further down where the drag has dropped in strength.

As deposition continues, a mound is built up. But when this happens the surface is no longer flat, and the flow over the up-stream face of the mound is accelerated to a greater velocity at the top. This acceleration of the surface flow prevents the drag from decreasing in value, and so tends to prevent further deposition of sand. Equilibrium sets in when the curvature of the face of the mound is such that the acceleration it produces in the surface flow is just sufficient to maintain the drag at a constant value from the border onwards, and hence to prevent further deposition. The hillock is now stable in shape. The final curvature of the up-stream face of the mound depends on the Reynolds' Number $V_* d/\nu$ of the flow, and it is an outcome of the theory that the face should be steeper for fine sand than for coarse. This is confirmed by observation.

It is doubtful if the above theory has any effective bearing on the profile of the impact ripple formed in air, since the surface drag is negligible compared with that caused by the grains in saltation high above the surface. But it seems very likely that it is applicable to dunes; for here the mound is on such a large scale that the whole sand movement, including the saltation, can be taken as a true surface effect.

11. RIPPLES IN SNOW

The inability of the descending grain in water to cause any appreciable disturbance of the bottom material is due to the density of the grain being but little greater than that of the surrounding fluid; whereas in air the grain is 2,000 times as dense. It would therefore seem to be impossible under any conditions of flow to reproduce in water the '*impact ripple*' as it is formed in air, except by increasing the relative density of the grain. One might for instance use steel shot.

On the other hand it is possible that the '*boundary-layer*' ripple which is formed in water may also occur in air under suitable conditions. A very light fluffy grain would be needed, which would alight on the surface without disturbing it.

Snow appears to form two kinds of ripple, according to the nature of the particles. When these consist of coarse hard ice granules the ripples are hardly to be distinguished from sand ripples in air, and have the same continuous transverse crests (Plate 8). But when the snow is fresh and consists of fluffy flakes, the pattern (Plate 9) resembles much more closely the water ripples shown in Plate 7. The resemblance may, of course, be found to have no significance, for the exact mechanism has in this case not yet been established. But the existence of two kinds of snow ripple certainly seems suggestive.

12. RIPPLES IN VERY FINE SAND

Deposits of sand of peak diameter less than 0·15 mm. are rare. Experiments with such a sand with a peak diameter of 0·08 mm. disclosed an interesting change in the ripple formation when the wind reached a certain critical strength.

The threshold wind gradient for this sand ($V_* = 15$) was very close to the minimum value. Light winds of any strength between $V_* = 15$ and $V_* = 25$ produced the ordinary wind ripple with its characteristic continuous crest (Plate 10*a*). The wavelength just above the threshold wind strength was less than 1 cm., but it conformed to the usual rule, increasing to about 1·5 cm. as the wind was raised.

When V_* exceeded 30, however, the surface began to rise up to form new ripples on a much larger scale (Plate 10*b*); and the former little ones faded away. These new ripples, as can be seen in the photograph, were discontinuous, and consisted of pockets surrounded by crescentic ridges.

It is possible that these tiny grains are so susceptible to air resistance that the mechanism of their movement lies on the border-line between the impact mechanism of larger sand grains in air and the direct fluid drag mechanism of sand in water. It may be significant that according to the theory mentioned in Chapter 5 (7), suspension, for this fine sand, should be quite appreciable at the wind strength at which the change in the ripple takes place. At low wind speeds we undoubtedly have saltation and the effects of grain impact predominating, and the observed ripples seem to be true impact ripples. At higher wind speeds, with an appreciable proportion of the total sand flow moving in suspension and so contributing nothing to the drag, it is possible that the drag due to the remaining saltation is not sufficient to keep the surface wind velocity below the threshold value. In this case the surface wind may set grains in motion by its direct action, as it does in water. If so we might expect to see the appearance of surface forms of a similar type to those in water.

REFERENCES

BAGNOLD, R. A. (1937). *Geogr. J.*, 89, p. 428

CORNISH, V. (1914). *Waves of Sand and Snow.* (T. Fisher Unwin) and numerous previous papers

PART III

LARGE-SCALE EFFECTS. SAND ACCUMULATION. DUNES. INTERNAL STRUCTURE, ETC.

Chapter 12

LARGE-SCALE PHENOMENA. THE CONDITIONS OF GROWTH OF A FLAT SAND SURFACE

1. LIMITATIONS TO THE EXPERIMENTAL STUDY OF DUNE FORMATION

IN this chapter we shall deal, as a preliminary to the consideration of real dunes, with the conditions under which sand deposition takes place on a flat surface under a wind of constant direction. Although the areas to be considered are far larger than that of a ripple, and although changes in the wind velocity are involved up to a greater height above the surface, experiments can nevertheless still be carried out on the straight floor of a wind tunnel. But we must remember that the sand on the floor is only the longitudinal section of an imaginary deposition area, and that wind-tunnel experiments can tell us little about the shape of the real area.

If the experimental deposit were allowed to grow so thick that its surface could no longer be treated as flat, the wind-tunnel method of investigation would break down altogether; for in order to avoid interference by the tunnel walls with the complicated air flow over and round the now curved sand surface, the tunnel would have to be made very large indeed.

Thus experiment becomes very difficult in the case of real dunes, and in the following two chapters we shall be forced to fall back largely on description and inference. We are immediately concerned, however, only with the conditions under which an initially flat patch of sand situated in an open stretch of country can accumulate sand and grow into a dune.

2. THE SUPPLY OF MATERIAL FOR DUNE-BUILDING. NATURE OF THE DESERT FLOOR

It is necessary before considering the growth of an incipient dune to form a clear idea of the sand supply, and of the kind of country it has to pass over in order to reach the dune.

In the case of coastal and riverine dunes the sand is produced elsewhere, is transported by the water current, and is deposited on the shore and left high and dry ready for the wind to carry it away. The grading of such sand has been pre-determined by the flow conditions in the water, and the material supplied at any one place is usually very uniform in grain size. Sea sand in particular is conspicuously free of large grains. This fact, together with the effects of moisture and the presence of vegetation, all play such an important part in the building of coastal and riverine dunes that a separate consideration of them will be omitted.

Desert dunes present a far simpler and at the same time more general case. The place of origin of the grains is usually fairly obvious—an escarpment or a series of depressions where wind erosion is actively taking place. Sometimes, however, the origin is not clear, owing to uncertainty as to the direction of the general long-period sand drift.

The grading of the sand made available for dune-building varies greatly with the type of rock from which it came. Where this has originated as a marine deposit or as an ancient field of coastal dunes, the range of grain size is narrow, and large semi-mobile grains infrequent. Where, on the other hand, the rock has been laid down as sandstone by successive fluvial deposits, it is likely to contain layers of coarse grains which, on disintegration, yield a sand of wide grading.

The most typical kind of country on which desert dunes are found is a flat erosion surface, so arid that the complications introduced by rainfall and vegetation are negligible. The usual erosion surface consists of pebbles or coarse grit, with larger rock fragments scattered about here and there. The pebbles may be entirely immovable, or they may be small enough to be moved by impact during moderate sand storms. *But a desert surface is never composed entirely of fine dune sand, unprotected by a layer of coarser grains.* Such a surface is confined entirely to the dunes themselves.

3. SAND STORAGE ON A PEBBLE FLOOR

The loose sand grains drift across this country and lodge among the pebbles in greater or fewer numbers according to the strength of the wind. The following wind-tunnel experiments will illustrate both the resulting storage effect and the important bearing which this has on the conditions of dune-building.

The imitation desert floor consists initially of a fine nearly uniform sand, mixed with a small proportion of pebbles about 4 mm. in diameter—too large to be moved by wind or sand action. A steady wind, just above the threshold strength, is made to blow.

As the sand is carried off down-wind, more and more pebbles are exposed. These project further and further out of the surface until they begin to form a wind shield which protects the sand between them. Eventually no more sand removal or movement takes place because the grains are completely protected. Even when a stream of sand is fed in at the tunnel mouth and passes over in saltation, no further changes occur in the loading of the surface, which is now quite stable to the particular wind strength operating.

The wind is now raised. This results in a fresh layer of sand being removed, so that the surface is still more denuded. Eventually a new stable condition is reached, when the sand movement again ceases.

When the wind is made to slacken, and the stream of sand is fed in at the tunnel mouth, the sand surface tends to build up again. Sand is deposited in the hollows between the pebbles until another stable condition is reached such that the sand is again only just screened by the now more submerged pebbles.

A pebble surface can therefore be regarded as a reservoir in which sand is stored during periods of gentle wind, and from which it is removed by a sudden storm.

4. DEPOSITION BY ACCRETION ON AN EXISTING PATCH OF BARE SAND

Now it will be recalled (Chapters 5 (5) and 6 (3)) that for any given wind the rate of sand flow over a surface containing pebbles is considerably greater than the maximum rate possible over a surface of plain sand. Hence at the beginning of a sudden increase in wind strength the surplus sand may be swept off the pebbles in a heavier stream than could pass over any patch of pebble-less sand which might happen to be lying immediately down-wind. The inevitable result must be a deposition of sand on the patch.

The following two experiments throw a useful light on the behaviour of such a patch of bare sand.

(*a*) *Gentle Wind.* The arrangement is sketched in Fig. 56. The sand bed is covered, as before, with a sprinkling of pebbles. On the down-wind half of this bed, except on the last metre, is spread a further layer of plain sand, which is meant to represent an incipient dune.

A gentle wind, say about 10 per cent. above the threshold strength, is made to blow from right to left. Sand removal from between the pebbles starts at a point near the tunnel entrance on

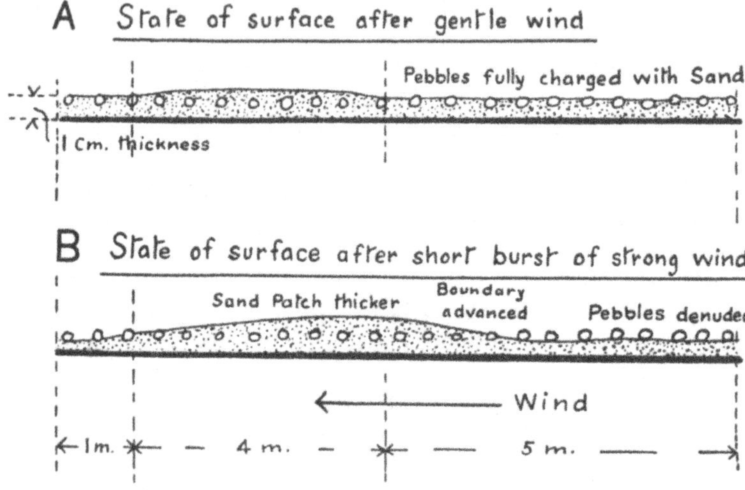

FIG. 56.—ACCRETION ON A SAND PATCH OF SAND FROM A PEBBLE-COVERED SURFACE UP-WIND

the right. As the pebble surface becomes stabilized, the point where movement begins shifts down-wind to the left. Soon the whole pebble surface is motionless, the removal area having passed on over the border of the sand patch, whose level now begins to fall. But meanwhile the down-wind border of the patch slowly advances, submerging the exposed pebbles on the extreme left as it does so.

From this experiment it appears that *under a gentle wind a patch of fine sand extends down-wind at the expense of its own thickness.*

(*b*) *Strong Wind.* The wind is now suddenly increased to four times the threshold strength, in imitation of the onset of a sand storm. Removal of further sand from among the pebbles up-wind begins again very violently. At the edge of the sand patch the intense bombardment due to the heavy oncoming saltation produces a very great disturbance of the surface grains. The excessive numbers ejected into the air so check the flow that a heavy accretion of sand takes place over the first two metres of the patch. Indeed the drag is so great that the back-pressure makes itself felt some distance up-wind of the border, with the result that deposition begins even before the border is reached, and the sand patch actually extends to windward.

Unfortunately the limited length of the tunnel prevents this action from continuing for long, because, owing to the shortness of the storage area up-wind, the sand supply runs out very quickly. (In the open this area would extend for a long distance, and heavy sand flow might continue for several hours.) As the oncoming sand flow decreases in intensity, the sand border begins to recede down-wind, sand being removed very rapidly by the bombardment of the remaining available grains left among the pebbles. Accretion still continues for a time further down the sand patch, but now only at the expense of its up-wind border. Later, when the pebble surface has become quite stable, the sand at the border is left undisturbed, but removal sets in over all the rest of the sand patch.

This experiment shows that *a strong wind causes an accretion of sand on an existing sand patch, together with an extension up-wind of the border ; but this action lasts only as long as there is a plentiful supply of sand stored on a pebbly up-wind surface.*

The rate of the deposition on the sand patch may be estimated from the following considerations. The intensity of the sand flow, for dune sand of normal size, is given by equation (9) of Chapter 5

$$q = C\frac{\rho}{g}V'^{3}_{*}$$

The constant C depends on the type of surface. If we give it a value C_1 for the sand flow q_1 over the pebbles, and a value C_2 for the flow q_2 over the sand patch, then the quantity q_d of sand deposited on unit width of the patch per second is given by

$$q_d = q_1 - q_2 = (C_1 - C_2)\frac{\rho}{g}V'^{3}_{*}$$

If C_1 is given a value of 3·5 (Chapter 5 (5)), and C_2 a value of 2 (Chapter 5 (3)), the rate of deposition is

$$q_d = 1{\cdot}5\frac{\rho}{g}V_*'^3$$

Thus nearly half the sand carried on to the dune, under ideal conditions of ample sand supply, should therefore be deposited upon it, the remainder being carried off over the down-wind pebble surface.

It will be noticed that the rate of deposition should decrease if C_2 has a larger value corresponding to a sand of a wider range of grain size. This is consistent with the observed fact that dunes composed of such sand are not found in nature.

5. EXPLANATION OF SAND ACCRETION ON A FLAT SURFACE IN TERMS OF THE WIND VELOCITY PICTURE. DISTINCTION BETWEEN 'GENTLE' AND 'STRONG' WINDS

The following rather idealized explanation is based on a slight extension of the wind velocity picture given in Chapter 4 (8), to which reference should be made.

In Fig. 57, P represents the level down among the pebbles at which the wind velocity is zero. Assuming that the drag of the sand movement over the pebbles is negligible compared with that over the sand surface, P may be taken as the focus through which pass all rays representing wind velocity distributions over the pebbles.

O is the corresponding level of zero velocity among the grains of the sand surface, for winds below the threshold of movement.

O′ is the focus for sand movement over the sand surface. The rays passing through O′ represent winds above the threshold gradient. The threshold wind for the sand surface is given by the ray OO′.

Consider first a very gentle wind PA as it passes from the pebble surface to the sand surface. The lowest layer of air is the first to be affected by the changed conditions, for the level of zero velocity must drop abruptly from P to O. The air at the level P which was stationary now begins to move. As the wind advances over the new surface the change in the velocity distribution is propagated upwards to the higher layers of air (Fig. 57, inset). The general effect is that the whole ground wind is allowed to speed up, because it blows over a smoother surface than before. But since the new ray OA′ passes to the left of O′,

PLATE 9

Photo : H. Hoek

RIPPLES IN FRESH FLUFFY SNOW

PLATE 10

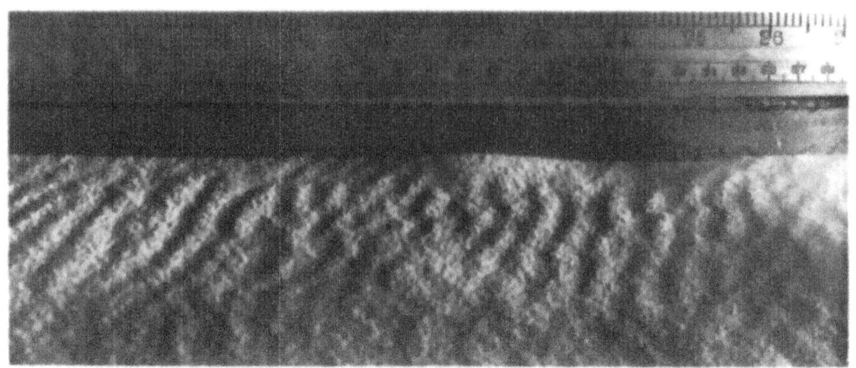

←——Direction of wind

a. VERY FINE SAND. RIPPLES FORMED BY A LIGHT WIND

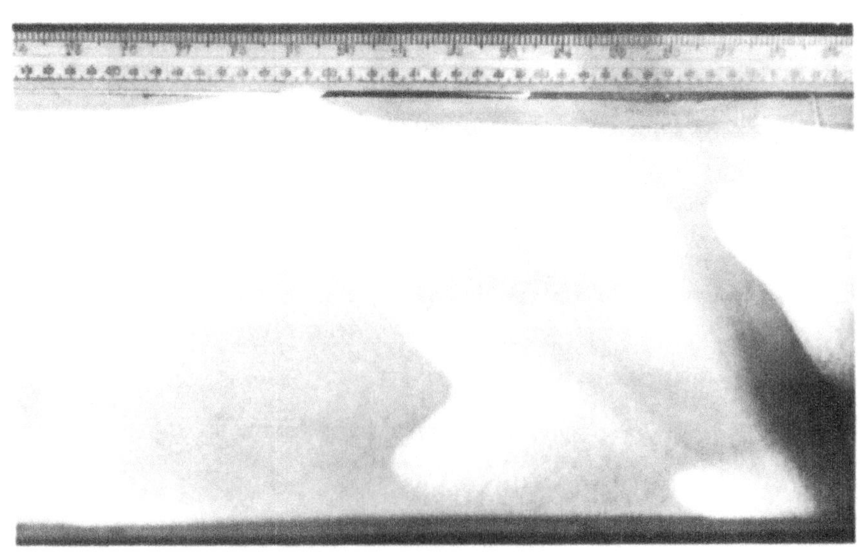

←——Direction of wind

b. VERY FINE SAND. NEW TYPE OF RIPPLE FORMED BY A SLIGHTLY STRONGER WIND THAN IN THE CASE OF *a*

i.e. since the wind gradient is less than the threshold value, no sand movement takes place.

Towards the end of the first part of the experiment described in the last section, the wind gradient, though above the threshold value for the open sand surface, was unable to move the sand among the pebbles because its speed near the surface was reduced by the large surface drag due to the pebbles. Over the pebbles the line PB represents such a wind. When this wind reaches the open sand the velocity at all heights tries to increase to a

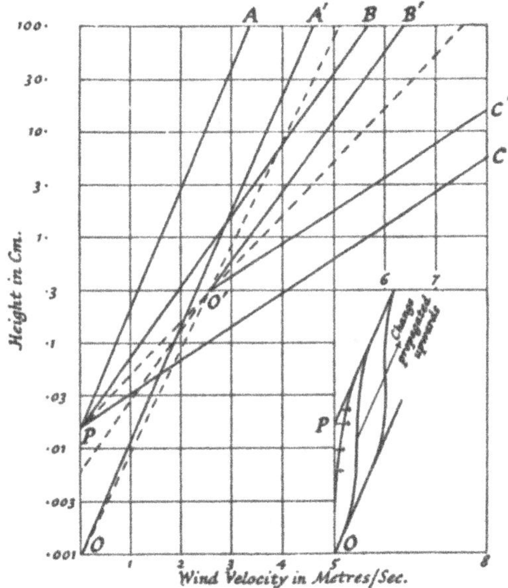

FIG. 57.—WIND VELOCITY CHANGES AT A PEBBLE-SAND BOUNDARY

parallel distribution through O, as in the first case. But it cannot do this because, owing to the onset of the sand movement and the extra drag due to it, no velocities at the level of O′ can exceed that of O′ itself. The wind velocity distribution over the open sand is therefore given by the ray O′B′.

The subsequent strong wind in experiment (*b*) is represented, over the pebbles, by the ray PC. Since, as before, no ray can pass to the right of O′ after the open sand is reached, the surface wind must be checked at the up-wind border, from PC to O′C.′

At the down-wind border of the sand patch the wind begins to revert to its former distribution, slowing down from O′B′ to

PB in the case of the gentle wind, and speeding up O′C′ to PC in the case of the strong wind. In the first case (gentle wind) the slowing down causes the sand streaming off the patch to be deposited among the pebbles, thus extending the patch down-wind; in the second case (strong wind) the down-wind pebble surface is denuded to a stable condition, and the sand passes over it unchanged.

It will be apparent from Fig. 57 that the critical wind strength below which sand is removed from the patch, and above which, under suitable conditions of sand storage up-wind, deposition tends to occur, is given by the line joining PO′. A wind of this gradient should charge the pebble surface to its maximum storage capacity; and thereafter any higher wind adds sand to the dune as long as plenty of sand is still available on the storage area. We will define a *strong wind*, therefore, as one whose gradient V_* is greater than that given by the line PO′. On the other hand any wind whose gradient lies between that of the threshold OO′ and that of the line PO′ tends to elongate the dune at the expense of its bulk. This will be called a *gentle wind*.

The height of P is the measure of the size and spacing of the pebbles, rocks, vegetation, or other surface roughnesses covering the surrounding ground not occupied by the dune. The figure shows that the larger these roughnesses are the greater must be the gradient above which the wind must rise before any dune-building can take place, and therefore the less likelihood there is that a dune will form in the locality. A surrounding surface of small pebbles would seem to be more favourable to dune growth than a stony one.

Several factors have been omitted from the above argument. For instance, the height of P must be affected by the partial filling up of the interspaces between the pebbles during the storage period. Again, the obstruction to the wind's passage created by the dunes themselves as they rise up into the third dimension must play a most important part in their subsequent life-history. This will be discussed in the next chapter, together with the changes in the grading of the oncoming sand brought about by the checking of the surface creep due to the increasing inclination of the surface. But the above picture may serve, when considered in conjunction with the rate at which sand is supplied from the source, and the direction and relative duration of the strong and gentle winds, to convey a useful idea of the principles which seem to be involved.

6. THE EFFECT OF VARYING WIND DIRECTION

The experimental process described in the past section cannot, as it stands, be a true imitation of nature. In fact it will not work more than once, unless the store of sand on the pebble area is replenished artificially. For during the long period required to carry as much sand on to the pebble area as was taken off it by the storm a truly uni-directional wind would have removed the sand patch altogether. It follows that in general a wind that remains truly constant in direction, even though it may vary in strength, can never give rise to an accumulation of sand, unless (*a*) the material is produced at the source at a greater rate than the wind can carry it over a sand surface, or (*b*) the sand stream

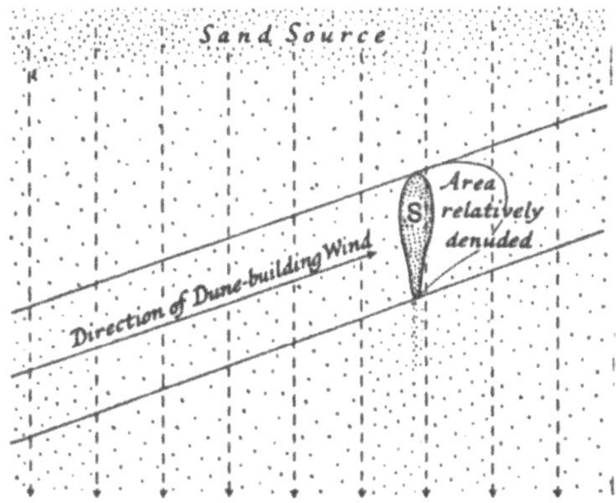

FIG. 58.—SAND ACCUMULATION BY WINDS FROM TWO DIRECTIONS

can somehow be made to move sideways so as to cause an over-concentration in a particular place. The first alternative does not seem to be worth considering. The second will be dealt with in the next section.

But in nature the wind does change in direction; and it is found that in the case of certain types of dune-field, the direction from which the storm winds blow differs greatly from the prevailing direction of the gentler winds.

Fig. 58 shows how the mechanism of our experimental sand accumulation might work under real conditions of varying wind direction. Suppose that the whole area of the figure represents a pebbly or a stony surface, and that S represents a patch of uninterrupted fine sand. The prevailing gentle winds blow in the direction of the dotted arrows, causing a drift of sand over the country from a wide source somewhere up-wind.

All that is now required for the progressive growth of the patch S in thickness is the occurrence of occasional storms from any *other* direction whatsoever.

For example, if the storm blows from the direction shown, the sand stored in the whole of the up-wind part of the zone bounded by the two continuous lines in the figure is available for dune-building; and a comparatively short period of gentle wind from the direction of the sand source will suffice to make good any resulting deficiency in the surface charge of sand among the pebbles.

During the period of gentle wind the dune will tend to string out in the direction of the dotted arrows, at the expense of some of the accretion of mass which it acquired from the previous storm.

While the storm lasted the dune collected a portion of the sand which would otherwise have been driven onward between the continuous lines in the figure. Hence it is apparent that the pebble surface to leeward of the dune has been left partially denuded. Conditions, therefore, for some distance to leeward of dunes, in the direction of the storm winds, should be adverse to the growth of any second sand patch which might exist there.

7. SAND DRIFT OVER A UNIFORM SURFACE IS UNSTABLE ACROSS A TRANSVERSE SECTION. SAND-STRIP FORMATION. DUNE-BUILDING BY A UNI-DIRECTIONAL WIND

The effect of the higher resistance offered to the wind by sand motion over a sandy surface compared with that offered by the motion over an immobile surface is manifested in another way. We have seen what happens when the border between sand and pebbles runs transversely to the direction of flow. We have now to consider such a border lying in the same direction as the wind. Fig. 59 represents the same general surface as that of Fig. 58, but the sand patch is shown on a larger scale. The wind blows only from the direction of the wide uniform source along the top of the figure.

When the wind is gentle, and the sand movement over the patch is small, the roughness of the pebbly or stony surface prevents the wind velocity over it from attaining as high a value as it attains over the smoother sand surface alongside. (Turning to Fig. 57, the velocity distributions over the pebble and sand surfaces are respectively shown by the rays PA or PB and the rays OA′ and P′B′.) There must therefore be a change in the surface wind velocity along the border. This causes eddies to be set up, as indicated in Fig. 59. If these could be made visible, and if the observer were to travel down the sand patch with the wind, their appearance would be similar to the eddies seen in sea water along a ship's side. The effect of the sense of rotation of these eddies probably tends towards a scattering of the sand from the patch outwards over the pebble surface; though with gentle winds the velocity differences are not large.

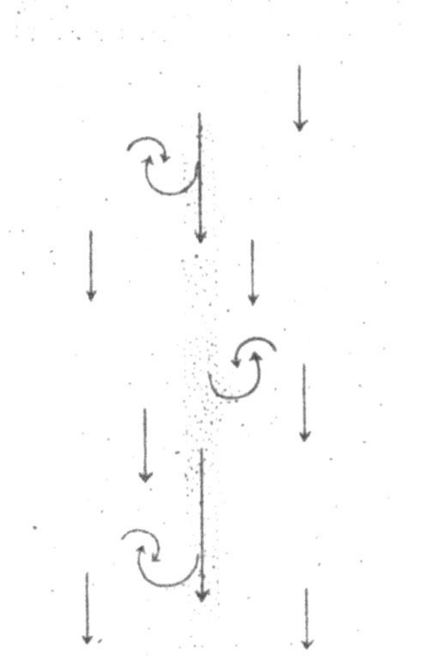

FIG. 59.—LONGITUDINAL SAND-PEBBLE BORDER. GENTLE WIND

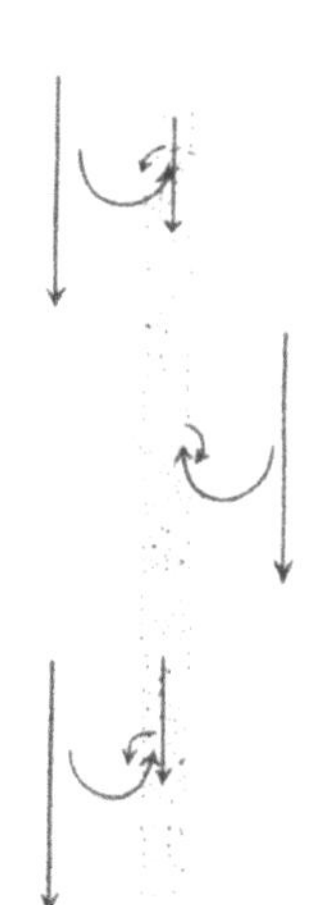

FIG. 60.—LONGITUDINAL SAND-PEBBLE BORDER. STRONG WIND

But a strong wind must produce just the opposite effect, and to a much more marked degree. For now the drag due to the intense sand movement along the sand patch has a far greater checking effect on the wind than has the roughness of the pebble surface next door. The velocities on either side of the border are shown in Fig. 57 by rays such as PC (pebble surface) and O′C′ (sand surface). The differences may be as great as 4 to 6 feet per second. The resulting eddies along the border should now be in the opposite sense (Fig. 60), for the sand moving down the pebble surface tends to be carried inwards, and to deposit under the slower-moving wind on the sand patch.

The effect is very similar to the deposition of bed material in a river in the slower-moving shallows near the banks.

Such a longitudinal border can be imitated in the wind tunnel by covering the whole floor with pebbles, and then burying one longitudinal half with sand, so that the edge of the sand strip runs down the middle of the floor. Under a gentle wind, the strip of sand advances down-wind as before, but the longitudinal edge also tends to spread out over the pebbles. A strong wind, accompanied by a stream of sand from further up, on the other hand, clears the pebble half of the floor, and at the same time increases the thickness of the sand strip on the other side.

It seems from this that *in a strong sand-laden wind a uniform drift of sand over a uniform rough surface has a transverse instability, so that sand tends to deposit in longitudinal strips.* For once a small chance concentration in any one place causes a temporary deposit of sand to cover the surface, this tends to grow thicker by collecting more sand *from each side.* This tendency is, of course, additional to that we have already dealt with whereby sand is deposited at the windward border.

In the open desert the result of this transverse instability may be seen in the peculiar appearance of a pebble-covered sand sheet when a storm has driven sand over it very heavily. Narrow longitudinal strips of new deposit 1 to 3 metres wide and 1 to 2 cm. thick are laid down parallel to one another, 40 to 60 metres apart for great distances. These strips can be seen in the photograph in Plate 6*a*, Chapter 11. When travelling over the great sand sheet of southern Egypt the writer crossed a succession of more than 200 of these sand strips laid out with great regularity on an otherwise perfectly featureless plain. It was noted that the individual strips were of limited length—averaging perhaps half a kilometre—and that the heads of new strips began in the spaces between the tails of others, as indicated in Fig. 61.

On more than one occasion the strips were observed in process of formation during a sand storm. When the storm was over, and the wind no longer sand-saturated, the strips of fine sand gradually disappeared, partly by scattering, and partly by the slow creep over them of the smaller of the pebbles from the surrounding surface (Chapters 11 (8), and 16 (7)). But it is probable that under occasional very favourable conditions a succession of storms from the same direction might build up one or more of the strips to such a thickness that it would outlast subsequent adverse weather periods and develop into a chain of dunes.

The regularity of the repetition of the strips strongly suggests some such large-scale rotary movement in the air stream as is shown in Fig. 61. It is interesting to note that longitudinal strips of fine material are also deposited under water, again only when the velocity of flow is raised above a certain value. Casey [1] has repeated them on a small scale in a laboratory flume, and in his paper gives some remarkable illustrations of them.

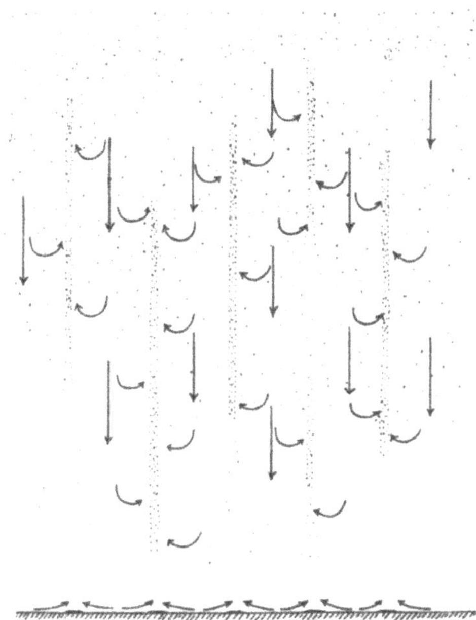

FIG. 61.—APPEARANCE OF NEW STRIPS OF FINE SAND DEPOSITED DURING A STORM ON THE SURFACE OF A UNIFORM SAND SHEET—WITH HYPOTHETICAL WIND CIRCULATION OVER THEM

But the echelon arrangement appears to be absent, possibly on account of the restriction caused by the flume walls. Casey, too, suggests that regular transverse flow components are set up within the fluid.

The formation of sand strips in air seems to be confined to a surface of absolute uniformity, such as a sand sheet covered with small pebbles of constant size. It is likely that the irregular roughness of the usual surface of an erosion desert would prevent

[1] Casey (1935). *Mitt. Preuss. versuch fur Wasserbau und Schiffbau.* Berlin.

the growth in the air stream of transverse currents sufficiently regular to produce any observable repetition of surface form.

8. SURROUNDING SURFACE NOT IMMOBILE. INHIBITION OF DUNE GROWTH BY THE SPREAD OF COARSE GRAINS OVER THE SAND SURFACE

In the foregoing sections the surrounding surface was assumed immobile, for simplicity. In many cases this is approximately true. A common type of desert floor consists, for instance, of water-borne pebbles 10 to 30 mm. in diameter, or larger. But in the most general case we must assume the presence of grains which, though they are too big to take part in the saltation, can nevertheless creep slowly over the surface under the bombardment they receive from the saltation (grains of 1 to 10 mm. diameter). Once a covering of such grains has spread over a fresh deposit of fine sand, the latter's power of collecting like material for its growth is much reduced, and may cease altogether. For, as we have seen, a covering of large grains increases the limiting rate at which fine sand can pass over and away from the surface. The dune is *killed*. This is no doubt the true explanation of the experimental and long-known fact that a dune can be stabilized and even made to shrink by sprinkling pebbles over it.

When the initial sand surface has grown up into a mound or dune its steepening slopes prevent the coarse grains from encroaching on to it. (Their tendency to climb up on to the dune is well shown by the thick accumulations of them that are so often found on the lower windward slopes.) But in the early stage when the dune surface is fairly flat an incipient dune must be very vulnerable to this form of attack. Continued growth can only be possible if the invaders are buried by fresh sand accretion before they can spread in sufficient numbers to stop further accretion from taking place.

The effect of the presence of coarse grains on a sandy desert is therefore somewhat analogous to that of oil on disturbed water. The coarse grains tend to inhibit the growth of dunes, and to encourage the gradual building up of flat or very gently undulating sand sheets.

9. FLUCTUATIONS IN THE RATE OF SAND MOVEMENT OVER A SAND SURFACE. THE MINIMUM SIZE OF DUNES

Having examined the various surrounding conditions which bear on the growth of an exposed patch of sand, as a whole, we will now turn to the relations between sand and wind movement at different points on the patch, assuming as before that the surface is nearly flat.

Reverting to the original wind-tunnel experiments described in Chapter 5, it will be remembered that the tunnel was divided into sections each of which was supported by spring balances, so that the rate of removal and deposition taking place on the sand floor in each section could be accurately measured. Therefrom the intensity of the sand flow q passing through each section could be deduced. Ultimately, at a sufficient distance from the mouth, q attains a certain definite equilibrium value depending only on the grain diameter and on the wind velocity gradient. But since it is not possible to arrange matters at the up-wind end so that the conditions there are the same as they are further down where an equilibrium has been set up between the wind and the sand flow, there is an unavoidable end-effect at the mouth, and the sand flow is not constant in the up-wind part of the tunnel.

When no sand is allowed to enter at the mouth, the sand flow q there is zero. But at a point near the mouth the first grains are dislodged by the direct pressure of the wind, and move forward. Each of these grains disturbs other grains, which, in their turn, begin to move. The sand flow becomes more intense as the distance increases from the point at which movement starts. As a consequence, owing to the extra drag caused by the sand saltation, the wind velocity close to the surface is less further down the tunnel than it is at the mouth.

But there must be a lag, at any given point, between the sand flow there and the full effect of its drag upon the wind velocity; for the drag, originating in the tiny eddies in the wake of each individual grain as it moves backwards relatively to the air, must take time to spread through the fluid and so to reduce the general velocity of the air molecules. Consequently, at the point at which the sand flow reaches a value equal to the steady rate it will eventually attain, the air is still moving faster than the corresponding steady velocity that it will eventually attain. Hence the sand flow goes on increasing for some distance further. The wind where this is happening becomes for a space overloaded with sand; but ultimately it is checked by the now increased drag, and deposits its overload on the surface. There is thus an initial removal of sand extending over a distance corresponding to the time taken by the wind velocity to respond to the change in the surface conditions. Owing to the failure of the wind to respond at once, too much sand is removed. The excess of sand in motion is deposited a little further down the tunnel.

This fluctuation of sand-flow intensity as the movement travels along the tunnel is shown in Fig. 62. Curve (*a*) shows the growth of the sand flow when no sand enters at the tunnel mouth. Curves (*b*) and (*c*) relate to entering sand streams of different intensities. It will be seen that the fluctuation increases in violence with the intensity of the incoming stream.

The fluctuation may even go through a second cycle further down the tunnel before the final equilibrium is established. In the wind tunnel this second cycle is feeble compared with the first, but the damping effect of the constant drag of the walls and roof may have a restraining influence. It is possible that

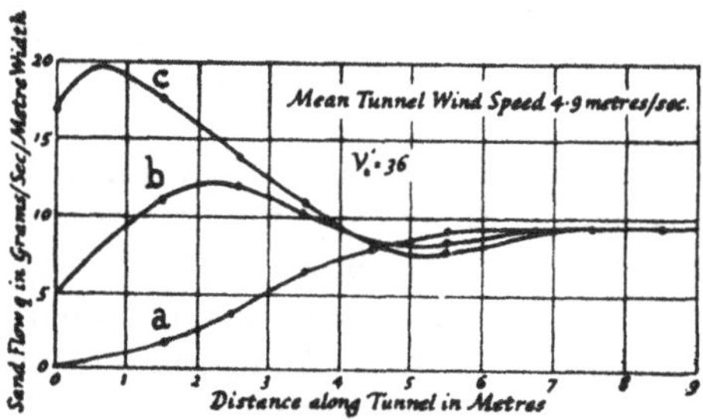

FIG. 62.—FLUCTUATIONS IN THE RATE OF SAND MOVEMENT

in the open these fluctuations might increase with the distance instead of dying away. *In general, however, it can be said that any change in the rate of sand flow produces a fluctuation downwind of it consisting of at least one cycle of removal followed by deposition* (*accretion*).

The sand used in these experiments had a nearly uniform grain diameter of 0·24 mm. It will be noted that in this case the sand flow took more than 7 metres to reach its steady equilibrium value. When sand of larger grain was tried the distance was longer. With a sand of 1·0 mm. diameter the flow showed little sign of approaching its maximum value even at the end of the tunnel 10 metres from the mouth. In the case of a sand of wide grading in which the fine grains tend to bounce off the bigger ones and the height of the saltation is consequently greater, there are indications that the wavelength of the fluctuation becomes much longer.

These experimental results show that *in order that the oncoming wind may be sufficiently checked to cause deposition to occur at all, the sand surface must extend over a certain minimum distance down-wind.* This is obvious if we imagine the sand patch reduced to a narrow transverse line. For now, the surface drag being in the nature of a force per unit area, and the sand area which gives rise to the additional drag of the sand movement being very small, the extra force offered to the wind would be negligible, and the patch would be immediately carried away. This consideration explains why attempts in the field to make artificial dunes have failed. They have not been big enough. From the curves of Fig. 62 it seems that a minimum length of 4 to 6 metres is required, and it is significant that the smallest true dune found in nature is of this size. It also illustrates the difficulty inherent in experimenting on a model scale with the formation and behaviour of fully grown dunes.

The question of the lag, in distance, between a change of surface conditions and the resulting change in the sand flow intensity seems amenable to approach from another direction. The change of surface condition must create in its lee a boundary layer (Chapter 4 (9)) whose thickness at any distance downwind of the border of change is the height to which the resulting change of wind velocity has spread upwards. By applying the established boundary-layer theory, regardless of the disturbing effect of the sand saltation, the following figures emerge. For a change of surface roughness at the border equivalent to the diameter of a sand grain—say 0·025 cm.—the layer of affected air should have risen to a height of 6 cm., which is of the right order for the height of the visible sand cloud when the grains are of uniform size, in a distance of 2·5 metres, which is again of the same order as the length of the fluctuations observed in the wind tunnel.

10. THE INFLUENCE OF VEGETATION

Physically, vegetation can be regarded as a special kind of surface roughness. The simplest case is that of a loose surface of dry sand on which sufficient rain falls at intervals, and is retained below, to cause the germination of wind-blown seeds and the growth of a uniform but thin distribution of light grass or other herbage. The grass blades, by projecting into the air stream, have the effect of raising the height k (Chapters 4 and 5) of the level above the surface at which the wind velocity is on an average zero, in just the same way as do the pebbles or stones we have previously dealt with.

The sand surface is therefore converted by the growing grass into the equivalent of one containing scattered pebbles, and it will tend to store oncoming sand between the grass blades. But there is this important difference; the blades being light and yielding, the sand grains do not bounce off them as they do off pebbles. Hence unlike a pebble or rock surface vegetation cannot increase the rate of sand flow over it relatively to that over bare sand—rather the reverse. So a patch of bare sand downwind of vegetation has no tendency to collect more sand. Again, as long as the vegetation is alive, the surface on which it grows cannot ever become fully charged with sand, for the grass grows higher as the sand around it accumulates. The result is that under all wind conditions the grassy surface acts as a continuous deposition area, and we get great undulating tracts of accumulated sand such as the *gozes* of Kordofan, which are devoid of steep-sided dunes.

11. THE PREVAILING SAND-DRIVING WIND. THE LONG-PERIOD SAND MOVEMENT AS A VECTOR-SUM OF MOVEMENTS DURING 'STRONG' AND 'GENTLE' WINDS

It will have become evident in the course of this chapter that the growth or otherwise of sand accumulations is intimately connected with the relative strength, duration, and direction of alternating periods of strong winds and gentle winds. And whereas in the last chapter we were concerned mostly with small-scale phenomena formed temporarily while the wind blew in one direction, we are now concerned with sand forms built up very slowly by many winds blowing from different directions.

We must therefore deal henceforth with imaginary winds, constant in strength and direction, which will be equivalent in their sand-moving effects to the real wind which 'bloweth where it listeth' for periods of years or decades.

Though existing meteorological records do not permit of useful numerical calculations being made for any specific cases, it will greatly simplify the ideas put forward in the following chapters if we can form a clear conception of how these imaginary *prevailing sand-driving winds* might be obtained from day-to-day measurements.

Now it was shown in Chapter 5 (4) that the rate of displacement of sand at any instant in the direction the wind happens to be blowing is given by an expression of the form $q = bV_*^3$, where the constant b depends on the type of surface and the grading of the sand. If we split the whole period T, be it 1 year or 10 years, into elements of time δt so short that the wind may be regarded as constant during each one, then the displacement m of sand during any element of time is given by

$$m = bV_*^3.\delta t \quad . \quad . \quad . \quad . \quad (1)$$

Since the displacement has a direction as well as an absolute magnitude it is a vector, and can be split up into northerly and easterly components

$$\left.\begin{aligned} m_N &= bV_*^3.\delta t.\cos\theta \\ \text{and} \qquad m_E &= bV_*^3.\delta t.\sin\theta \end{aligned}\right\} \quad . \quad . \quad . \quad . \quad (2)$$

where θ is the leeward bearing of the wind, and where negative values of m indicate southerly and westerly directions.

The total northerly and easterly sand displacements during the whole long period T can then be found by simply adding together all the little elements m_N and m_E, and we have

$$\left.\begin{aligned} M_N &= b\delta t\Sigma V_*^3.\cos\theta \\ M_E &= b\delta t\Sigma V_*^3.\sin\theta \end{aligned}\right\} \quad . \quad . \quad . \quad . \quad (3)$$

The magnitude M of the whole resultant displacement is obtained by adding M_N and M_E together vectorially, so that

$$M = \sqrt{M_N^2 + M_E^2} \quad . \quad . \quad . \quad . \quad (4)$$

If M is divided by the whole time T, we get a vector $Q = M/T$ which gives the *mean* rate of sand flow over the long period, corresponding to the *instantaneous* rate q.

The mean direction in which this mean sand flow has taken place is given by

$$\Theta = \tan^{-1}\frac{M_E}{M_N} \quad . \quad . \quad . \quad . \quad (5)$$

and this is therefore the direction of the true prevailing, sand-driving wind.

Since this imaginary wind is defined as that which would have the same sand-moving effect as the real wind if it blew steadily for the whole period T, its strength, in terms of its gradient $\mathbf{V}_*$, is given by

$$Q = b\mathbf{V}_*^3$$

$$\text{whence} \qquad \mathbf{V}_* = \sqrt[3]{\frac{Q}{b}} \quad . \quad . \quad . \quad . \quad (6)$$

The summation indicated in equation (3) is quite straightforward, and can be done from wind records as usually kept. The period δt can be made equal to the usual period of a few hours between observations, the bearing θ is that recorded, and V_* could be obtained from the velocity records by applying a suitable factor.

In years to come records will doubtless be available from an adequate number of stations around the great desert areas for an accurate computation of this kind to be made. The result would throw very valuable light not only on the present trend of sand movement, but also on the climatic changes which have taken place during recent geological time. For instance, areas where the value of Q is found to be a minimum or to be zero should coincide with existing dune fields and sand seas. If they do not, the discrepancy would indicate a change in the prevailing wind.

We have just defined the *overall* value of the prevailing sand-flow vector Q as the vector-sum, over a long period, of the short-period elements caused by sand-moving winds of *all* strengths. But it is more important for our immediate purpose to be able to consider separately the *two components* of the overall value of Q which are due respectively to the strong, *dune-building winds*, and to the *gentle winds*.

We will therefore introduce two new vectors ${}_sQ$ and ${}_gQ$ to represent these components. When added together they make up the overall rate of sand flow Q.

'Strong' winds and 'gentle' winds have been defined in our special restricted sense in Section 5, both in terms of their effects and in terms of the texture of the surfaces over which they blow. A strong wind is one whose gradient exceeds that of the line PO′ in Fig. 57, and which causes an accretion of more sand upon a sand surface. It is the dune-building wind. A gentle wind has a gradient less than that of PO′ but greater than the threshold gradient OO′. It drives sand off a dune on to the surrounding country, causing the dune to extend down-wind in the process.

To obtain ${}_sQ$ in magnitude and direction it is merely necessary to form the corresponding partial sand displacements ${}_sM_N$ and ${}_sM_E$ by summing $V_*^3 \cos\theta$ and $V_*^3 \sin\theta$ for those winds only which exceed the critical gradient V_{*_c} given by the line PO′ in Fig. 57. The resulting displacement ${}_sM$ when divided by the total time ${}_sT$ during which the strong winds have blown gives us the magnitude of the required vector ${}_sQ$. Its direction is given by

$$ {}_s\theta = \tan^{-1}\frac{{}_sM_E}{{}_sM_N} $$

Similarly ${}_gQ$ is obtained by summing $V_*^3 \cos\theta$ and $V_*^3 \sin\theta$ for those winds whose gradients lie between those of the lines PO′ and OO′ in Fig. 57.

The prevailing strong-wind and gentle-wind sand-flow vectors ${}_sQ$ and ${}_gQ$ can be added together by the ordinary method of the 'parallelogram of forces' to form a 'resultant' which in this case is simply the overall rate of sand flow due to all winds lumped together for the whole period.

The directions of these two component vectors may almost coincide, or they may be very different, according to the climate of the geographical area considered. The wind may blow from the same quarter during mild and stormy periods alike, or mild winds may blow from one prevailing quarter and storms from quite another. The suggestion will be elaborated in the following chapters that it is the relative angle between the directions of the mild winds and the storms that determines more than anything else the type of dune which is found in various parts of the world.

Before leaving this subject it may be as well to emphasize again the great importance of taking the relative strength of the wind into consideration whenever sand movement is concerned. For owing to the fact that the *cube of the wind velocity* enters into the expression for the sand flow Q, a single day's storm may move more sand than several weeks or months of calmer weather.

REFERENCE

BAGNOLD, R. A. (1937). *Geogr. J.*, 89

Chapter 13

LARGE-SCALE PHENOMENA. SAND SHADOWS AND DRIFTS. GENERAL CONSIDERATIONS REGARDING DUNE SHAPE

1. TYPES OF SAND ACCUMULATION

THE existing descriptive literature on wind-blown sand formations is large, and is unfortunately scattered among a host of publications ; much of it deals only with small areas where special local conditions prevail. The value of the conclusions drawn as to the precise agencies in operation is limited by an almost entire lack of reliable long-period records concerning both the strength and direction of the wind, and concerning the growth and movement of the dunes. Moreover the problem of investigating the growth of large-scale sand phenomena by means of models is a most difficult one. Having, however, described the physical ideas which appear to underlie sand movement by wind, it may be useful to depart temporarily from the experimental basis of the rest of the present work in order to examine, with these ideas as a background, the main observed characteristics of the various types of sand formation which are found in nature.

These can conveniently be classified as follows, according to the special conditions which appear to give rise to them.

A. Deposits caused directly by fixed obstructions in the path of the sand-driving wind ; for example by bushes, rocks or cliffs. These *sand shadows* and *sand drifts* are dependent for their continued existence on the presence of the obstacle, and cannot move away from it.

B. True Dunes. A single dune may be defined as a mound or hill of sand which rises to a single summit. Dunes may exist alone or attached to one another in colonies or dune chains. Unlike shadows and drifts, dunes can exist independently of any fixed surface feature, and do, in fact, reach their most perfect development on flat featureless country. Although capable of movement from place to place, they are able to retain their own

PLATE 11

BARCHAN DUNES

PLATE 12

a. AN ASYMMETRICAL SEIF DUNE CHAIN, SHOWING THE VESTIGIAL BARCHAN WINGS ON THE LEE SIDE (SOUTH LIBYAN DESERT)

b. 'TEAR-DROP' FORM OF SEIF DUNE CHAIN. PROBABLY DUE TO WINDS DIFFERING IN DIRECTION BY MORE THAN 90°

characteristic shape. A special feature of all dunes which have attained a certain stage of development is the *slip-face*, where the slope of the dune surface reaches the limit of steepness imposed by the *angle of shear* of the deposited material.

Dunes assume two fundamental shapes: (i) the *barchan* or crescentic dune, and (ii) the longitudinal dune, whose arabic name *seif* or 'sword' will be used hereafter for brevity, in default of any universally recognized name. The simplest forms of either of these two dune types are seldom found except in an erosion desert; for in coastal and riverine regions their essential features are usually masked by the confusion of form introduced by moisture and vegetation together with special sand conditions (comparative uniformity of grain size). Except under rare conditions provided by local surface relief, the two types rarely if ever occur together in the same geographical area. Since no distinctive difference in the material has been found, the dune type appears to be determined by the character of the wind—by its relative periods of variation in strength and direction, or in more precise terms, by the coincidence or otherwise of the direction of the vectors ${}_sQ$ and ${}_gQ$ of the preceding Section.

C. Coarse-grained residues or platforms built up and left behind by the passage of a long-continued succession of seif dunes along the same path. I have called them *Whalebacks*.

D. Gentle large-scale undulations apparently associated with slight present, past, or periodic rainfall and its resulting light intermittent vegetation (e.g. the *Gozes* of Kordofan).

E. Sand sheets.

2. SAND SHADOWS BEHIND OBSTACLES

The material is deposited to form a sand shadow when the wind velocity is locally checked by an obstacle in its path. It will be enough to take one simple example—a single sharp-cornered obstacle such as a wood packing-case standing by itself on a flat open sand sheet.

Since we are now dealing with air streams which are deflected from the straight path, it must be borne in mind that the direction of travel of the air and of the sand grains will not necessarily coincide. The sand grains are not readily deflected by sudden changes in the direction of the air stream, and therefore tend to pass straight on. For this reason it will be as well to consider separately the flow of air and of sand round the obstacle.

The air both in front and behind the obstacle is divided into two parts by a somewhat ill-defined *surface of discontinuity* whose approximate shape is sketched in plan and elevation in Fig. 63*a* by dotted lines. Outside this surface the air stream flows smoothly by; but the volume within the *wind shadow* of the obstacle is filled with swirls and vortices of air whose *average forward velocity is less than that of the air stream outside.* As we go down-wind from the obstacle the forward velocity of the air inside the shadow gradually increases and the shadow fades away to merge eventually with the general flow of the wind.

The sand grains which strike the obstacle rebound off it and

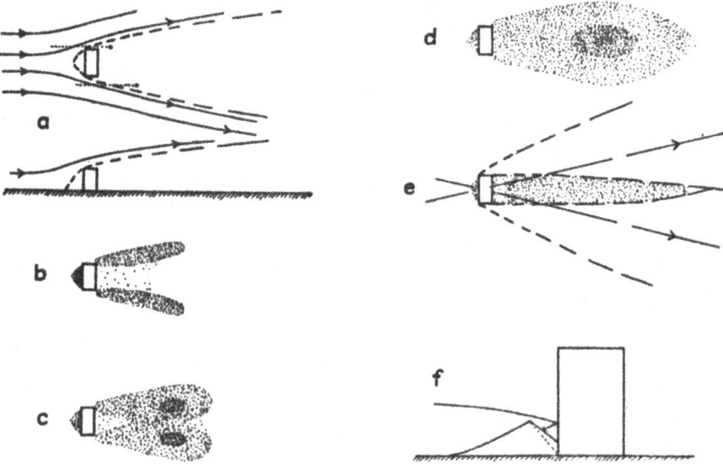

FIG. 63.—FORMATION OF A SAND SHADOW

come to rest in the relatively stagnant air in front (Fig. 63*f*). When the resulting heap has grown up so that its slopes stand at the limiting angle of repose (about 34°) all additional material slides down the slopes to join the sand stream passing along the side of the obstacle.

The grains of this stream, as will be seen from Fig. 63*a*, pass straight through the surface of discontinuity into the zone of lesser forward wind velocity inside. Here they therefore tend to settle.

Successive stages in the growth of the shadow are sketched in Fig. 63*b*, *c*, and *d*. The two wings gradually coalesce as the swirls of air within the wind shadow carry the grains towards the middle.

The above refers to an ideal wind which is truly constant in direction. Usually the shape of the shadow is modified to something more like that shown in Fig. 63*e*. Here the wind is supposed to swing between two limiting directions which are indicated by the arrows. The sand shadow is confined to the space occupied by the overlap between the two limiting wind shadows.

It should be noted that as sand cannot stand at an angle steeper than the angle of repose, the height of the sand shadow is always limited by the size of the ground plan of the wind shadow in which it is formed. Any sand which slips down the sides and protrudes beyond the boundary of the wind shadow is very soon swept away by the stronger wind outside. The size of deposit is therefore very sensitive to the shape of the bottom of the obstacle. A round boulder, or a bush beneath which a strong current of air can blow, will allow the formation of little or no sand shadow.

3. SAND DRIFTS BETWEEN OBSTACLES

A sand shadow is, as its name implies, an accumulation formed in the shelter of, and immediately behind, an obstacle. A *drift*, on the other hand, is formed in the lee of a gap between two obstacles, and is due to ' funnelling ', or the concentration of the sand stream on the windward side from a broad front to a narrower one.

Fig. 64 represents two sections of a low wall with a gap between them. The wind as it flows initially is sketched in Fig. 64*a*. It goes over the top of the walls as well as through the gap. But the oncoming sand is unable to rise over the walls (whose extremities always remain unburied owing to their vertical ends). Hence the sand which arrives over a wide frontage drifts sideways and is concentrated to pass through the gap. The sand flow through the gap must therefore exceed in intensity the equilibrium flow in the open.

The wind through the gap is also stronger ; but a short distance down-wind its velocity begins to slacken as the air stream merges with the general flow, so it is inevitable that the surplus sand must be dropped out of the air stream to form a growing deposit. The early stage is sketched in Fig. 64*b*. At a later stage the deposit has risen to such a height as to become, of itself, an additional obstacle round which the wind is again deflected. Further oncoming sand, being deflected to a lesser degree, tends to pass straight on, and is deposited on the drift, in the comparative shelter of its lee side. The limit of growth is reached when the frontage of the drift, off which sand can stream away at the equilibrium rate, becomes equal to the frontage of the up-wind collecting area, i.e. the frontage between the wall centres.

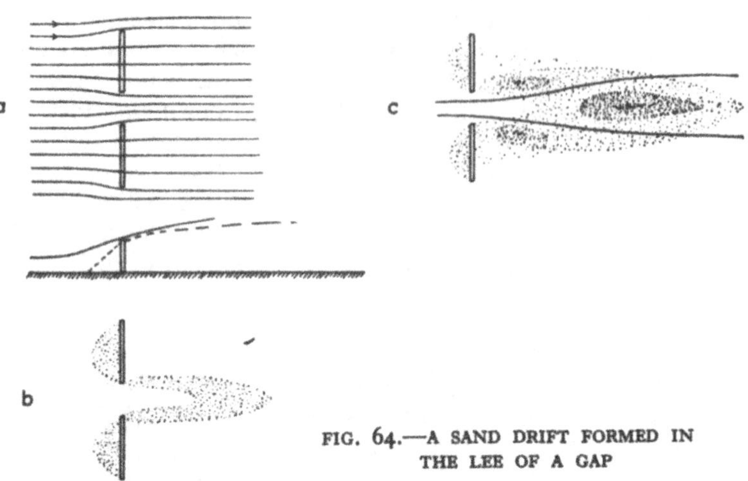

FIG. 64.—A SAND DRIFT FORMED IN THE LEE OF A GAP

4. SAND DRIFTS BELOW CLIFFS

A sand shadow is also formed whenever a sand-bearing wind sweeps over the brink of a sudden fall in the ground (Fig. 65). Here the grains fall through the boundary surface of the wind shadow into the comparatively sheltered zone below, where they settle. In plan, if the surface of the ground above were perfectly uniform, a continuous sand bed would be formed below. But if, as is more usual, the cliff edge is indented, by drainage channels for instance, the wind tends to converge into the re-entrants, carrying with it a more concentrated stream of sand. Hence, in general, the sand deposit below is more pronounced in some places than in others, and consists of a series of tongues jutting out into the plain which, we will suppose, extends to the right of the figure. These deposits are therefore combinations of shadows and drifts.

The form assumed by the sand accumulation below the cliff depends on the long-period distribution of the wind's velocity and direction. For instance, if the prevailing sand-bearing wind is parallel or nearly parallel to the line of the cliffs, there can be no large drifts at all, for the sheltering effect is small and the sand is swept away along the foot of the cliffs to some other locality.

The sand accumulation is a maximum, on the other hand, when the prevailing wind blows from off the plateau at right angles to the cliffs. For now the space immediately beneath the cliffs is exposed to no wind whose net long-period effect is to carry sand away. It is completely sheltered from the main outward wind current which blows overhead; and though violent gusts sweep along the cliffs, they do so in either direction at random,

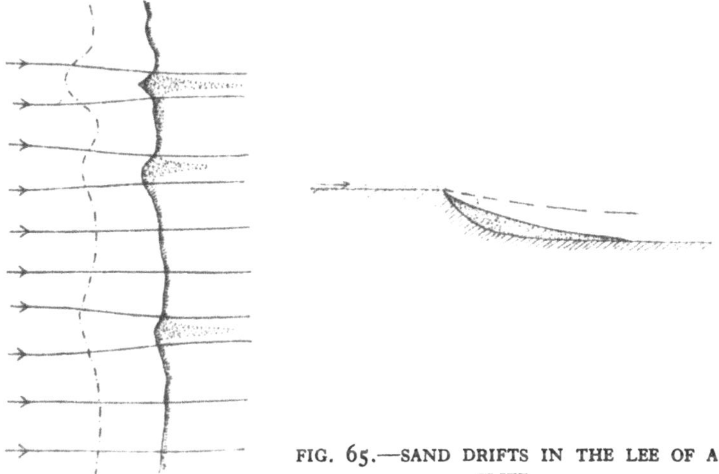

FIG. 65.—SAND DRIFTS IN THE LEE OF A CLIFF

and so cause no general drift of sand to some other locality. In other words, the vector Q is zero beneath the cliff.

These lateral gusts drive the accumulated sand to and fro, and in so doing cause the larger drifts to grow at the expense of the smaller ones (owing to the tendency for sand to accumulate where a sand surface already exists).

As the big drifts grow higher, their crests begin to be influenced by the forward movement—away from the cliffs—of the main wind stream blowing overhead. They therefore begin to string out longitudinally into the plain.

5. THE INFLUENCE OF CROSS-WINDS ON DUNE SHAPE SUGGESTED BY THE BEHAVIOUR OF UNDER-CLIFF SAND DRIFTS

A typical example of such a well-developed drift is shown in Fig. 66. The main sand-bearing wind is supposed uni-directional, and blows outwards over the cliff during strong and gentle periods alike. Using the conception of the 'prevailing strong- and gentle-wind vectors' $_sQ$ and $_gQ$ evolved in Chapter 12 (11), the distribution of the wind effects is shown by the diagram at the bottom of the figure. Here the heavy lines represent $_sQ$ and the light lines $_gQ$. Above the cliffs the directions of these two coincide (diagram *a*).

Beneath the cliff we have a totally different wind régime, which, however, gradually reverts to the original one as we go out into the plain (diagram *e*). Immediately underneath there is no

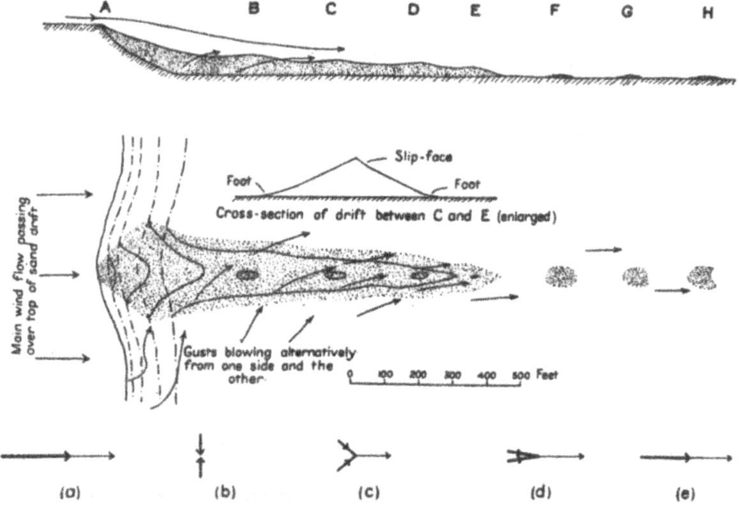

FIG. 66.—A SEIF-LIKE DRIFT IN THE LEE OF A CLIFF BREAKING UP INTO MOUNDS AND BARCHAN DUNES AS IT EXTENDS INTO OPEN COUNTRY

outward wind at all (though the sand supply is still maintained from overhead). And since there is no net long-period wind from any direction, the effects of the alternate gusts can be shown diagrammatically by two equal and opposite vectors $_sQ_1$ and $_sQ_2$ which mutually cancel one another (diagram *b*).

Further out, where the outward wind overhead begins to be felt on the surface of the drift, the wind effects are as indicated in diagrams *c* and *d*.

Referring to the picture of the drift itself in Fig. 66, it will be seen that far out (F to H) where the wind has once more become uni-directional, the drift assumes a very different form from that closer in where the cliff causes cross-winds to blow. Near the cliff the drift is a single continuous tongue composed of a regular succession of summits, identical with the arrangement of a self or longitudinal dune chain. But in the open it has split up into isolated mounds which finally display the crescentic form typical of the barchan dune.

Numerous instances of this phenomenon can be observed in any desert area where the barchan dune type prevails in open country. These, together with other evidence which will be cited later, lead me [1] to put forward the following hypothesis, which will be elaborated in the succeeding chapters dealing with true dunes in open country:

The longitudinal or seif dune occurs when the wind régime is such that the strong winds blow from a quarter other than that of the general drift of sand caused by the more persistent gentle winds. In other words, when the vectors ${}_sQ$ and ${}_gQ$ differ in direction. The conditions of sand accumulation are therefore essentially those described in Chapter 12 (6).

The barchan dune on the other hand occurs when the wind is nearly uni-directional: i.e. when ${}_sQ$ and ${}_gQ$ nearly coincide. The conditions are those described in Chapter 12 (7).

6. TRUE DUNES AS DEFORMABLE WIND OBSTACLES. GENERAL CONSIDERATIONS AFFECTING THE SHAPE THEY ASSUME. THE LONGITUDINAL PROFILE

We have dealt with the observed effects of fixed obstacles in the path of the wind on the movement of sand carried along by it, and with the shapes of the resulting sand accumulations. We can now turn to those cases where the obstacle itself is a loose deformable sand accumulation—a true dune—free to move, to grow, to divide, or to be blown away altogether.

At the outset the difficulty appears that since a single isolated dune can alter its form in three dimensions at once, the effect of the wind on the shape of, say, a longitudinal cross-section is influenced by the shape of the transverse section, and by the consequent diversion of the wind stream round the sides of the dune.

It is simplest, therefore, to deal first with the longitudinal cross-section of a hypothetical dune which is so long that the end-effects can be neglected, when it is exposed to a transverse uni-

[1] For the original idea I am indebted to Mr. J. L. Capes of Fuad-el-Awal University, Egypt.

directional wind. We can then consider why such a transverse dune is likely to be unstable, and to break up into isolated barchan dunes. In the next chapter we shall deal with the shape and movement of such isolated dunes; and thence we shall pass to their fate when the wind begins to blow from more than one direction, i.e. when, according to the above hypothesis, they become transformed into seif dune chains.

It should be borne in mind that the explanations given have not been verified by experiment, but are deductions from the general body of experimental fact described in earlier chapters, and applied to the large-scale natural phenomena of which the author has made a considerable study.

Now the steady flow of a fluid in uniform motion past a transverse obstacle totally immersed in it has received much attention, owing to its important bearing on aircraft design, &c. And in

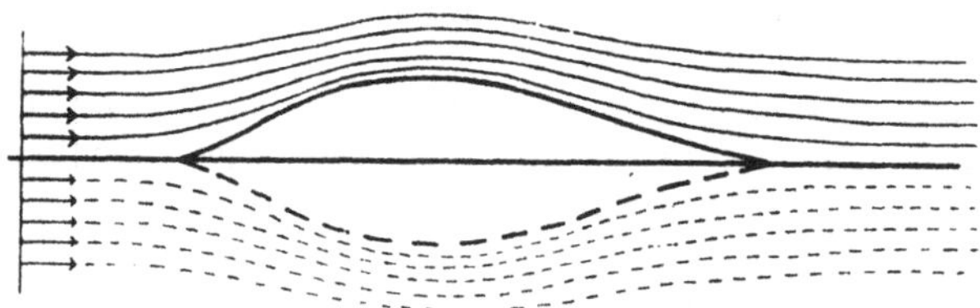

FIG. 67.—FLOW PAST A SYMMETRICAL STREAMLINE OBSTACLE

the case of a rounded symmetrical obstacle it is clear that we can split the system into two halves, as shown in Fig. 67, by a frictionless plate running longitudinally through the axis of symmetry, without affecting the flow on either side. Provided that the friction of the ground could be disregarded, one-half of the system might then represent flat ground with our transverse dune lying on it. But unfortunately the ground friction cannot be disregarded; and the flow of the air over the ground is therefore not uniform, for the velocity increases with the height above the surface. Hence the flow of the wind round the half obstacle lying on the real ground is not the same as that round each half of the whole obstacle if this were suspended above the ground. Very little research has been devoted to air flow over a rough mound lying on flat rough ground.

Nevertheless it is certain that the value of the drag velocity V_* at the surface changes from point to point over the profile of the mound. This is because the fluid flow is no longer uniform.

The air speed above the surface increases on the windward face, and decreases again over the lee face; and as mentioned in connexion with water ripples in Chapter 11, the surface value of the drag velocity is greater wherever the flow is accelerated, so it is greater on the windward face than on the level plain up-wind. Similarly on the lee side V_* falls to a lower value because the fast-moving air from over the summit is being retarded by the divergence of the flow. V_* slowly rises again to its steady value somewhere down-wind of the mound. Therefore, since the rate of sand movement is a function of V_*, the result, in general, is a removal of sand from the windward slope and deposition on the lee slope.

It should be noticed here that in the case of flow over curved surfaces the drag velocity V_* at the surface has not necessarily the same value as that found by measuring the velocity gradient above the surface. At the rounded summit of a large dune, however, where the curvature is very flat and the air velocity nearly steady, the two values are found in practice to coincide fairly well, at any rate up to heights of one or two metres.

(*a*) *The effect of gentle winds.* From the ideas put forward in Chapter 12, (4) and (5), it seems necessary to consider the effects of 'gentle' and 'strong' winds separately. The term 'gentle wind' as applied to dune formation is defined as a wind whose gradient is such that the intensity of the sand movement which it causes over the dune surface is less than that required to give the surface an equivalent roughness equal to the real roughness of the surrounding country.

The drag is a maximum at some point B (Fig. 68) on the windward face where the acceleration of the wind is a maximum. So, as the wind strengthens from a calm, sand movement starts at B. Once started, it continues to increase in intensity, owing to the lag (Chapter 12 (9)) between cause and effect for a certain distance BC, even though V_* has fallen to a lower value. At C deposition sets in, and at D, further down the lee slope, the drag velocity V_* has fallen to such a low value that no further sand movement takes place. The net result is that sand is removed from the upper part of the windward face, which consequently gets flatter, and deposited on the lee face.

As the wind increases in strength, the starting-point B of the removal moves down the windward face towards the foot A, and the stopping-point D moves down the lee slope towards the lee foot E. At a certain wind strength, D advances beyond E, and sand streams off the dune. At a still higher wind strength, sand begins to be picked up from the surface up-wind of the dune and swept on to it. Between these two wind strengths the dune clearly loses sand. And in all gentle winds the windward face tends to get flatter, and the dune tends to lengthen.

It should be noted that if the dune is so small that the lag distance between B and C brings the point C beyond the lee edge E there will be no deposition on the dune at all, and it will very soon be blown away.

(*b*) *The effect of a strong wind.* In a strong wind the sand movement on the dune surface is so intense that the resistance it opposes to the air stream is equivalent to that of a surface

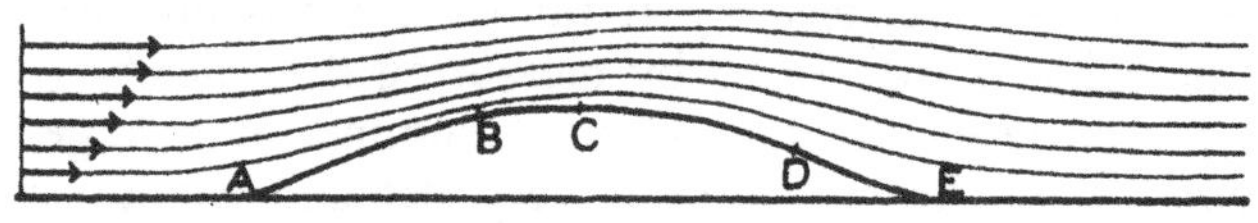

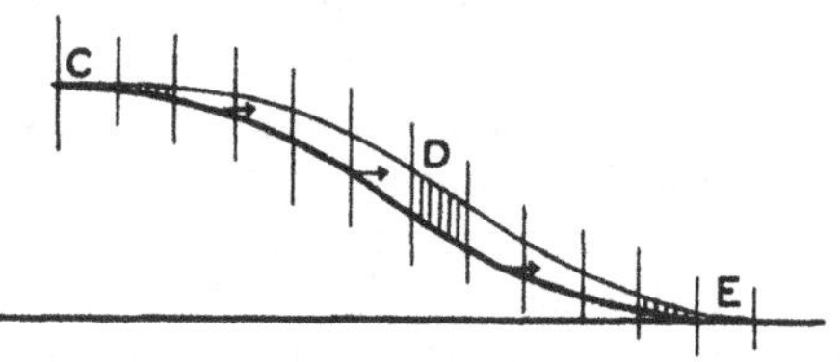

FIG. 68.—FLOW OF WIND OVER A DUNE OF ROUNDED PROFILE

roughness greater than that of the open pebbly country up-wind; and the bottom layer of air is therefore checked at the dune foot A. The conditions are similar to those obtaining on a very much smaller scale on the up-stream faces of the hillocks formed under water which were discussed in Chapter 11 (10). The drag is very heavy at the boundary A, and would fall again to the open-country value if the ground beyond were flat. But the curvature of the dune, and the resulting acceleration of the wind up it, maintains the drag at a high value from A onwards up to the summit. It is quite possible that the final profile of the up-wind face may be amenable to calculation on the lines suggested in the section referred to. If so the inclination of the face would seem to depend only on the wind gradient and the size of the sand grains. There is much scope for further research on this point.

If no sand arrives from up-wind, removal takes place from the whole of the windward face, which therefore advances down-wind. Deposition occurs on the lee face, but since sand is carried away off the lee foot E the dune must shrink in size as it advances.

If, however, the country up-wind of the dune is well charged with sand, the mechanism discussed in Chapter 12 permits of the arrival of sand at a greater rate than that at which it can be carried away to leeward. When this happens the dune grows fatter as it advances.

(*c*) *Long-period mean wind. Relation between rate of sand flow over the dune, and the shape of the dune.* Though it is impossible without a great deal more experimental work to predict the effect on the dune of a temporary wind of any particular strength, yet some interesting deductions can be made from purely geometrical

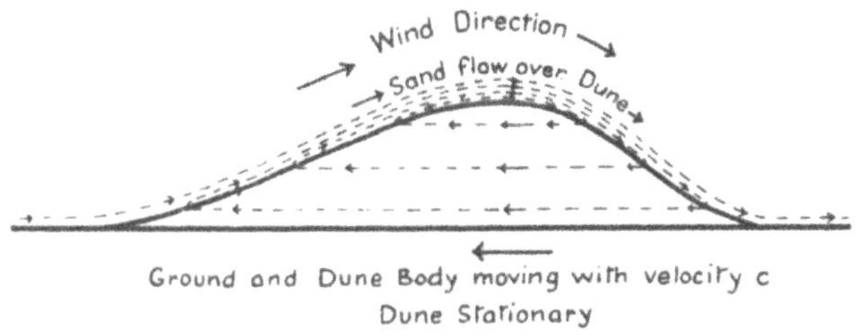

FIG. 69.—CIRCULATION OF SAND OVER AND THROUGH A DUNE ADVANCING WITHOUT CHANGE OF SHAPE OR SIZE

considerations if we postulate that the dune is, on average over a long period, moving steadily down-wind without change of shape or size.

Suppose an imaginary observer moves down-wind with the dune from left to right, and measures distances always from its windward foot (Fig. 69). Then if the dune profile is in reality advancing with a mean velocity c, the whole of the sand in the body of it, which is really stationary, will appear to the observer to be moving from right to left at this velocity.

It is clear that since the dune remains unchanged in shape and size, all the sand which emerges across the windward surface must be immediately removed by the wind, carried forward over the summit, and distributed as a deposit on the lee side. The sand movement can be represented by streamlines as shown in the figure.

It will be seen that the sand flow q up the windward side must increase in intensity towards the summit, and decrease again as we go down the lee side. Further, the rate of removal from any small area AE (Fig. 70) is given by $Q_E - Q_A$; and if we denote this by dQ, we know that in unit time a weight of sand dQ has been removed from the area. If γ is the specific weight of sand in bulk, the volume of this removed sand is dQ/γ. This volume is represented by the area of the parallelogram ABDE in the figure, which is equal to that of the rectangle ABEF.

Now this volume of sand must, if the dune remains constant in shape, be exactly equal to that of the sand which has emerged

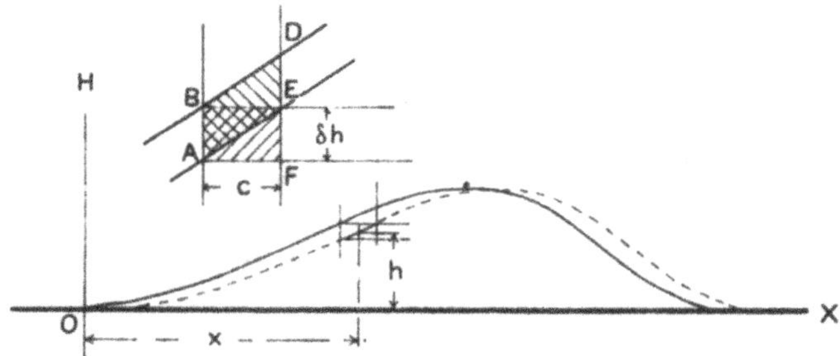

FIG. 70.—RELATIONS BETWEEN RATE OF SAND REMOVAL, RATE OF DUNE ADVANCE, AND INCLINATION OF SURFACE

during this unit time from the surface between the levels of F and E while the dune has advanced a distance AF = c.

Calling this small difference of level dh, we therefore have the relation

$$\frac{dQ}{\gamma} = cdh \quad . \quad . \quad . \quad . \quad (1)$$

Since EF/AF is equal to the tangent dh/dx of the angle of inclination α of the surface at the point considered, we can substitute $dx \tan \alpha$ for dh in equation (1), so that

$$\frac{dQ}{dx} = \gamma c \tan \alpha \quad . \quad . \quad . \quad . \quad (2)$$

dQ/dx is the rate of sand removal (or deposition) per unit area (measured horizontally) at any point, positive values indicating removal and negative values deposition. Hence we have the general relation that *the rate of removal or deposition per unit area at any point on the surface is proportional to the tangent of the angle of inclination of the surface at that point* (since $\tan \alpha$ is negative over the downward lee slope dQ/dx must also be negative there, i.e. there must be deposition).

From this relation it is clear that (1) the rate of sand removal or deposition is constant over any area of the surface which lies at a constant angle; (2) *there can be neither removal nor deposition at the summit where* $\tan \alpha$ *is zero*; and (3) *the rate is a maximum where the surface angle is steepest.*

It should be noted that all the above relations are purely geometrical and have no reference to the distribution of the wind flow. And since it is the wind flow over the dune which directly determines the value of Q at any point, we can make no exact deductions as to the particular dune shape which will be in equilibrium with any given wind.

(*d*) *Formation of the slip-face.* The rate of deposition dQ/dx is zero at the summit, reaches a maximum somewhere on the lee slope, and thereafter falls off to zero again at the extreme leeward foot. It seems likely that the distance between the summit and the point of maximum deposition depends on the lag, mentioned in Chapter 12 (9) between a change in the wind condition and the corresponding change in the sand movement. If this is true, since the lag distance may be expected to remain nearly constant, the point of maximum deposition should get relatively closer to the summit as the dune grows in size. Consequently the upper part of the lee face should tend to advance faster than the lower, and the face should steepen.

There is an essential element of instability in this small tendency, because a steepening of the slope so affects the wind flow that the tendency is greatly accentuated. For as the slope steepens, the wind experiences an increasing difficulty in deflecting downwards sufficiently rapidly to follow the surface. The surface therefore becomes increasingly sheltered. Deposition is thereby hastened, with the result that the slope becomes steeper still (Fig. 71*a*).

Finally, when the surface reaches the maximum angle of repose of 34°, the mass of the deposit suddenly shears along a plane which is inclined a few degrees less steeply (the angle of shear). An avalanche takes place, as shown in Figs. 71*b* and 71*c*.

At the top of the shear plane there is an abrupt break in the continuity of the surface. The wind, being now completely unable to flow smoothly over the surface, does its best to con-

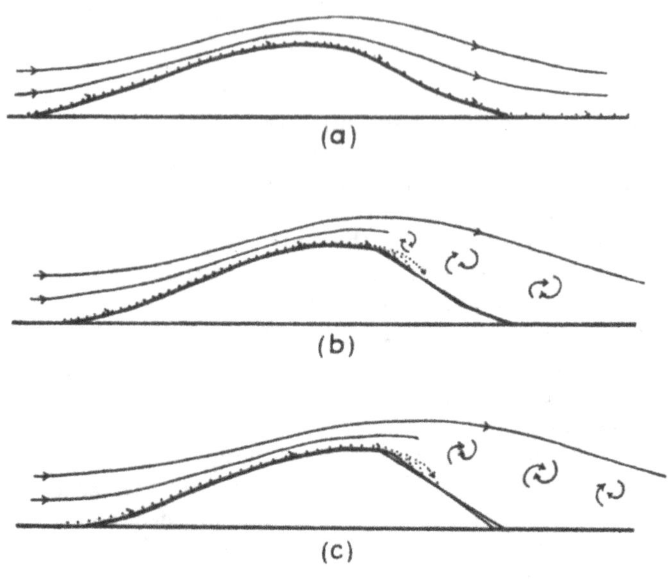

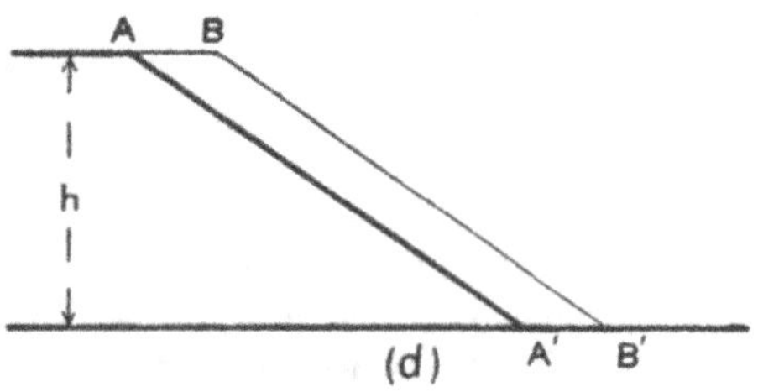

FIG. 71.—FORMATION OF A SLIP-FACE

tinue the streamline form by creating a wind shadow similar to that described in Section 2. The dune has formed a slip-face.

The sand grains coming over the crest fall like snow flakes through the comparatively still air inside the wind shadow.

They build up the surface by sedimentation till the angle again reaches 34°, when another avalanche occurs.

The action is closely analogous to the successive formation and breaking off of snow cornices. In the case of snow, however, the greater cohesion between the particles admits of a far bulkier accumulation at the crest before rupture occurs. Also, whereas only a small portion of the driving snow goes to build up the cornice, the rest owing to its lightness being carried off elsewhere by the wind, in the case of sand the *whole* of the material in motion falls on to the surface of the slip-face and is trapped there.

The critical size which the sand mound must attain before the slip-face is formed would seem to depend on the lag-distance, i.e. the distance travelled by the sand between the point where the wind slackens in strength and that at which deposition sets in. The wind-tunnel experiments described in Chapter 12 (9) rather indicate that the lag-distance is greater for coarse sands and for sands of a wide range of grain size than for fine uniform sands. Hence we should expect that the critical size of the mound should be smaller for fine uniform sands than for others. This seems to be borne out by observation in the desert. But the whole question of the lag-distance requires further investigation. It also appears that a certain minimum height must be attained before a permanent slip-face can be established. This will be discussed in Chapter 14 (3).

(*e*) *The effect of the slip-face. Its rate of advance.* The establishment of the slip-face has a profound effect on the subsequent life history of the dune. From its transient existence as a collection of grains, deriving a precarious nourishment from the small excess of the oncoming over the departing sand movement during occasional storms, the dune, by the action of the slip-face, *henceforth becomes a trap for all the sand which is driven over the brink of the face by winds of any strength whatever.* The only qualifications to this statement are (i) that the height of the face must exceed a certain minimum, and (ii) the wind must blow from such a direction relatively to the slip-face that the face is toc sheltered for sand movement to take place over it.

The slip-face advances by a series of discontinuous jerks as each successive avalanche encroaches a few centimetres over the bare ground to leeward. The rate of advance depends on the vertical height of the face, and on the rate of sand movement over the brink. Since the inclination of the face is fixed and known, the rate of advance is very easily found.

In Fig. 71*d* the line AA′ represents a section through the slip-face, and BB′ another section one unit of time later when the dune has advanced a distance AB. If we consider a slice of the dune of unit width perpendicularly to the paper, it is clear that the volume represented by the area AA′B′B contains all the sand which has passed across unit width of the brink in unit time; i.e. it contains a weight Q of sand, where Q is the rate of sand flow at the brink.

Now the volume AA′B′B is equal to the distance advanced, AB, multiplied by the height h. Hence if γ is the specific weight of loosely packed sand in bulk, we have $AB \times h = Q/\gamma$, and therefore since AB is the distance c advanced in unit time, the rate of advance is given by

$$c = Q/\gamma h \qquad . \quad . \quad . \quad . \quad (3)$$

In other words, ***the rate of advance of the dune must vary directly as the rate of sand movement over the brink, and inversely as the height of the slip-face.***

Provided the advance is measured in the same direction as the sand-flow vector Q and the face is so sheltered that no transverse sand movement occurs across it, the above simple and exact relation holds good for any horizontal angle between the slip-face and the wind, and whether the ground trace is curved or straight.

As an important corollary; if the height is not constant along the length of the slip-face, the face cannot retain a constant ground plan as it advances unless the value of Q at every point along the brink is always proportional to the height of the face at that point. For if Q remains the same everywhere, the low portions of the face must advance faster than the high portions.

We have now obtained from purely geometrical considerations two independent expressions for the rate of advance c. From equation (2) we have

$$c = \frac{1}{\gamma}\frac{dQ}{dx}\cot\alpha$$

which holds for all points on the dune where slipping does not take place—i.e. where the sand stays where it is deposited. And from equation (3) we have

$$c = \frac{1}{\gamma}\frac{Q}{h}$$

for the slip-face only. Hence, if the dune is to advance without change of shape, c must be the same in both cases ; and therefore

$$\frac{dQ}{dx}\cot \alpha = \frac{Q}{h}$$

So that the angle α of the surface just above the brink must be given by

$$\tan \alpha = \frac{h}{Q}\frac{dQ}{dx} \quad . \quad . \quad . \quad . \quad (4)$$

7. THE INSTABILITY OF A LONG TRANSVERSE DUNE

Small- and large-scale sand forms in air differ from one another in two important respects ; (i) the coarsest grains are found at the crests of ripples, and the finest in the troughs, whereas it is the finest grains which collect at the tops of dunes, and the coarsest which collect at the bottoms ; (ii) ripples always run transversely to the wind direction, whereas dunes, though they may be isolated or longitudinal, are never transverse to the wind.

These two differences, in the bulk configurations, and in the arrangement of the grains composing them, appear to be intimately connected, and to be inherent in the mechanism of the grain motion in the two cases.

In the case of the ripple, reasons have already been put forward (Chapter 11 (9)) why the transverse alignment should be the most stable ; but let us consider the matter from another angle. Suppose that at any point along the ripple the crest happens by chance to be a little lower than elsewhere, so that a small gap occurs. This should give rise to two independent local changes : (i) The local wind velocity through the gap increases slightly by ' funnelling '. (ii) The rate of advance of those grains in surface creep which are being knocked up the slope of the ripple becomes slower on the less steep slope leading up to the gap than it is elsewhere. This has nothing to do with any change in the wind velocity, but is due to the very sensitive dependence of the rate of surface creep on the angle of incidence between the impelling bombardment and the bombarded surface (Chapter 11, (3) and (4)). Since a slowing up of the movement necessarily implies a local congestion of traffic, the result must be that grains accumulate in the gap until it has risen to the general level of the crest line.

In the case of the dune, we have effect (i), i.e. a local increase of wind velocity through the gap, without effect (ii). For, in the dune, we are dealing not with a local accumulation of the surface creep, but with an accumulation of the whole sand movement, of which the surface creep forms but a fifth part or less. Moreover the rate of surface creep depends not upon the general large-scale slope which now concerns us, but only on the relative tilt of the small ripple face to inclination of the characteristic paths of the saltating grains. The rate of the whole sand movement is controlled entirely by the surface wind strength, and not to any appreciable extent by the inclination of the surface (except in so far as changes of inclination affect the surface wind strength).

If a small chance lowering occurs in the crest line of a long

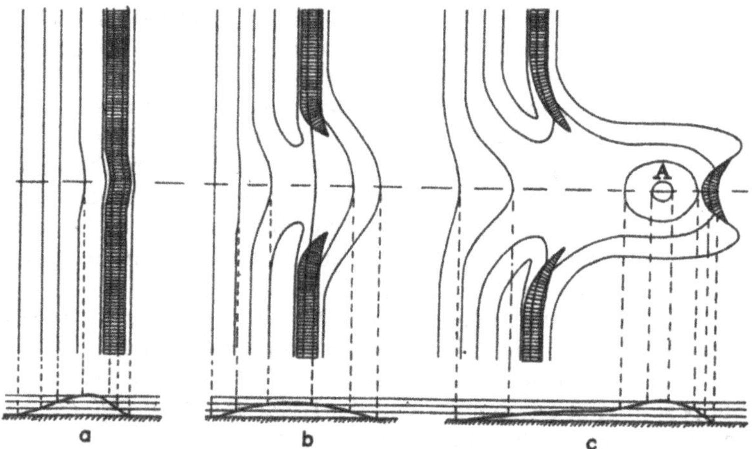

FIG. 72.—PROBABLE SUCCESSIVE STAGES IN THE BREAK-UP OF A CONTINUOUS DUNE BROUGHT ABOUT BY A TRANSVERSE WIND

transverse dune, the local increase of wind velocity through the gap causes a rise in the rate of sand movement there, with a consequent removal of sand from the surface of the gap. The gap gets bigger, and a *blow-out* is formed.

Fig. 72 is a diagrammatic sketch of the probable result. The increase in the sand flow at the gap must, from what has been said in the last section, cause the lee side there to advance faster than elsewhere. At the same time the state of affairs becomes very similar to that of the drift between two obstacles which was discussed in Section 3, where, as we saw, a concentration of the sand flow produced a separate sand accumulation on the lee side.

In that case the deposit was limited in size by the dimensions of the two fixed obstructions, and could not, unless these were very large, attain the minimum size necessary for its separate existence as a dune. But in the case of the accumulation at A in Fig. 72 the whole scale is larger, and the system is free to seek its own equilibrium formation.

As the accumulation at A grows bigger it must eventually build up a slip-face of its own, whereby it will trap for its further growth most of the sand which passes over it. A dune has, in fact, been born.

For some considerable time the height of the new isolated slip-face must be lower than that of the rest of the ridge behind, and so the new face must advance faster. The new dune therefore moves away down-wind and starts an independent existence.

The same instability must occur at other places along the ridge. Consequently the ridge must break up into a number of isolated dunes, whose shape we will now consider.

Chapter 14

THE BARCHAN DUNE

1. THE CRESCENTIC OR BARCHAN DUNE. THE OBSERVED WIND DISTRIBUTION OVER IT

IN the preceding chapter we examined the longitudinal cross-section, cut parallel to a uni-directional wind, of an imaginary transverse dune whose length was so great that the end-effects could be neglected. We saw that as this cross-section grows bigger there comes a time when the initial rounded shape is no longer stable; the top advances faster than the leeward foot, and a slip-face is formed.

We have now to apply the conclusions reached regarding the action and movement of the slip-face to the case of an isolated sand mound whose *transverse* section is short and rounded. And, moreover, in what follows it must be remembered that $\mathbf{V}_*$ and Q, which were both defined in Chapter 12 (11), refer to the *long-period-mean* values of the drag velocity and the sand-flow intensity, as distinct from the *instantaneous* values V_* and q.

Unfortunately neither theory nor adequate experimental measurements are available to define the exact distribution of the wind over and round such an obstacle. But it is certain that the streamlines must be pressed closest together about the summit, and must separate horizontally to some extent as they pass over the flanks. The distribution is indicated approximately in Fig. 73.

On account of this distribution it is probable that the drag velocity should increase from its constant open-country value to a maximum in the neighbourhood of the summit. A few measurements made by the writer show, however, that the increase is small. On the lee side of the transverse crest line AB there is a sharp fall in the drag velocity occasioned by the sheltering effect of the body of the dune. Qualitative evidence of this is provided by the ripple wavelength, which gets progressively smaller as we pass down-wind from the crest line AB towards the leeward wing-tips.

As regards the empty space within the 'bite' of the slip-face repeated observations carried out with smoke candles during winds of all degrees of strength show conclusively that, as long as the wind blows outwards over the brink of the face, the space to leeward of it is an almost perfect wind shadow. The air is stagnant; and though there is a slight tendency for reverse currents to move inwards along the floor, these are rarely strong enough, even during violent storms, to cause appreciable sand movement.

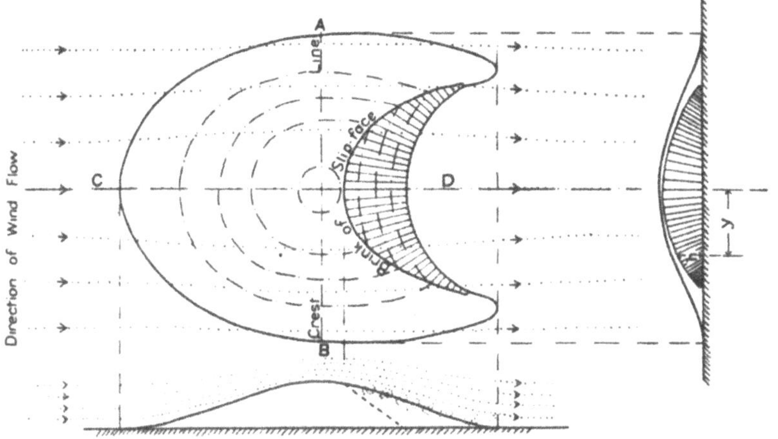

FIG. 73.—THE BARCHAN DUNE. APPROXIMATE WIND DISTRIBUTION, AND POSITION OF THE SLIP-FACE

As far as the wind is concerned, therefore, we can regard the dune as a complete circular, or elliptical mound whose surface is continued over the 'bite' by an imaginary 'surface of discontinuity'.

We will now assume that an unknown slip-face exists somewhere in the mound, and will try and predict its shape and position from the further assumption that the dune advances without change of form. The small lateral diversion of the wind stream across the transverse section will be neglected for the time being, and as a first approximation the streamlines will be taken as parallel.

2. THE SHAPE AND POSITION OF THE SLIP-FACE

With these assumptions the geometrical relations found in Chapter 13, (6*c*) and (6*e*), can be applied. The rate of advance c is constant everywhere, and the sand flow Q over the brink of the slip-face at every point along it is proportional to the height of the face. It is also known that Q at any point is proportional to the cube of the drag velocity of the wind, as measured a short distance up-wind of that point.

Whatever may be the shape of the slip-face, it is clear that at its extremities the height of the brink must be very small, since the dune's height is zero everywhere at the periphery. If we suppose the face to run straight across the dune just in front of the summit, the low extremities would be exposed to a sand flow very nearly as strong as that at the summit. The extremities would therefore advance more rapidly than the centre, and the face would become concave.

But as the extremities advance, they pass into regions which are more and more sheltered by the bulk of the dune, where the drag velocity is less, and the sand flow very much less, than they are near the transverse diameter. The relative advance of the wings of the slip-face ceases when the brink has everywhere reached a line such that $Q/\gamma h =$ the dune's speed c. Whence, by equation (9) of Chapter 5, the drag velocity at the brink is

$$\mathbf{V}_* = \sqrt[3]{\frac{c\gamma h}{b}} \quad . \quad . \quad . \quad . \quad . \quad (1)$$

where $$b = C\frac{\rho}{g}\sqrt{\frac{d}{D}} \text{ (Chapter 5 (3))}.$$

The fore-and-aft position of the centre of the face in relation to the summit depends on the distribution of the sand deposition rate dQ/dx along the axis of x. Since this is a function of the wind distribution, which in turn depends on the shape of the windward slope, very little can be said about it. The distance between the brink and the summit is sometimes very short indeed, and the summit may become a sharp ridge separating the windward face from the slip-face. In general, however, the summit is fairly flat, and the surface curves gently forwards and downwards to the brink. The angle of the upper surface at the brink is given by equation (4) of Chapter 13. It varies from 0° to 25°, and 10° is very common. By the above equation it should be possible to calculate the deposition rate dQ/dx at the brink from measurements of the rate of advance c, the angle α, and the height h. Since dQ/dx must be zero at the summit, some useful light would be thrown by such a calculation on the variation of the deposition rate with the distance along the surface.

3. THE MINIMUM HEIGHT OF THE SLIP-FACE

An interesting point arises at the extreme tips of the slip-face of a barchan dune. If the height h of the brink were to decrease continuously to zero, equation (1) of the last section could not hold good unless $\mathbf{V}_*$ were also zero; that is, unless the slip-face terminated in a region of absolute shelter. But observation shows that there is no point on the rounded surface of a dune which is so sheltered that sand movement does not take place. Consequently, if equation (1) is correct, the slip-face must end suddenly when its height falls below a certain limit. This is just what is found to happen.

That there must be a minimum height limit to any slip-face is obvious if we consider the trajectories of the sand grains after they have passed over the brink (Fig. 74). On the level surface the mean range of the grain path is equal to the wavelength

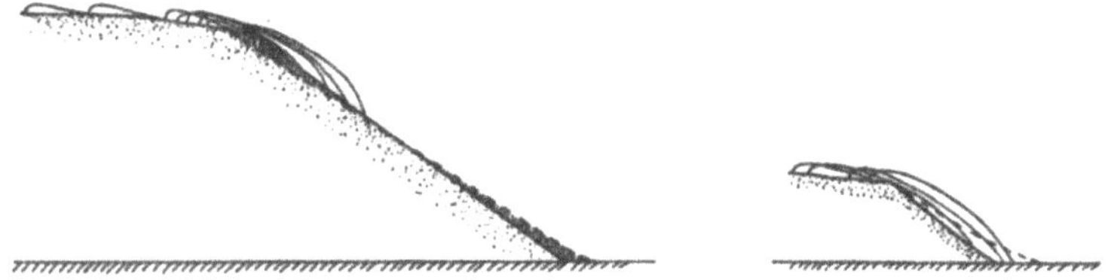

FIG. 74.—MINIMUM HEIGHT OF SLIP-FACE DETERMINED BY THE GRAIN PATH

of the ripple (Chapter 5 (2)). If the surface suddenly drops away, the grains, continuing their fall, enter the stagnant zone in the lee of the brink, and come to rest on the slope within a few wavelengths of the top. If the foot of the slope is too near the level where maximum deposition takes place, the slope can never become steep enough to slip. The limiting condition is given by equation (2) of Chapter 13, when the surface angle α is equal to the angle of repose.

Thus, since the average ripple wavelength, which is a measure of the mean paths of a grain on the level, is about 12 cm., we should expect the limiting height of the slip-face to be of the order of 30 cm.; this seems to agree very well with observation. The height in any particular case should depend on the strength of the wind and on the size of the grains; and it appears to be true that the lowest slip-faces are found on the lee side of dunes composed of very fine uniform sand, and in localities where the dunes are partially sheltered by bushes or by large dunes to windward.

4. THE TRAILING WING-TIPS. THE LATERAL SAND MOVEMENT AWAY FROM THE AXIS. SAND LEAVES THE DUNE IN TWO STREAMS

Beyond the ends of the slip-face (Fig. 73) the inner slopes of the sand wings become rapidly less steep, till at the extreme wing-tips the dune dwindles to a mere sprinkling of sand over the ground. From a consideration of the conditions necessary for stability, it seems likely that the unlimited extension of these wing-tips is prevented by the increase which takes place in the surface wind strength as the shelter afforded by the dune becomes less effective at greater distances. The trailing sand fringe must mark the position of minimum $\mathbf{V}_*$, in the lee of which its increasing value would cause removal instead of deposition if the fringe extended too far.

Of the whole transverse width of the dune, sand can only stream away to leeward from these narrow trailing wing-tips, and from the outer edge between the tips and the flanks A and B. *The total transverse width from which sand can stream away is only about one-third of the whole width that receives sand from up-wind.*

If the dune is advancing without change of mass, no sand whatever can be added from up-wind to any sections lying between the limits of the slip-face, since no sand can leave the face. Hence all the oncoming sand, supposedly distributed uniformly across a transverse section, must be diverted outwards, as it passes over the dune surface, and must leave from the sides only. This diversion of sand from the centre to the sides is brought about partly by the direct action of the small outward component of the wind, and partly by the action of gravity.

It will be evident that there must be a considerable increase of intensity between the oncoming sand movement and the leeward stream from the narrow wing-tips. The long-period-mean intensity Q to leeward of the tips must be some three times its value to windward. The most favourable positions for the birth of a new dune would therefore seem to be somewhere directly to leeward of the wing-tips. This no doubt explains the diagonal or echelon arrangement of the dunes in a barchan field.

5. NON-UNIFORM DISTRIBUTION OF SAND SUPPLY. COMPLEX BARCHANS. FULJIS

As an example of the application of the foregoing ideas to special cases it is instructive to examine the conditions under which more complex barchan forms may exist. Fig. 75 shows one of the simplest of the many forms which are found—a double barchan.

It consists of two summits A and B separated by a very slight re-entrant on the windward side, and by a col C at the crest. The slip-face is continuous, and is low and convex in the middle. Such a dune may or may not be stable. If it is stable, and is advancing without change of shape or size, we can deduce something of the special conditions which must obtain.

(*a*) *Wind conditions.* The value of Q at the centre D of the lower, convex, part of the slip-face must be less than it is at the higher parts E and F of the concave brink. The wind must therefore be less strong at D ; otherwise D would advance faster. D has already found the most stable position by advancing, and at the same time falling, into a region of greater shelter. But

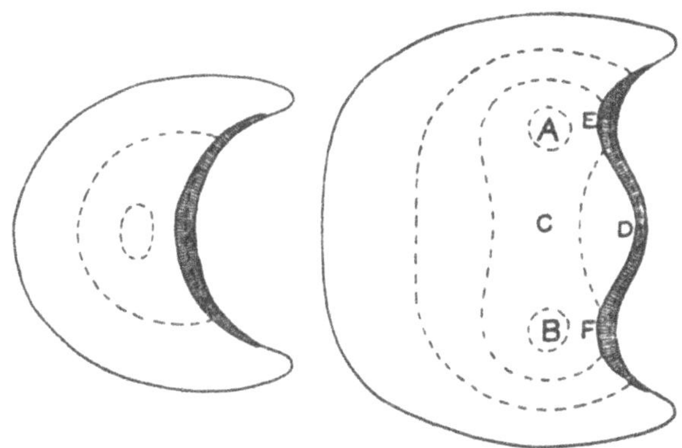

FIG. 75.—DOUBLE BARCHAN CAUSED BY THE PRESENCE OF A DUNE TO WINDWARD

unless the wind is also weaker in the centre than over the summits A and B the funnelling effect should remove sand from the col C and should tend to split the dune into two, as in the case discussed in Chapter 13 (7). We therefore look to windward for a something which is causing this uneven wind distribution.

(*b*) *Sand conditions.* The existence of two summits must prevent the total diversion of the oncoming sand stream from the centre to the sides which is necessary for complete stability, because some of the sand must be carried through the col by the funnelling effect there. And so we are again forced to conclude that if the dune really is stable in size something to windward must be withholding the oncoming sand stream from reaching the middle of the dune.

In nature we nearly always find that the complication in the dune outline is due to the presence of another dune [1] immediately to windward. In the case considered, the bulk of this second dune provides the necessary wind shelter in the middle, and its slip-face prevents the arrival of sand there. For complete stability over a long period this second dune must of course be advancing at the same rate as the one in front, and it must therefore be of the same height. For temporary stability, the windward obstacle may be a low hill in the middle, or a pair of hills one on each side.

But there is rarely if ever any evidence of real stability. The dune may in fact have become too broad, for some reason, and may be in the act of splitting in half.

If the dune to windward is low, and has been advancing faster than the one in front, it may have got so close that its wings have joined up with the foot of the leeward dune. In this case the hollow formed by its slip-face may be almost circular in shape, and may suggest at first sight that it is caused by a rotary swirling action on the part of the wind. But there is no evidence that such large-scale swirls seriously affect the shape of dunes. These inter-dune hollows are known in northern Arabia as *Fuljis*. They occur wherever a string of barchans are pressing closely on one another.

6. THE SIZE AND HEIGHT OF BARCHANS, AND THEIR RATE OF ADVANCE

The relative length, width, and height of barchans vary greatly. The maximum length and width of existing dunes is about 400 metres. The height of these very big dunes does not, however, increase in proportion to the girth. The maximum height seems to be about 30 metres.

As regards the relative rate of advance of a group of dunes of different heights in the same uniform meteorological area, care must be taken to bring all the variable factors into account. While it seems difficult to escape from the conclusion reached in Chapter 13 (6*e*), that the rate of advance c must vary according to the relation $c\mathrm{H} = \mathrm{Q}/\gamma$, or $c = \mathrm{Q}/\gamma\mathrm{H}$, as long as the slip-face traps all the sand passing over the brink, it is clear that c will not vary inversely as the height H of the summit unless the long-period-mean rate Q of the sand flow over the summit is constant for all the dunes in the group.

[1] An excellent though unintentional illustration of a double barchan with its causatory barchan to windward is given in Fig. 106 of Bosworth's book—see reference at end of chapter.

Now the value of Q at the summit depends on the drag velocity $\mathbf{V}_*$ at the summit; and it also depends, though to a smaller extent, on the grading of the sand grains. Though $\mathbf{V}_*$ may be constant over a wide area of open country and up to a considerable height above the ground, it has already been pointed out that its local value over surfaces which project upwards into levels of faster-moving wind must be greater than near the ground. The amount of the increase will depend on the shape of the projection, and could only be determined by experiment and careful measurement, but there must be an increase. Hence the product cH of dune speed and dune height, which would be constant for all dunes of the group if Q were constant, should be greater for high dunes than for low ones.

Many short-period estimates have been made of the rate of advance of single isolated barchans in various parts of the world, but since the essential factors governing the movement have not hitherto been recognized, the records are too incomplete to be of much value in checking the above relation between height, wind, and dune speed. Beadnell,[1] however, gives figures for a period of a year for the movement of five barchans of different heights in the same area (Kharga Oasis, Egypt) from which values for cH can be compared.

Dune	Height H (metres)	Total Advance (metres)	c, in metres per hour	cH
a	20	10·9	0·00124	0·025
b	17	10·8	0·00123	0·021
c	11	16·2	0·0018	0·0198
d	10·5	18·8	0·00215	0·0226
e	4	18·4	0·0021	0·0084

It will be seen that except in the case of dune *d* the value of cH gets progressively smaller as the height falls. The slight increase in the speed of dune *d* might indicate that its surface was becoming lower. Similarly the relative slowness of dune *e* might indicate that it was in process of building up its summit at the expense of sand which would otherwise have streamed over the brink of the slip-face and added fresh material on the lee side.

Though he recorded no figures for the actual wind velocities from hour to hour during the year, Beadnell gives enough infor-

[1] Beadnell, H. J. L. (1910). *Geogr. J.*, 35, p. 379.

mation to enable an independent estimate to be made of the value of cH from the wind data only. I have arranged his information into the following table.

	A Sand movement on dunes only	B Sand driving across country and on to dunes	C Sand storms	Total days
	5·8 to 10 metres/sec.	10 to 13·5 metres/sec.	13·5 to 15·7 metres/sec.	
North wind	178	90	13	281
South wind	10	10	2	22
Cross-winds	28	5	1	34
Total days	216	105	16	337
			Calm days	29
				365

The figures refer to the numbers of days of 12 hours daylight, and Mr. Beadnell tells me that it was very rare indeed for any appreciable wind to blow at night.

It will be seen that the wind was almost uni-directional. If we neglect the 34 days of cross-winds we can arrive at a fair estimate of the value of the mean rate Q of sand movement for the whole year, as follows:

	A	B	C	
Estimated mean wind velocity for categories A, B, and C	7·9	11·3	14	
q, in tons (m) per hour, from Fig. 22, Chapter 5	0·035	0·22	0·53	
No. of hours of north wind, less no. of hours south wind	2015	960	132	
q × no. of hours net north wind = total weight moved in year	70	211	70	Total, 351

The mean rate of sand flow Q is therefore equal to

$$\frac{351}{365 \times 24} = 0{\cdot}04 \text{ tons per hour per metre width.}$$

And the corresponding mean sand-driving wind velocity throughout the year, from Fig. 22, is 8·1 metres/sec.

Taking a value of 1·7 for γ we obtain from the equation $cH = Q/\gamma$ a value for cH of 0·023 metres²/hour, which is in remarkable agreement with the actual measured value already given in the table on page 215.

As regards the rapid movement of barchans during short periods of storm wind, the speed is very simply found provided the dune is not growing or shrinking. In the case of a dune 15 metres high in movement by a wind of 30 miles per hour or 13·5 metres/sec., q is found from Fig. 22 to be 0·46 tons per hour. Hence

$$c = \frac{q}{\gamma H} = \frac{0{\cdot}46}{1{\cdot}7 \times 15} \text{ metres per hour}$$

or 1·8 cm. per hour. On the other hand the maximum speed in the same wind is attained by a dune of the minimum height necessary for its slip-face to trap all the sand that passes over —say 40 cm. Here $c = 67$ cm. per hour.

It seems likely that a dune that is shrinking moves faster, and one that is growing less fast, than the rate calculated as above, even though the heights are the same and the wind constant for both.

7. THE EFFECT OF WINDS FROM THE REVERSE DIRECTION

Although it is highly probable that the barchan dune is only stable when the wind blows always along one axis, this does not exclude winds from the opposite direction. The observed effect of such a wind is indicated in Fig. 76. Violent removal occurs

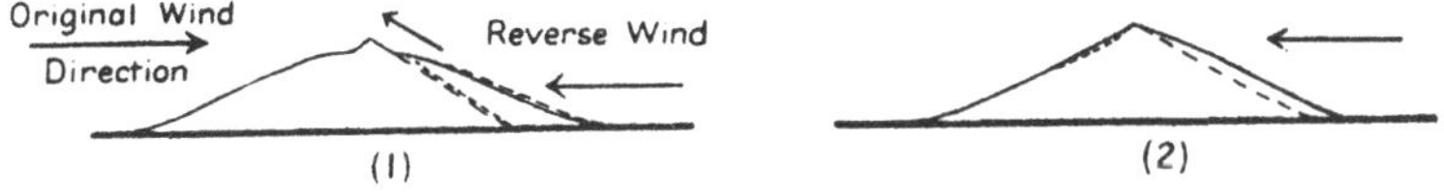

FIG. 76.—EFFECT OF A REVERSE WIND

on the upper part of the slip-face, and a new slip-face is formed, facing the other way.

The original slip-face may temporarily disappear as such because the sand now stands at an angle less than the angle of shear. For a considerable period during the restoration brought about by the return of the former wind there may be no slip-face at all, and the dune exists as a rounded mound.

8. BARCHAN BELTS

All dunes tend to occur in belts or chains, whose direction coincides with that of the resultant long-period sand vector Q (Chapter 12 (11)). The lateral position of the belt at right angles to Q coincides with a line along which the stream of oncoming sand has a maximum intensity. On the other hand, as we go along the line of the belt we should expect the point of greatest sand accumulation—where the dunes are most closely packed—to be found where either (*a*) the magnitude of Q for the particular belt is a minimum; just as the densest road traffic occurs where the vehicles are moving slowest: or (*b*) where the belt passes through a region of maximum sand supply; a road junction, on the same analogy.

Over the younger, up-wind, portion of the belt's length, where the sand supply is ample, the dunes are growing bigger as they advance, so that their speed must be decreasing. As a consequence we should expect this portion of the belt to consist of closely packed dunes which have overtaken one another, as sketched in Fig. 77. This is generally found to be the case.

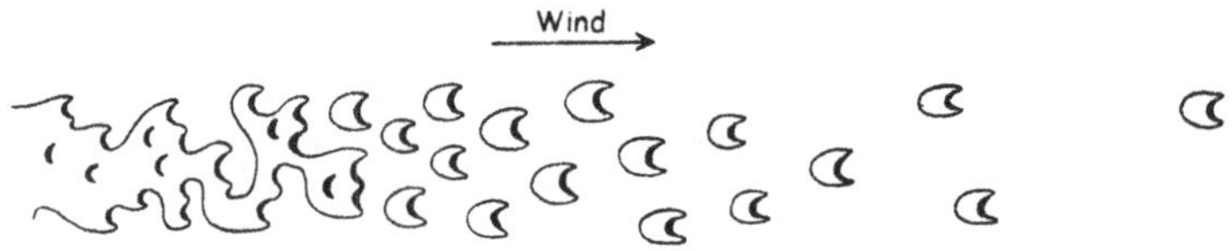

FIG. 77.—A TYPICAL BELT OF BARCHANS (NOT TO SCALE)

Further down-wind, where the sand supply has fallen off, and the dunes have ceased to grow, there should be a tendency to disperse; because the dunes which happen to be slightly smaller than their neighbours will gradually outstrip them.

Over an open stretch of desert, where no surface features have interfered with their march, it is usual for the spacing between the dunes to increase towards the down-wind end of the belt. The length of the belt and the position of the end dune may be determined by either of two possible factors. If the size of the dunes is found to dwindle to nothing at the end of the belt, it is likely that the position of the last dune depends upon the progressive failure of the sand supply as the distance from the source increases. In this case the movement may have been going on for an indefinite time.

But it is more common for barchan belts to terminate because the frequency of their occurrence dwindles to nothing rather than their size. The end dunes are only slightly smaller than those in the middle of the belt, but are separated by far greater distances from one another. In this case it is possible that the final dunes are the original ones which were born at the period when increasing desiccation first started the supply of driving sand from the source.

This opens up interesting possibilities for estimating the dates of climatic changes in desert areas. For instance, the barchan belts in the lee of, and presumably originating from, the oasis depressions of southern Egypt and northern Sudan average about 120 km. in length, and their average height does not exceed 10 metres. If the dunes travelled at the same rate, in proportion to their height, as Beadnell's dunes in Kharga Oasis, the time taken by the terminal dunes to reach their present positions should not be greatly in excess of 7,000 [1] years. This brings us to 5000 B.C., which is a not unreasonable date for the abandonment of the Libyan Desert by the pre-Dynastic folk who are known to have migrated to the Nile Valley.

Further westward in the same desert the barchan belts are longer. Though the survey is still incomplete, portions of what seems to be one continuous belt have been crossed by the writer at points separated by more than 300 km. But here, since the whole of the surrounding area is sandy, the source may not have lain entirely to windward, and the terminal dunes may have come into being anywhere along the belt. The width of such a belt may exceed 12 km.

In some cases the dunes do not separate out towards the end of the belt, but remain close-packed throughout its length. The belt then often ends in a collection of mounds devoid of slip-faces, and these mounds finally merge into vague undulations. The most likely cause of this is clearly a progressive decrease in the value of Q due to a gradual change in the meteorological conditions from one end of the belt to the other. On a smaller scale, the termination of a dune belt in a confused sand accumula-

[1] J. Ball (*Geogr. J.*, 70, p. 214), using a similar rate of advance derived from Beadnell's figures, arrived at a rough estimate of 35,000 years for the age of the 350 km. length of the Abu Moharik dune chain further north. Since, however, this great dune system consists of seifs and not of barchans, the above estimate seems to be of rather doubtful significance (see Chapter 15 (3)).

tion is generally due to a local decrease in Q caused by wind obstacles such as trees or other vegetation.

Both the spacing and the size of the barchans, though each is very constant at any one point in the belt, vary greatly in different places, and it seems unlikely for this reason that either are determined by any large-scale dynamical wind-sand reaction such as accounts for the wavelength of ripples. It seems more probable that the size-spacing ratio depends on the variation of the value of cH with the rate of growth or shrinkage. Several factors must affect this: the intensity of the sand supply in relation to the wind velocity; the wind velocity and its variation with time; the presence or absence of temporary or permanent vegetation; and the grading of the sand, in particular the relative proportions of the large semi-mobile grains which tend to inhibit dune-building.

It is likely that these large grains, by the protection afforded to the windward dune foot by their accumulation upon it, delay the advance of the dune and so exert a strong influence on the size attained. Observation shows, too, that in general an absence of coarse grains on the floor is associated with a close packing of the barchans, and a plentiful supply with large spacing. In coastal and riverine dunes, for which the sand supply is water-borne and the grain grading consequently more uniform, large isolated dunes are seldom found.

The effect of vegetation is not only to break up the orderly arrangement, but to limit the dune size to that of the open spaces between the vegetated patches. This is particularly evident in coastal sand accumulations. Nor, in desert country, must the possible effect be neglected of a recently vanished covering of light grass or other fitful herbage. It is not impossible that the vague mounds in which the leeward ends of the dune chains sometimes terminate are evidence of the advance of the chain into a geographical area of greater rainfall frequency.

As regards the supply of dune-building sand for the continued growth of the long desert barchan chains, it seems necessary, if we accept the hypothesis that a nearly uni-directional wind is necessary for barchan formation, to postulate a sideways transportation of sand from the open country towards the lines of greatest surface drag, by the mechanism outlined in Chapter 12, Section 7. An account was there given of the formation over a featureless sand sheet of narrow longitudinal strips of new sand deposit during one uni-directional storm. In the case of an existing dune chain the increased surface drag along the line of the

PLATE 13

a. EGYPTIAN SAND SEA. LAT. 27°, LONG. 26°. TOP OF AN OPEN WHALEBACK, SHOWING THE END OF A LONG SUPERIMPOSED SEIF DUNE CHAIN RUNNING ALONG ONE EDGE OF THE WHALEBACK. FACING SOUTH

b. EGYPTIAN SAND SEA. LAT. 25°, LONG. 25° 30′. LOOKING NORTH

PLATE 14

a. ACCRETION LAYERS PARALLEL TO THE FORMER *WIND* SURFACE DISCLOSED BY WATER SEEPAGE. THE DEPOSIT IS VERY COMPACT AND RIGID

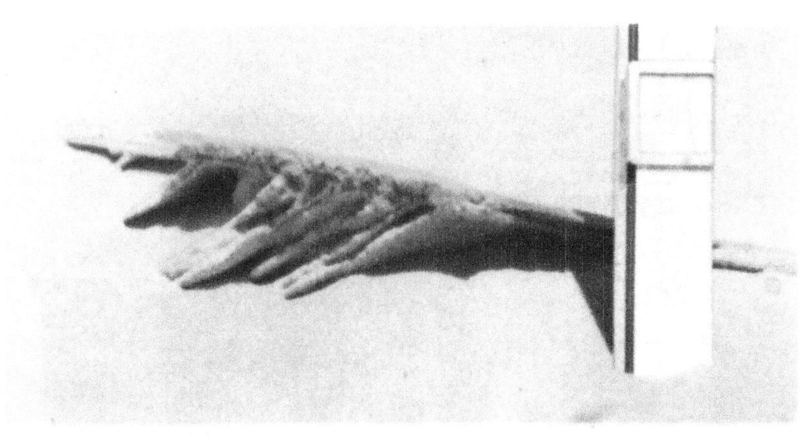

b. AVALANCHE LAYERS PARALLEL TO THE FORMER *SLIP-FACE*. THE DEPOSIT HAS THE CONSISTENCY OF A QUICK-SAND

chain must be much more pronounced because we have now not only the drag due to the moving sand, but also the permanent 'form-drag' due to the large-scale irregularities of the dunes themselves. And just as in a river the finer particles in motion tend to be deposited in the shallows near the banks where the increased effect of the surface drag slows down the water flow, so in the case of long dune chains the finer material must tend to drift towards them. A lane between two parallel chains in this respect resembles the bed of a river.

9. ICE BARCHANS

Moss [1] has described in detail the formation of small barchan dunes composed of very cold ice crystals. The dimensions varied between 3 metres long and 5 wide to 10 metres long and 12 wide. The rate of advance was about 1 cm. per minute, in a wind averaging 15 miles per hour at an unspecified height. The shape appeared to vary with the size and grading of the grains. In the young dune the grain size ranged from 1 to 3 mm., and the width between the wings exceeded the total length. As the dune advanced, the grains split into spicules 1 mm. long, and the dune lengthened to a cigar shape. Since, however, there seems to have been considerable cementing between the surface grains, even at the low temperature of − 30° C., the shape of the dune was probably influenced as much by this as by the true interaction of the wind and the ice grains. The slip-face was absent, possibly because the dunes were below the critical size needed for its formation.

The dunes were only formed when the wind, though variable in strength, was absolutely constant in direction. These conditions agree exactly with those already put forward as necessary for the formation of barchans in sand.

Similar ice barchans have been described by Cornish [2] and others.

REFERENCES

BEADNELL, H. J. L. (1909). *An Egyptian Oasis.* (John Murray)

BOSWORTH, T. O. (1922). *Geology and Palaeontology of North-west Peru.* (Macmillan, London)

CORNISH, V. (1934). *Ocean Waves.* (Cambridge)

— — (1914). *Waves of Sand and Snow.* (T. Fisher Unwin)

HUME, W. S. (1928). *Geology of Egypt.* Vol. 1

[1] Moss, R. (1938). *Geogr. J.*, 92, p. 215.

[2] Cornish, V. (1934). *Ocean Waves.* (Cambridge.)

Chapter 15

THE LONGITUDINAL OR SEIF DUNE. WHALE-BACKS AND MISCELLANEOUS FORMS

1. THE TRANSITION FROM THE BARCHAN TO THE SEIF DUNE FORMS

IN the barchan dune the straightforward relationships between the rate of sand movement, the speed of advance, the surface angle, and the height were all based on three assumptions : (*a*) that the wind is uni-directional, (*b*) that the rate of sand supply is symmetrical on either side of the longitudinal axis, and (*c*) that the surface of the slip-face is in complete shelter, so that the face traps all the sand passing over its brink. When these assumptions become untenable, no simple deductions can be drawn as to the stability of the resulting sand forms.

In the case of the seif dune not only are reliable data as to the size, repetition distance, and movement at present very meagre, but no clear explanation has so far presented itself of why the seif form should emerge *ab initio* as sand accumulates. It seems possible, however, to gain some insight into the formation of this continuous chain-like dune system by considering the probable fate of an isolated barchan when the conditions assumed above no longer obtain.

We will suppose that the prevailing directions of the gentle and strong winds fail to coincide ; so that ${}_gQ$ and ${}_sQ$ of chapter 12 (11) are not in the same straight line. The prevailing gentle wind *g* which blows along the axis of the dune is interrupted at times by sand-bearing storm winds from a new direction *s* (Fig. 78).

Fig. 78*a* shows the original barchan formed by a steady wind from the direction *g*. Fig. 78*b* represents the probable result of a sequence of storms from the new direction *s*. The windward wing A has advanced in the new direction and at the same time has grown fatter by a heavy deposit of fresh sand. If this wind were to continue indefinitely the barchan would no doubt assume a new symmetry about the axis *s* ; the wing B would atrophy, and a new wing would appear at C.

But the wind now returns to the more settled bearing *g*. Symmetry is restored on the windward side of the barchan: but on the lee side the wing A has outgrown the limits of stability. Having swollen in size, and having extended to leeward, its curvature is less than before and its surface is therefore less sheltered from the wind *g* by the body of the dune. And since the action of a gentle wind over a flat surface causes the lee side of a sand patch to extend down-wind at the expense of its height (Chapter 12 (4)), we can reasonably expect a low tongue of sand to be formed to leeward of A, as is indicated in Fig. 78*c*.

It should be noted that this tongue is neither stable nor permanent, and a long continuance of the wind *g* should cause such

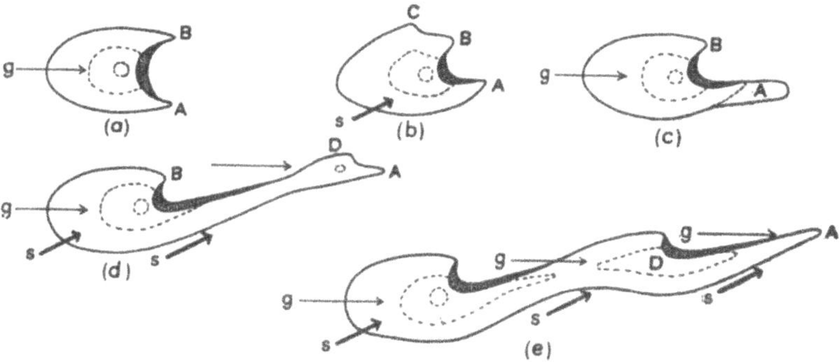

FIG. 78.—TRANSITION FROM BARCHAN TO SEIF DUNE FORM DUE TO A BI-DIRECTIONAL WIND

an extension and shrinkage in height that the whole of the excess length of the wing A would eventually disappear, so that the dune would regain its original symmetry.

During the next stormy season the wing A has another period of growth. The process continues thus until a critical stage is reached when the tip has advanced to D, where it enters the stream of sand which flows to leeward from the wing-tip B. It here receives a sand supply during both wind régimes, and consequently begins to grow more rapidly than the connecting arm behind it. A new dune is formed (Fig. 78*d*). In time the operation is repeated to leeward, till eventually a great chain comes in being, similar to that shown in the photograph (Plate 12*a*, which was taken from the lee side facing the vestigial barchan wings B).

Though the actual transition forms suggested in Fig. 78 do exist and have been examined by the author, the above tentative explanation of the growth of a seif dune chain should certainly not be taken as implying that all such chains have originated as barchans. It may help, however, by providing a basis for further work both on the action of two alternating wind régimes and on the mechanism which controls the repetition distance between the succeeding summits.

2. THE SEIF SHAPE VARIES ACCORDING TO THE PREVAILING LONG-PERIOD WIND RÉGIME

The detailed shape of the seif dune assumes several different sub-types according to the particular long-period wind régime which prevails in the observed area. But the essential feature common to all is a single continuous ridge which swells and rises at regular intervals to form a chain of summits.

In some areas the directions of the storm winds are such that storms blow towards the dune from either side of the main

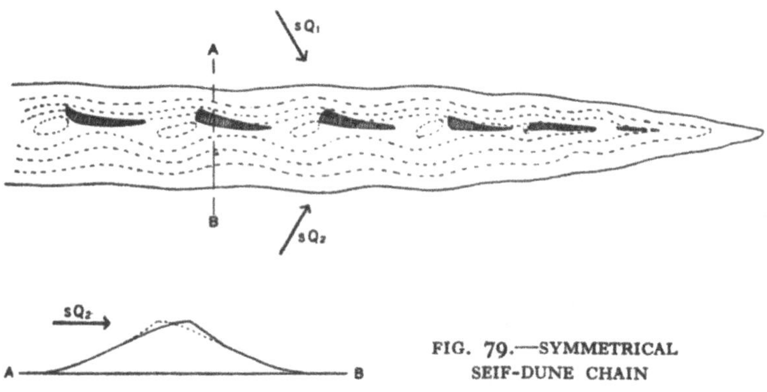

FIG. 79.—SYMMETRICAL SEIF-DUNE CHAIN

resultant axis. A simple case is shown diagrammatically in Fig. 79. Here the vector ${}_sQ$ is split into two parts ${}_sQ_1$ and ${}_sQ_2$. The seif form is now very nearly symmetrical, and no trace of the barchan form remains. The form may be compared with that of the ideal sand drift shown in Fig. 66, Chapter 13.

It will be noted that the seif dune differs most markedly from the barchan in that its slip-face, instead of running mainly transverse to the prevailing wind, runs parallel with it. In the seif dune the slip-face lies always on the side away from that of the prevailing cross-wind. Hence, in the case of the symmetrical dune, the slip-face is a temporary phenomenon which is formed and reformed on either side according to the direction from which the cross-wind happens to blow. It is low in relation to the total height of the dune, and occupies only the upper part of the slope, from the longitudinal crest downwards.

In cases where one or both of the storm vectors ${}_sQ_1$ and ${}_sQ_2$ blow from bearings differing from that of the resultant prevailing wind by more than 90°, the slip-face may exist only in short stretches along the connecting ridges ; and the summits may have the appearance of tear-drops (Plate 12*b*).

3. MOVEMENT OF THE SEIF DUNE

The arrangement of the slip-face is such that it traps most of the sand driven over the crest by the cross-winds, but has little effect on the flow ${}_gQ$ along the length of the chain, except when the dune shape is very unsymmetrical. It is likely, therefore, that the chain grows in height and width by trapping sand during the periods of strong cross-winds, and extends lengthwise during the longer periods of more settled conditions when the wind blows down the chain.

Apart from the growth of the chain in cross-section there are three different movements to be considered. (*a*) The extension of the chain towards the leeward end of the chain. (*b*) A longitudinal displacement of the summits along the chain. (*c*) A transverse shift on the part of the whole chain due to the transverse component of the resultant cross-wind.

Practically no numerical data are available regarding any of these movements or the winds which cause them. Nor is it known for certain whether the chain extends by a general onward march on the part of the summits, or by the addition of new summits at the leeward end. Probably both occur together.

The few observations made in Egypt on the rate of extension of the seif dune chains were so discordant, from one chain to another, that interest in the subject seems to have flagged. For while the end of one chain was found after a period of years to have advanced rapidly, another in the same area had hardly moved at all. It has even been suggested that the movement of the point of the seif is so sensitive to the texture of the desert floor that the grooves made by the wheels of travellers' cars around the end of the dune have encouraged it to advance more quickly than it would otherwise have done. This may indeed be true. At all events one gains the impression that the seif-dune chains behave like glaciers, in that their advance is fitful and uncertain. Speeds of scores of metres a year appear to be quite common, but such speeds bear no relation to the size or the length of the dune chain behind.

Observation of the movement of the individual summits, as distinct from the advance of the point of the chain, is difficult; for there is no way, short of paying frequent and regular visits to one summit for a long period of time, of identifying any particular one. In the case of summits well back from the extending end of the chain, the movement appears to be very slow.

The lateral movement of a well-developed dune chain is certainly extremely small. In the case of the symmetrical dune there is no likelihood of any long-period movement at all. In the unsymmetrical dune where the slip-face is on one side only, and where at first sight it might be thought that some advance is inevitable, it is quite possible that much of the new sand deposited by a cross-wind is removed again by the subsequent longitudinal wind. It is also possible that deposition may take place equally on both sides, so that though the slip-face advances laterally on one side, the centre of the cross-section remains where it was, and the net result is general growth without lateral movement. Whatever the reason, there is some archaeological and other evidence that the lateral movement of the base of a well-established dune is almost negligible, except perhaps over very long periods of time (see Section 5).

4. GROWTH OF A SEIF DUNE. GRADING OF SAND OVER THE CROSS-SECTION. FORMATION OF A PLINTH OF COARSE SAND AT THE BASE

Fig. 80 shows successive stages in the growth of the cross-section. The direct evidence on which it is based will be discussed in the next chapter. The dune is supposed nearly symmetrical, but has shifted a little to the right during its growth under the action of a slightly dominant wind from the left. The main reversal of the slip-face is probably an annual phenomenon, but the many hundreds or thousands of alternate phases in the building up of the dune have been reduced to six in the diagram for the sake of simplicity.

The smallest and oldest section formed part of the original

point of the dune chain, which may be considered as advancing out of the plane of the paper, and growing as it does so.

It is probable that the quantity of sand moved from one side to the other during each half-phase increases somewhat as the crest rises upwards into faster-moving wind currents; but since the area of the largest cross-section may be a thousand times that of the smallest, it is clear that if the periodicity of the reversals remains constant, the smallest section must have moved by more than its own width during each period, whereas the present section does not shift its base at all. This same differential movement of the base must also act at the present time when the size of the section varies along the length of the chain. It probably accounts for the observed fact that the small narrow leeward extremities of long seif chains are often out of alignment with the massive dunes of the chain behind.

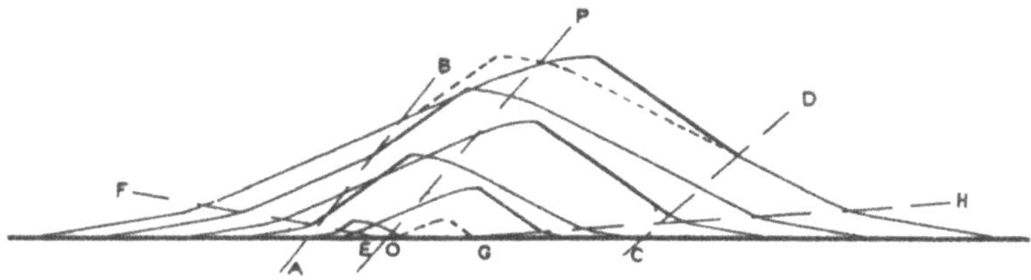

FIG. 80.—THE GROWTH OF THE CROSS-SECTION OF A SEIF DUNE

It will be seen that the process of the building up of a seif dune is very different from that of the barchan. And hence a marked difference is to be expected both in the internal structure of the dune and in the grading of the sand through the cross-section. The internal structure of dunes will be discussed in the next chapter.

The grading of the material composing an isolated *barchan* dune is nearly homogeneous from the summit downwards to within a height above the ground of the order of 5 per cent. of that of the summit. Below this there may or may not exist on the windward side, according to the nature of the surrounding country, a fringe of coarse grains and small pebbles whose slow movement has been held up by the dune. But since on the lee side the advancing barchan pours fresh sand from the summit down the slip-face directly on to the bare ground, the whole of the under-portion of the dune is composed purely of this material from the upper dune, unmixed with any coarser grains than can be driven in surface creep up the windward slope. The very coarse material on the windward side is therefore only superficial, and none of it has emerged from under the dune. Most of it is left behind as the dune advances, and forms a wake of removal ridges.

In the case of the *seif* dune, however, the conditions are quite different. For if the body of the dune does not move in the direction of, but rather moves at right angles to, the sand-supplying winds, all the material too coarse to be driven up over the crest of the dune collects at the foot—on either side equally in the symmetrical case, unequally in other cases.

Of the finer grains which are small enough to rise to the crest, the largest are again sorted out by gravity and roll furthest as they avalanche down the slip-face. As the slip-face shifts from side to side this winnowing action continues, with the result that the coarser of the more mobile grains which have once succeeded in reaching the crest, tend to collect at the foot of the slip-face. Here, as the dune grows bigger, they are buried by others and never emerge again.

The generalized seif dune can be divided into five parts by radial boundaries which appear at the surface as abrupt changes in the surface angle (Fig. 80). The boundaries are also surfaces of constant grading and constant mean grain diameter.

The whole of the central core lying between the boundaries AB and CD has taken part at some time or other in the alternating lateral movement, and most of the material has been subjected to avalanching down a slip-face. The mean grain diameter, which is constant over AB and CD, becomes gradually less towards the centre line OP. Here the diameter is a minimum.

The two zones AB/EF and CB/GH have been deposited entirely by accretion, and the sand has never avalanched. The mean grain diameter is nearly constant in these zones.

Throughout the whole mass lying between EF and GH the grading is regular (Chapters 9 and 10). The arms of the logarithmic grading curves steepen progressively towards the centre line. Along the boundaries EF and GH the grading is sometimes so wide that the sand contains grains of different sizes in nearly equal proportions over a great range of diameters.

Below EF and GH the grading is no longer regular, for grains of much larger size are present. These bottom zones represent the long-continued accumulation of grit and small pebbles from the surrounding desert floor. The surface slope of these zones is usually only a few degrees, and their structure is very similar to that of a sand sheet. Their relative size depends of course on the material available. They may not be present at all.

It seems desirable to give a distinguishing name to all that lower and outer portion of the dune beyond the slip-face boundaries AB and CD which has never been subjected to sand avalanches. The term 'Plinth' is suggested tentatively.

5. SEIF DUNE CHAINS. SIZE, LENGTH, AND ALIGNMENT

In comparison with isolated barchans, seif dunes, and the continuous orderly chains which they form, may grow to enormous dimensions. Many dune summits in the Egyptian Sand Sea attain a height of 100 metres. The highest dunes in existence appear to be some in Southern Iran, which are said to rise to 210 metres [1] above their bases (700 feet). The transverse width at the base is of the order of six times the height.

As might be expected from the ideas suggested in Section 1, the repetition distance between successive summits varies greatly with the stage of development and with the wind régime which gives the dune its characteristic shape. Along the same chain the distance between summits decreases with the dune height. The maximum repetition distance seems to be in the neighbourhood of 500 metres, and the minimum about 20 metres. An average figure for the ratio of repetition distance to dune height may be put at 6 to 1.

Seif chains run remarkably straight for great distances. The direction depends entirely on the long-period wind régime, and scarcely at all on local surface features. The largest and longest chains occur on featureless country, but they are often found to have crept over low scarps and into cliff-girt depressions without serious change of direction or form.

A single chain seems to correspond as regards individuality of shape and movement with an isolated barchan. Each chain has a broad massive stern to windward and its leeward end dwindles to a sharp point. The chain may be a short one consisting of but three or four summits, or it may run without interruption for 60 or 100 km.

Though the same line of advance may be followed by successive chains, end to end, for far greater distances, the individual chains retain their identity, and are separated from one another by gaps.

[1] Gabriel, A. (1938). *Geogr. J.*, 92, p. 195.

6. WHALEBACKS OR SAND LEVEES. THE EGYPTIAN SAND SEA

These gaps may constitute complete breaks in the line, so that the point of one chain is separated from the stern of the next by a ' street ' of bare desert floor. This happens when the dunes are small and have formed no appreciable plinths. But other instances occur, notably in the Egyptian Sand Sea, where the plinths have grown to such a vast size that the dunes which surmount them are small in proportion. Here we find what appear to be continuous plinths 1 to 3 kilometres in width and perhaps 50 metres high running in straight lines for distances of the order of 300 kilometres. The existing dune chains lie end to

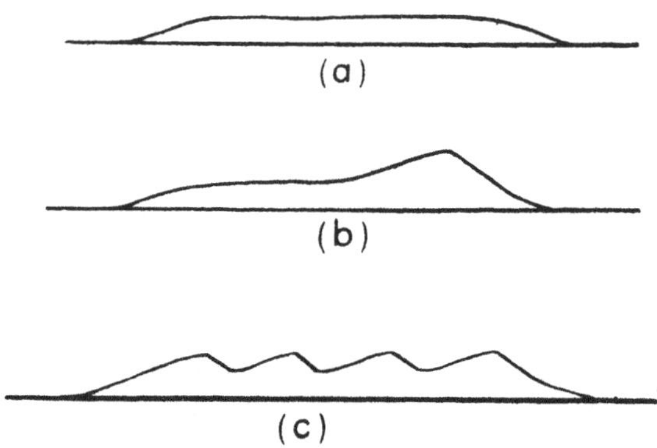

FIG. 81.—TRANSVERSE SECTION ACROSS WHALEBACK

(*a*) Gap between dune chains
(*b*) Single superimposed dune chain
(*c*) Multiple dune chains

end along them, separated by gaps where the cross-section may be likened to that of a rounded ' levee ' or ' whaleback ' (Fig. 81*a*).

The lateral position of the dune chain on the whaleback may vary from area to area along its length according to gradual changes in the geographical distribution of the winds. The chain may run along one edge as shown in Fig. 81*b* and in the photograph, Plate 13*a*.

Sometimes, however, the whole width of the whaleback is occupied by two, three, or four parallel chains side by side (Fig. 81*c*). The general appearance, internal structure, and grain grading of these huge formations suggests strongly that each is the residue which has been left behind by the march either of a single former dune chain of a far greater size than any now existing, or of an age-long procession of successive chains of the present size which have travelled down the same line.

It seems probable that the gradual shift in the relative position of the dune chains on the whalebacks, which is very noticeable as one travels for 600 km. through the great Sand Sea of western Egypt along the immense corridors which separate the parallel dune lines, may provide interesting evidence of geographical changes in the wind régime. The general direction of the whalebacks over this great length is SSE., with a slight trend towards due south at the southern end; and it is likely that this constancy of direction indicates the persistence of the present gentle winds from the north or NNW. over a very long period of past time. In the north, between Lat. 29° and Lat. 26°, the dunes lie along the eastern edges of the whalebacks as in Plate 13*a*, and suggest the action of dune-building storm winds from the west. (Though meteorological records in the open desert are lacking, the consensus of opinion certainly favours the prevalence of westerly storms in this area.)

About Lat. 25° two or more chains of dunes lie side by side on a single whaleback, and there is a tendency for the whole multiple dune system to keep to the western edge of the underlying mass. Further south each dune system becomes more complex. The chains are shorter, and do not always run parallel to the main line of the system. We seem to see here the effect of the Sudanese wind régime with its southerly and easterly storm winds.

The photograph in Plate 13*b* was taken facing north at Lat. 25°, Long. 25° 30′. It shows one of the major dune systems which runs for several hundred kilometres north and south. Four short dune chains abreast can be distinguished, each running NW. and SE. On the right is seen another similar system, separated by a corridor of bare rock some 5 km. wide. The Sand Sea is here some 250 km. wide, and contains more than fifty such dune systems side by side.

7. THE TRANSVERSE REPETITION DISTANCE BETWEEN SEIF DUNE CHAINS

In localities where the windward source of the sand supply is distributed over a wide front, many chains of seif dunes may be formed side by side. Since they all result from the same wind régime they run almost exactly parallel to each other. When the lateral distance separating them is of the same order as their length, there appears to be little or no interaction between the position and the rate of growth or extension of one chain and those of its neighbour. They live independent lives and are affected only by the local rate of sand supply and by the surface texture of the ground over which they travel.

But in the case of a large dune field there certainly does exist some mechanism which acts on a grand scale to maintain in any one area a fairly definite and constant lateral distance between the chains. No particular repetition distance seems to be favoured more than any other, and for dunes of any given size the corridors between them may be 10 km. or 1 km. wide. But the width is approximately the same over a large area, so that the chains, or, on the largest scale the multiple dune systems, all lie parallel to one another and are evenly spaced, thus giving the country an extraordinary aspect of geometrical order unseen elsewhere in nature except on a microscopic scale.

There can be little doubt that while the mean spacing is probably a statistical effect dependent on the sand supply, the uniformity is caused by some such secondary transverse circulation in the longitudinal wind as that suggested in Chapter 12 (7), and Fig. 61.

8. THE FORMATION OF BARCHANS IN THE LONGITUDINAL TROUGHS BETWEEN MULTIPLE SEIF CHAINS, WHERE THE EFFECT OF CROSS-WINDS IS EXCLUDED

Strong evidence in favour of the hypothesis which was put forward at the end of Chapter 12, (5), that the barchan dune-type can only occur when the wind is nearly uni-directional, is to be found among the close-packed multiple seif chains mentioned in Section 6. Diagonal or cross-winds can affect the upper crests of the interior chains of the multiple system sufficiently to maintain the seif form, but the narrow longitudinal troughs between the chains are sheltered from all winds except those which blow up or down them. Here and there, at the bottoms of the deepest troughs, in an area of country where the barchan type is otherwise completely absent, are found small but perfectly formed barchan dunes. Excellent examples are to be seen close to the spot from which the photograph in Plate 13*b* was taken. The occurrence of these barchans seems to prove conclusively that neither the grading of the sand nor its material nor the texture of the underlying desert floor can have anything to do with the determination of the dune type, which must therefore be entirely a matter of wind régime.

9. DUNE SYSTEMS AND WIND DIRECTION

The importance of a study of the orientation of the dune chains, whether seif or barchan, composing the major dune system of the world, for the sake of the light it must shed on the direction of the prevailing continental winds, has been stressed of late by several writers, notably by Aufrère [1] and by Madigan.[2]

Unfortunately meteorological data are meagre in the vast arid regions where the sand systems are most fully developed, and in no case as yet has the velocity of the wind been taken into account in the computation of the prevailing wind direction. The usual 'wind rose' diagram is compiled only from data as to the number of periods in the year during which the wind blew from each point of the compass, irrespectively of its strength. Since a single day's high wind from one direction can move more sand than many weeks of gentle wind from some other direction, the correlation of wind data and dune direction cannot progress much further until the velocity is taken into consideration. Unfortunately, too, it is only recently that either explorers or cartographers have begun to note carefully the directions in which the dune systems run; and even now it is rare to find mention made of whether the system is composed of the seif or the barchan dune type.

Information on both meteorology and dune direction is most complete in the case of the Australian deserts, and has been summarized in an important paper by Madigan. Here, as in large areas in North Africa and Serindia, the seif dune type predominates. Indeed in Australia the barchan is almost non-existent. The similarity in appearance between the maps and aerial photos of the straight, parallel, and regularly spaced seif chains of the Australian deserts given by Madigan, and the Egyptian 1/500,000 maps of the Sand Sea, is most striking. The maps are almost indistinguishable from one another, as also they are from the dune maps of the French Sahara. This is the more remarkable because (*a*) in the Australian case the country is by no means devoid of vegetation whereas in Egypt there is none whatever, and (*b*) the Australian systems are young, the corridors between them are sand-free and the dunes are but one-seventh of the height and width of these in the Sand Sea, where the

[1] Aufrère, L. (1928). *Report of Proc.* (*12th*) *Internat. Geogr. Congr.* Cambridge.

— — (1931). *Ann. de Geogr.*, 40, pp. 312–85.

[2] Madigan, C. T. (1936). *Geogr. Rev.*, 26, pp. 205–27.

accumulation of sand has proceeded to such a degree that the desert floor even in the corridors is buried to an unknown depth.

It seems most difficult to escape from the conclusion that both the large-scale character of the dune field and the small-scale shape of the individual dunes are determined by the character of the wind régime and by that alone. Evidence has already been put forward in favour of the view that the barchan only occurs where the wind is nearly uni-directional. For this we have (*a*) wind records in Kharga Oasis (Chapter 14 (6)), where the barchan is the only dune form present; (*b*) observations on the occurrence of ice barchans (Chapter 14 (9)); (*c*) the occurrence of barchans in the hollows between close ranges of seif dunes, where there is protection from all winds except those blowing along the line of the seif ranges, in a region totally devoid of other barchans in the open (Chapter 15 (8)).

As evidence, on the other hand, that the seif type of dune needs cross-winds for its continuance, we have (*a*) in Chapter 13 (5) that in regions where only the barchan type exists in open country, the seif type is found under cliffs which run transversely to the wind direction. These cliffs give rise to transverse gusts and at the same time protect the dune from the steady effect of the prevailing wind. The following evidence also seems very suggestive:

(*b*) In studying the literature on the subject of the correspondence of wind and seif dune directions—the papers of Aufrère on the Saharan, and of Madigan on the Australian dunes, both already referred to, and papers by Beadnell,[1] Wingate [2] and others on the Egyptian Sand Sea, one curious fact emerges. In all three cases, although it is now agreed that the dune direction corresponds more or less with that of the prevailing wind, there has been considerable disagreement in the past as to the direction of the prevailing wind. The early observers in each case held that it blew at right angles to the dune direction, whereas later observations over a longer period show that it blows parallel to the dunes. On the above hypothesis the explanation is simple. Both are right, since cross-winds are essential for seif formation. Moreover, if the hypothesis is correct that the cross-winds, though lasting for a shorter time, should be stronger in intensity than the longitudinal winds, it is natural that the early explorers would have noted the former rather than the latter.

(*c*) In the case of the Australian seif dunes the 'wind rose'

[1] Beadnell, H. J. L. (1934). *Geogr. J.*, 84, p. 337.
[2] Wingate, O. (1934). *Geogr. J.*, 83, p. 292.

diagrams published in Madigan's paper speak for themselves. At no single meteorological station can the winds be classed as in any sense uni-directional. The nearest approach is at Alice Springs, where the wind blows from the prevailing direction and its opposite for 160 days in the year, and at Port Headland, where the figure is 180. These may be compared with Beadnell's figures for the barchan country round Kharga Oasis, where the wind blew along the prevailing axis for 303 days in the year, and of the remainder 29 were calm.

(*d*) It is admittedly dangerous to argue from the particular to the general, but the following fact appears to be explainable in no other way than by the bi-directional hypothesis of seif dune formation. The whole dune system of north-east Africa makes a vast wheel round from a NNW.–SSE. axis in the north, through the true N. and S. to an axis running ENE.–WSW. in the south. The dune chains lie on arcs of circles centred roughly in the neighbourhood of Lat. 23° N., Long. 25° E., and the radii vary from zero to 800 km. Near the centre of this great system are to be found groups of well-formed and mutually parallel seif chains which have been carefully mapped by the Egyptian Survey Department. But groups lying only a few kilometres from one another differ in direction by more than 50°. Again the explanation seems simple. We have but to assume that in this region the distinction between strong and gentle wind is not well marked, and that by a slight change in their relative velocities they take each other's places.

REFERENCES

BALL, J. *Geogr. J.*, 70, pp. 211–20

DESIO, A. (1939). *Missione Scientifica della Reale Accademia d'Italia a Cufra* (1931—IX). (Rome. Reale Accademia d'Italia.) Vol. II

JORDANS (1876). *Physische Geographie und Meteorologie der libyschen Wuste.* (Cassel)

KADAR, L. (1934). *Geogr. J.*, 83, p. 470

GAUTIER, E. F. (1928). *Le Sahara.* (Payot, Paris) and numerous other publications

Chapter 16

THE INTERNAL STRUCTURE OF SAND DEPOSITS

1. CONSISTENCY OF THE DEPOSITED MATERIAL

HAVING dealt with the movement of sand grains over the surface, with the resulting surface forms both on a small and on a large scale, and to some extent with the grading of the sand deposits laid down under constant controlled conditions, it remains to discuss the arrangement of the grains when they come finally to rest, and the evidence which can be thereby obtained as to the structure of the deposit.

Fortunately a very simple method of examination is available; and it is possible to corroborate in large measure by direct observation the rather speculative deductions of the last two chapters as to the mode of growth of full-scale dunes.

No one who has travelled in dune country can have failed to be struck by the sudden and often very disconcerting changes in the supporting properties of the material, whether underfoot or under the wheels of a car. A heavily loaded vehicle can often be driven for long distances over the rounded tops of dunes without disturbing the surface to a greater depth than that of the ripple trough—a matter of a centimetre or so. The underlying substance is exceedingly resistant to normally applied pressures. A scraping movement of the fingers will, however, prove at once that the firmness cannot be explained by cohesion or cementing between the grains. The grains are quite loose, but are packed together in a peculiar way.

Then, without any warning being given by a change in the appearance of the surface, the wheels drop suddenly into a soft yielding mass through which a six-foot rod can be thrust with one hand without effort. Sometimes these dry quicksands are so unstable that by bringing the weight of one's body to bear sharply by a small jump, a real circular wave can be made to radiate outwards for several metres. Yet no difference is perceptible between the appearance of samples taken from these quicksands and from the firm ground nearby. Further, an

PLATE 15

STRATIFICATION OF ANCIENT SAND DEPOSITS IN THE NUBIAN SANDSTONE

PLATE 16

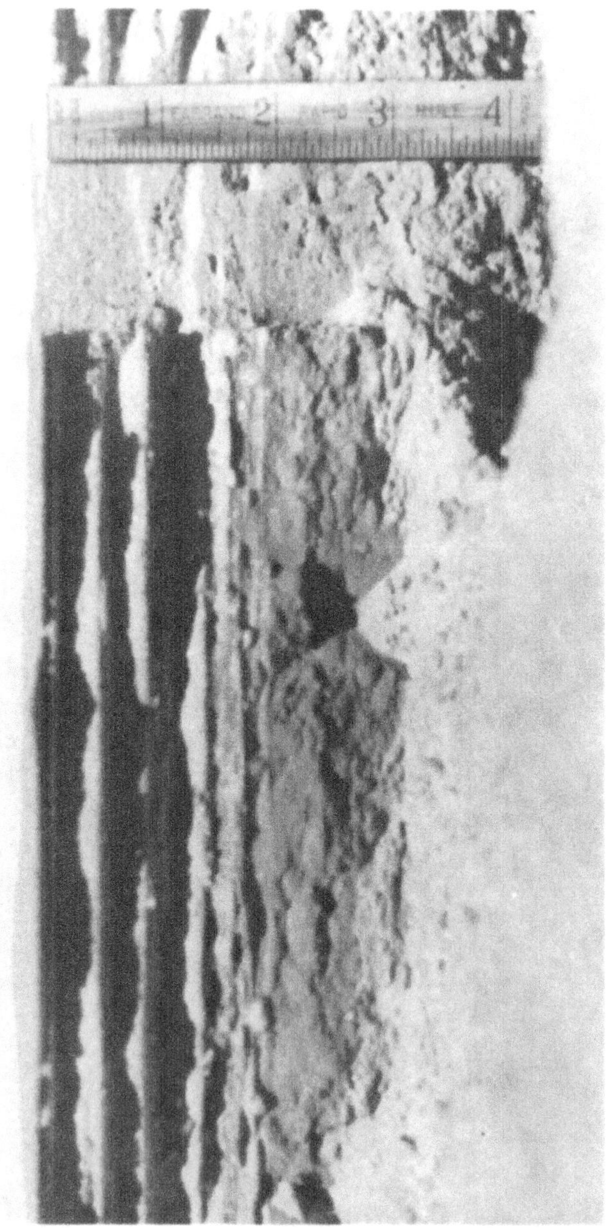

LAMINATED STRUCTURE OF A SAND SHEET

analysis of the samples very often shows no appreciable difference in the bulk grading.

The soft areas or 'pools' are found only to occur either in actual dunes, or in sand country which is likely to have been built up by the passage of former dunes. Their positions are apparently haphazard on any one dune, but they appear in the same places in every dune in a given dune field; and this clearly points to some intimate connexion between the soft pools and the past history of the dunes.

2. LAMINAR STRUCTURE REVEALED BY THE DIFFERENTIAL RATE OF WATER SEEPAGE THROUGH LAYERS OF VARYING GRAIN GRADING [1]

The chief difficulty in investigating the internal arrangement of a sand deposit has been that the material is so homogeneous that even when wetted to prevent collapse a cut section reveals next to nothing. The method which has been used with great success by the writer depends on two experimental facts: (*a*) all deposits of wind-blown sand are found to consist of narrow layers or laminae, a few millimetres thick, in each of which the grading varies very slightly from one side to the other as regards the proportion of fine material present: (*b*) if water is allowed to seep through clean sand, the wetted front travels faster through the material as the proportion of fine material is increased.

Hence, if a small quantity of water—a pint or less—is allowed to seep slowly downwards through the top surface, and the yet unwetted sand is soon afterwards scooped away from in front of the advancing wetness, the layers through which the water has travelled faster and farther will stand out sideways as thin wafers, while the loose dry sand between them and ahead of the water in the remaining layers falls away and is removed.

The method is extremely sensitive; but in order to obtain the best results some discretion must be used as to the quantity of water applied to any one spot and the time allowed before exposing the wetted front.

3. STRUCTURE OF BEDS DEPOSITED BY ACCRETION. THEIR FIRMNESS. SIMILARITY TO WIND-PACKED SNOW

It may be well at this point to refer back to Chapter 10, wherein accretion was defined in Section 1, and the grading changes were summarized in Section 4. Accretion is the type of deposition which occurs during sand movement over a smooth continuous

[1] Bagnold, R. A. (1938). *Nature*, 142, p. 403.

sand surface when the wind fails to carry away from any point as much sand as it carries to that point.

At the beginning of a period of wind during which the accretion occurs, the finest material exposed on the up-wind storage surface is the first to be set in motion, and is the first to be deposited. Subsequently, as the supply of fine grains runs short, the peak size of the oncoming sand slowly increases. Hence if any one rise and fall of wind produces deposition at all, it must add to the existing surface a new layer which is finest at the bottom and becomes coarser towards the new top surface.

Similarly whenever removal takes place the exposed top surface again tends to become coarser. Subsequent accretion lays on the old coarse surface a new coating of sand which is again finer below than on the top. And so on.

Each succeeding layer is usually only a few millimetres thick, so that any direct sampling made in an attempt to detect the change of grain diameter would probably fail. Moreover, in the case of dune sand the peak diameter shifts so little that the different layers are undetectable by eye. It is only here and there, at widely separated levels where prolonged removal has probably taken place, that observably coarser layers are seen.

The fine structure is, however, at once displayed by the water seepage method. The section shown in Plate 14*a* was taken on the side of a dune. It will be seen that the layers average 2 to 3 mm. in thickness. It is also apparent that the surface, which must clearly have coincided with each layer as it was formed, has been cut through by a new removal surface, and that one single additional layer has since been added.

It may be mentioned that in this particular case the wet mass was afterwards cleaved with a knife, and no sign of the stratification could be seen.

In every instance where the internal structure of a firm unyielding sand deposit has been tested in the field by the above method, the same narrow layers appeared, running parallel to the successive surfaces over which the sand was driven by the wind. Further, the remarkable firmness of the accretion deposit is invariably reproduced in the wind tunnel. Hence it seems certain that the firmness is due to the particular manner in which the individual sand grains are fitted into their final resting-places by the sand movement over the growing surface, and that the action builds up an aggregate having the greatest possible density.

Since any disturbance must cause such a compact mass to

increase its volume (dilatation), it follows that the mass must behave as a rigid body to a force applied perpendicularly to the surface. Final rupture can only take place when the force becomes so great that the whole body of the deposit shears sideways and upwards.

The accretion sand deposit may be compared with deposits of wind-packed snow, which appear to be formed under very similar conditions. But in this case it is likely that the peculiar hardness of the crust is due to a secondary effect. For if, as Seligman [1] suggests, some cementing also takes place at every point of contact between grain and grain, the exceptional close-packing of the accretion mechanism should produce a maximum number of contact points per unit volume of the material.

4. GRADING CHANGES DUE TO SHEARING. STRUCTURE OF AN AVALANCHED ENCROACHMENT DEPOSIT

Many interesting experiments can be made with sand of which each grade has been dyed a distinguishing colour. The rearrangement of the grains according to their size, which takes place whenever ripples are formed by a wind, can be shown very well by this means (Chapter 11 (5)).

The same method can be used to demonstrate the grading changes which occur when relative motion between the grains takes place by shearing. If about 1 cm. thickness of well-mixed sand, coloured in this way, is spread out on a flat inclined board, and the board is tapped repeatedly so that the sand slips downwards a little at each tap, it is found that the grades very quickly separate out. The coarsest grains rise to the top, and the finest sink through the material to the bottom. At the same time shearing takes place throughout the whole mass, so that the top layers travel faster than the bottom ones. As a result the layers underneath, containing the finer grains, tend to be left behind. Successive layers become exposed along the upper edge of the slipping mass, and the distinguishing colours appear as clear horizontal bands.

That the fine material tends to collect at the surface of shear can be shown better by tipping a well-mixed heap of coloured sand until the lower inclined side of the heap shears away. The freshly exposed surface of the remainder of the heap is seen to bear the colour of the finest grade present.

[1] Seligman, G. (1936). *Snow Structure and Ski Fields.* (Macmillan.)

These experiments show that whenever shearing takes place (*a*) the peak diameter of the sand along the surface of shear becomes smaller than that of the unsheared mass, and (*b*) the peak diameter of the sheared material after it has come to rest is greater at the bottom than at the top of the slip-face.

Here again, as in the previous section, the diameter change from the outer to the inner surface of any sheared layer, though usually undetectable to the eye, is always from large to small.

When the method of water seepage is applied to the slip-faces of dunes, the shear plane made by each successive avalanche can be made clearly visible. Furthermore, all those portions of the internal mass of a dune which have been built up, perhaps long ago, by sand avalanches slipping down an advancing slip-face, can be readily distinguished by the constant angle at which they must have stood.

Plate 14*b* shows the successive slip-face surfaces as they appeared after a little water had been applied at a point about 10 cm. behind the exposed section. The photograph was taken at a place a few metres away from the site of Plate 14*a*. It is clear that (*a*) the old slip-face of the dune had been advancing from right to left, and (*b*) subsequent accretion has begun to take place, probably after a new top surface has been carved out by removal.

The structure of the modern sand deposits shown in Plate 14 may be compared with that of the very ancient sand deposits in the Nubian Sandstone in Plate 15.

The important fact emerges that the existence of these old slip-faces close below the present surface is invariably disclosed whenever the tests are applied to the 'pools' of quicksand described in Section 1. *These dry quicksands are in fact simply deposits formed by the advance of old slip-faces.* They therefore afford sure evidence of the presence of former dunes, even though there may be no dunes in the vicinity at the present time.

The looseness and instability of the deposit is due to the manner in which the grains have come to rest, as was the firmness of the accretion deposit. But here, instead of being fitted selectively into the most secure positions by the gentle agitation of the surface caused by the bombardment of the saltation, the grains are piled anyhow, as a result of avalanching. Large spaces exist between the grains, and the density of the mass is relatively low. Consequently an applied pressure tends to encourage a relative movement of the grains into an arrangement of closer packing and therefore of smaller volume. It is probable, too, that the expulsion of air which must accompany the shrinkage of volume converts the mass momentarily into a semi-fluid condition.

If a layer of accretion overlies the soft encroachment deposit the degree of solidity of the surface evidently depends on the thickness of the accretion. 10 or 20 cm. may be necessary to bear the pressure of a loaded car or a heavy footfall.

5. STRUCTURE OF A BARCHAN DUNE

If sufficient labour were available to dismantle a dune, the whole of its past history, during the time the lee slope has taken to travel forwards from the position of the present windward edge, could be disclosed by an examination of its internal structure. Indeed, much can be discovered very quickly by noting the structure at selected spots immediately below the existing surface; or even by merely walking over it, noting the boundary lines between the firm and soft areas.

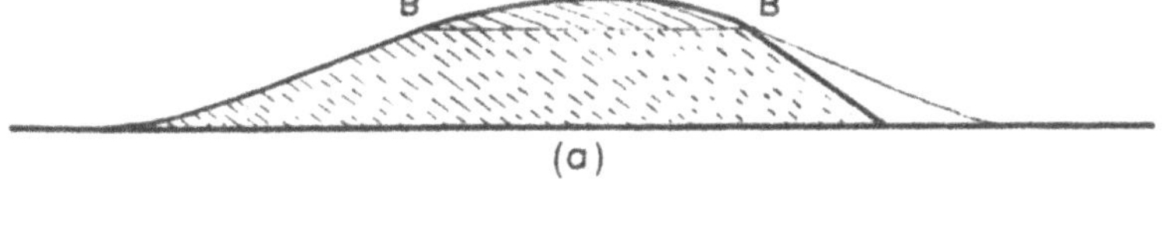

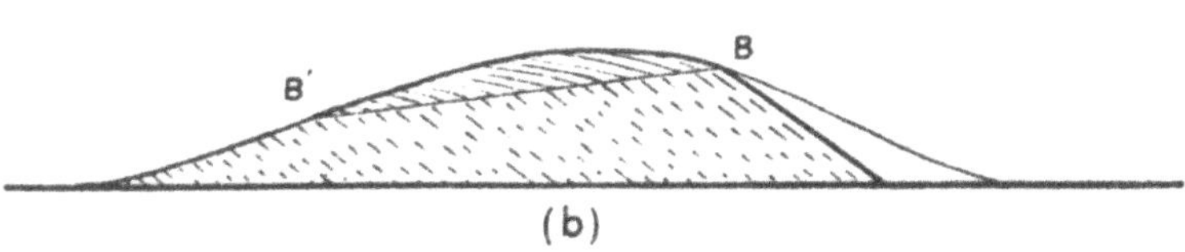

FIG. 82.—ARRANGEMENT OF ACCRETION (CONTINUOUS LINES) AND ENCROACHMENT DEPOSITS (BROKEN LINES) IN A BARCHAN DUNE

Fig. 82*a* shows an ideal longitudinal section through the summit of a barchan whose slip-face has been advancing without change of height. Since the brink B has moved horizontally, it follows that none of the sand above its path B′B has ever avalanched, and all the superstructure must have been built up by accretion. The top of the dune is therefore firm. On the windward side the surface below B′ is an exposure of the main encroachment deposit formed by avalanches of sand down the slip-face. All this surface should be soft. If, however, firm patches do occur, they are evidence of a temporary up-wind movement of the dune by an accretion of sand on the windward side.

In Fig. 82*b* the dune has been growing as it advances; so the windward exposure of the old slip-face brink at B′ is below the level of the present brink B. Similarly a progressive lowering of the slip-face will be disclosed by the existence of avalanche structure at a higher level at B′ than at B.

Reverse slip-faces formed during bouts of wind from the opposite direction can be distinguished at once by direction of the sloping shear-planes.

6. STRUCTURE OF SEIFS AND WHALEBACKS

In a nearly symmetrical seif dune, where the slip-face shifts alternately from one side to the other, the structure is necessarily more complicated. Fig. 83 shows an ideal case in which growth has proceeded in a perfectly regular manner. Actually of course the successive stages must be very irregular, but the few tests already made by the author certainly confirm that the general arrangement is as indicated in the figure.

It will be seen that the whole of the middle zone of the dune

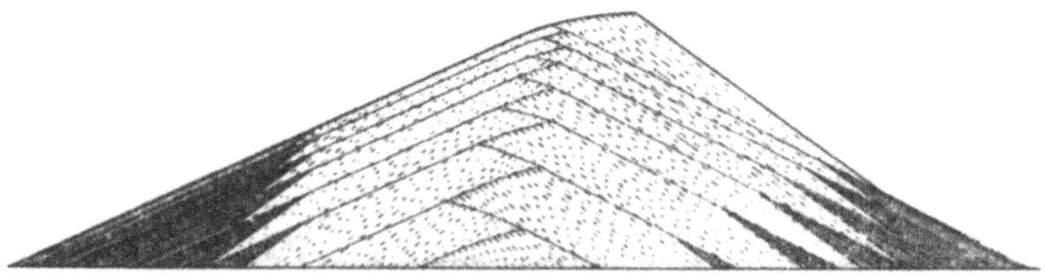

FIG. 83.—ARRANGEMENT OF ACCRETION AND ENCROACHMENT DEPOSITS IN A SEIF DUNE

consists of soft avalanched sand, and that the boundary lines AB and CD of Fig. 80 are in reality transition zones where the surface consistency is doubtful. The whole of the plinth is a very firm accretion deposit.

It is interesting to apply these general ideas to a speculation as to the probable internal structure of the huge whalebacks of the northern part of the Egyptian Sand Sea. The evidence is unfortunately very scanty. The dune chains lie along the eastern edge of the main sand banks, as in Fig. 81*b*. The terrace B

(Fig. 84) which is sometimes as much as a kilometre wide, is uniformly firm except at the bottoms of local shallow depressions in its surface. A belt A of very soft sand runs continuously along the western brow of each whaleback for a distance of nearly 200 km. Below this belt the plinth of the whaleback is firm.

The soft belt can only be accounted for by the former existence of a chain of dunes along the western side. And since the present surface at A is a considerable height above the ground, it is likely that the primitive dune chain was built up by nearly equal cross-

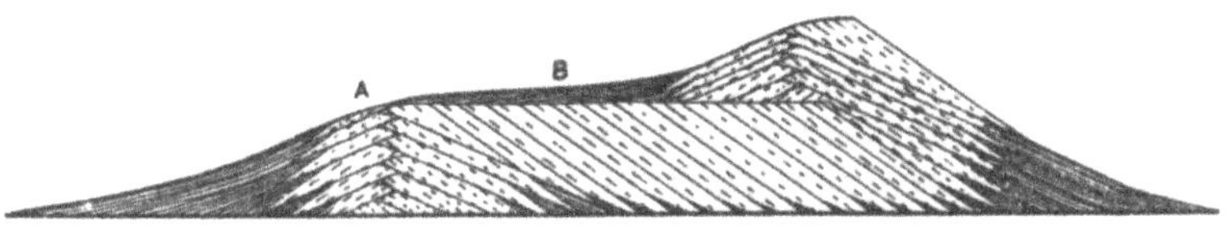

FIG. 84.—SUPPOSED INTERNAL STRUCTURE OF THE WHALEBACKS OF THE EGYPTIAN SAND SEA

winds from either flank, so that it grew high without much lateral movement.

We might suppose that there then came a change in the wind régime, and that westerly storms became dominant. As a result the slip-face on the lee side advanced eastwards for a considerable distance, and formed the lower terrace B.

Finally it may be supposed that the former wind régime returned, easterly storms banked up fresh sand on the east side, and a new period of dune-building began.

Without further evidence the above reconstruction is of course mere speculation ; it may, however, help to stimulate interest in this remarkable region, and to suggest lines along which a study of dunes may be usefully linked with climatology.

7. STRUCTURE AND GROWTH OF SAND SHEETS

Very large areas of desert country consist of sheets of flat or gently undulating sand. The exposed surface bears upon it an even sprinkling of coarse grains or small pebbles, and is almost devoid of ripples (Chapter 11 (8)).

The material below is usually very firm, and will stand to a vertical face round the sides of a test hole. It consists of layers of fine sand separated by single layers of pebbles similar to those found on the surface.

In the case of the vast level plains of sand sheet which are scattered over the North African desert, the thickness of this upper laminated structure is small. Within 10 cm. or less there is usually found, either pure or mixed with fine sand, an underlayer of red ferruginous powder. Below this again, at varying depths there may be other layers of clean yellow sand and possibly of the red material also. The whole structure strongly suggests periodical floodings separated by very long intervals of time.

But if, as seems likely, both the extreme flatness of the country and the occurrence of the bands of dry laterized mud are due to the action of water, how and under what conditions have the sand-pebble laminae been built up ? The answer is most probably given by the observed formation, during sand storms, of the long narrow parallel strips of fine sand described in Chapter 12 (7).

These temporary deposits are of the order of 1 cm. thick. After the storm is over removal sets in, and the whole of the new unprotected deposit disappears. In places, however, especially at the up-wind end of each strip, a scattering of pebbles has been driven up and over the deposit. If the distribution of these pebbles is sufficiently dense they will afford permanent protection to the sand underneath, and a new addition to the structure of the sand sheet will have come into being.

But this formation of a new layer requires a supply of extra pebbles, since the pebbles of the former protective covering are now buried. The extra pebbles can only come from the old surface up-wind; and unless this already contains pebbles in greater density than is needed to protect the underlying sand[1] there can clearly be no net addition of sand to the sheet.

It seems, therefore, that the formation of a new permanent layer of sand depends on the very gradual accumulation of a surplus of surface pebbles. The supply comes presumably from the disintegration of local rock projections, and the pebbles travel very slowly. Hence the formation of a new layer must be a very rare phenomenon. This is borne out by the fact that so few successive layers are found.

Plate 16 shows a section through a sand sheet in south-western

[1] Experiment (Bagnold (1937), *Geogr. J.*, 89, p. 421) shows that under a moderate wind complete protection of the underlying sand is afforded by a pebble distribution whose projected area is less than 10 per cent. of the whole. This may be compared with the corresponding figure of 5 per cent. for sand in water. (Colebrook, C. F., and White, C. M. (1937), *Proc. Roy. Soc. A.*, 161, p. 367.)

Egypt. The section was made by the seepage method immediately after a sand storm had added a half-inch layer of sand to the surface. It will be seen that only three previous layers had been established above the old mud surface.

Incidentally the photograph shows on the right how little of the existing detail is brought out by the usual method of cleaving a wetted mass of the material.

8. WATER RETENTION AND VEGETATION DEPENDENT ON THE INTERNAL STRUCTURE

It is well known that considerable moisture is often found close below the surfaces of dunes even in very arid countries, and even though the spot may be far above the level of the desert floor. An explanation is unfortunately still to be found in text-books to the effect that sand has some miraculous power of 'drawing up water by capillary attraction' from the underground water table to an unspecified height.

There is no evidence whatever for this idea; and experiment shows that if a column of sand, either enclosed in a tube or exposed as an open heap, is supplied at its base with an unlimited amount of water, the surface tension of the grains is unable to cause any moisture to rise higher than 40 cm. at the most. Nor can evaporation from below and re-condensation above be called upon to explain the presence of water high up in the dune. For the raising of water requires work to be done, and this work can only be provided by thermal changes within the body of the dune. And sand is such a poor conductor of heat that even the violent diurnal temperature changes which occur in the desert are inappreciable at a depth of 20 cm. below the surface.

In reality the moisture is due to rare showers of rain; and it is this very uniformity of temperature within the dune which, by preventing evaporation, retains the water for years underneath the surface. For water can only evaporate if the air in contact with it is unsaturated with vapour; directly saturation is reached no further evaporation can take place, and as long as the saturated air between the sand grains remains unchanged no water can be lost. In the upper 20 cm., however, the air is continually being changed, because the warmth of the daytime drives some of the expanding and water-laden air out of the dune, while fresh dry air is sucked in during the nightly cooling and contraction.

Two closely allied phenomena still call, however, for explanation. (*a*) Live grasses, or more frequently the remains of dead grass, is found in small patches on a dune surface which is otherwise quite devoid of any sign of life. (*b*) Moisture below the surface is more often found where there are indications of occasional plant life than elsewhere. The distribution is on far too small a scale to be accounted for by rain showers having fallen on one spot and not on another.

The explanation is indicated by a third phenomenon. Both the vegetated patches and those under which there is moisture are found to consist nearly always of soft sand, whereas the surrounding barren areas are firm underfoot. Tests so far made appear to show definitely that, at any rate where roots have not unduly disturbed the sand structure, both vegetated and moist areas are built up of steeply sloping encroachment laminae ; and that in the barren areas the accretion laminae run parallel to the surface, or nearly so. As an imitation of a rain shower the seepage test clearly demonstrates the differential action of the two kinds of structure. When applied to the accretion deposit the water runs rapidly sideways along the surface layers which contain fine material, and is prevented from sinking downwards by the relatively non-conducting layers from which the fine material is absent. The moisture remains close to the surface and soon evaporates. On the encroachment deposit, on the other hand, the water goes downwards along the old shear-planes and almost immediately reaches such a depth that subsequent evaporation is negligible.

Chapter 17

'SINGING SANDS'

NO work on the behaviour of dry sand can be deemed complete without some account of the so-called 'song of the sands'. I had started a research into this curious phenomenon in the summer of 1939, but it was interrupted by the outbreak of war and by my consequent departure on active service abroad. The following remarks, written at the publisher's suggestion after the completion of this book, may serve the purpose of summarizing the present state of our knowledge on the subject. There is as yet no real explanation of the mechanism by which the sounds are produced.

Sound-making sands are found in two types of locality: on the sea shore and on the slip-faces of desert dunes and drifts. Both the frequency of the sound emitted and the attendant circumstances differ considerably in the two cases, so it will be as well to deal with them separately.

1. 'WHISTLING' BEACH SAND

This is found on sea beaches in various parts of the world. It occurs in the British Isles on the Island of Eigg, and on the coast of North Wales. The sound, a squeak or whistle at a frequency of between 800 and 1,200 vibrations per second, is produced by any rapid disturbance of the dry top layer, such as is caused by walking over it, sweeping it quickly with the palm of the hand, or plunging a stick vertically into it. Conditions are usually best just above the high-water level, and when the sand has recently dried out after a shower of rain.

Although the existence of whistling sands has long been known, and although the phenomenon has been described and discussed in many scattered publications, no comparative analyses either chemical or mechanical of sands from the different localities, appear to have been made. In the samples I have seen the grains were fairly uniform in size with a mean diameter of the order of

0·3 mm. They were rounded but not markedly so, and from their appearance were assumed to be quartz. The sand from North Wales was entirely free from other material but that from Eigg contained grains which were clearly not quartz.

When the sand is removed from the beach for experiment, &c., the sound-making property does not last. In some sands it is more permanent than in others, but in all cases it appears that the sound is louder and more easily produced immediately after the sand has been washed and dried. The property afterwards fades. This fading may be due to a contamination of the sand by dust particles, or to some change in the physical state of the grains' own surfaces. Heat is not essential during the drying process, nor, indeed, is any great degree of dryness necessary. The surface grains will often whistle even though the sand 2 cm. below is still wet.

Carus Wilson and others have observed that the sound is best produced when the sand is contained in a shallow vessel with a smooth round bottom, such as a porcelain mortar. The use, however, of any container which has a period of sound vibration of its own should be avoided, because it has been found that in this case the sound emitted is apt to assume the frequency of the container, instead of characterizing some inherent quality in the sand itself. It is possible that the sound emitted by sand in a resonant container is a different phenomenon, and is merely a 'bow-string' effect arising from an intermittent frictional force acting on the grains in contact with the vibrating wall. I have produced this possible spurious effect both in a porcelain mortar and in a steel cylinder by using the artificial glass sand with very spherical grains which is known commercially as 'frozen dew', but I have never yet been able to get a sound out of this material in a non-resonant container. To ensure that we are dealing with the true effect the whole movement of the sand grains should be restricted to the body of the sand itself, and it should be arranged that no movement occurs between the boundary grains and the container walls.

The true whistle can be produced with least effort by giving the sand mass a light stab with the end of a pencil. The noise seems to start immediately the striker meets the sand surface. The speed of the stimulating motion must exceed a certain minimum value which, in the case of the North Wales sand, seems to be about 90 cm./sec. or 3 ft./sec. Unfortunately this is too fast for the eye to see what kind of movement takes place in the surrounding sand; i.e. whether it is of the 'viscous fluid' type, or whether the sand slides over a series of definite shear planes.

The note emitted varies according to the speed and circumstances of the stimulating movement. In the course of some preliminary experiments which I had hoped to elaborate later, the plunger consisted of a small steel cylinder 2 cm. in diameter containing a pair of quartz piezo-crystals.[1] These were connected through a D.C. amplifier to a cathode-ray oscillograph, so that the spot on the screen traced, against a horizontal time scale, a true curve showing the mechanical force with which the movement of the plunger was resisted by the sand ahead of it. When the plunger was at rest the spot traced a central horizontal line representing zero force. Movement of the plunger at less than the critical speed caused a displacement of this line upwards, corresponding to a steady resisting force. Directly the sound started, the tracing line changed to a pure sine curve of remarkably constant frequency and amplitude. The frequency of the sand vibration could be increased from a minimum of about 800 per second to a maximum of 1,200 by raising the speed of the plunger. The intensity of the force on the plunger head during one cycle of the vibration ranged from zero to twice the steady value obtaining before the vibration started.

These rough experiments seem to show that: (*a*) All the grains concerned in the vibration were acting in complete unison. For the force vibration over the whole of the plunger head gave a pure single sine curve on the oscillograph. (*b*) The plunger head being flat, the grains in the stagnant zone just ahead of the plunger must have moved with it during its advance through the sand mass, and can have had practically no mutual motion. It is therefore very unlikely that the source of the vibration could have been within this zone. The zone may have consisted of a cone of sand jutting out in front of the plunger, and the vibration may have originated from a shearing movement along the surface of the cone; or, as seems more likely from observations on the distortion of the same sand at a slower speed, there may have been no shear surface at all, and the displacement of the sand may have consisted of a general fluid motion within the whole mass. In any case, since the entire force on the plunger head was relieved and sank to zero instantaneously over its whole surface during one part of

[1] The apparatus had been used for a previous research, and had been found almost aperiodic. Details are given in the *Journal of the Institution of Civil Engineers*, Vol. 12, pp. 204–5.

the oscillation, it is clear that we have to deal with something akin to an oscillation of fluid pressure throughout a considerable volume of the surrounding sand.

2. THE 'SONG' OR BOOMING OF DESERT SANDS

We now pass from the squeaks made by small quantities of beach sand when trodden underfoot, to the great sound which in some remote places startles the silence of the desert. Native tales have woven it into fantasy; sometimes it is the song of sirens who lure travellers to a waterless doom; sometimes it is said to come upwards from bells still tolling underground in a sand-engulfed monastery; or maybe it is merely the anger of the jinn! But the legends, as collected by the late Lord Curzon,[1] are hardly more astonishing than the thing itself. I have heard it in south-western Egypt 300 miles from the nearest habitation. On two occasions it happened on a still night, suddenly—a vibrant booming so loud that I had to shout to be heard by my companion. Soon other sources, set going by the disturbance, joined their music to the first, with so close a note that a slow beat was clearly recognized. This weird chorus went on for more than five minutes continuously before silence returned and the ground ceased to tremble.

The sound came always from the lower part of a sand avalanche as it flowed down the slip-face of a high dune or drift. The avalanche might start spontaneously, as in the occurrence just described, either during a sand storm or afterwards when surface temperature changes make the slope unstable. Or it could be started artificially with a push of the hand or foot. In the natural case the sound only started when the foremost sand of the avalanche had begun to be checked by the change of slope near the bottom, and the sand above was telescoping into it. The rippled appearance of the movement was then strongly reminiscent of a rush of water as seen in slow motion.

As in the case of whistling beach sand the phenomenon is very rare, and happens only in certain places where, presumably, the sand has some peculiar property. The thought obviously occurs to one that a comparison of samples of the sands from all the sites, both shore and desert, would very soon disclose some common characteristic which would in turn suggest the mechanism involved in the sound production. But not only has no characteristic so far been found common to both whistling and booming sands,

[1] *Tales of Travel*, pp. 261–339.

but the latter does not seem to possess any special distinguishing character at all.

The grains are certainly uniform in size, but not more so than those of many silent sands. In the valuable account by Lewis [1] of the white 'roaring' sands of the Kalahari Desert stress is laid on the probable importance of the complete lack of very fine particles among the sand grains. This observation tallies with his statement that the sands roar best when freshly dry after a shower of rain, for this presumably has the effect of washing the fine material out. It also tallies with the idea that beach sands whistle best after rain. But it is completely at variance with my own experience in the Libyan Desert.[2] For the vocal material here, instead of being cleaner than usual, is on the contrary dirtier. The surfaces of the clear colourless quartz grains are not only heavily stained with red oxide of iron, but in two instances were caked around with tiny lumps of it. Rainfall is most unlikely in this area to have anything to do with the vocal quality of the sand, since the ground is appreciably wetted only once or twice in a decade.

That marked roundness is also not an essential quality is shown by the photomicrograph in Fig. 7 of Lewis's paper. This point is supported to some extent by the apparent fact already noted that the true sound cannot be made to occur even with the almost perfectly spherical glass material of very constant grain size. At present all we can safely say about the sand itself is that (*a*) the grains must be reasonably rounded and reasonably uniform in size, and (*b*) the grains in all cases appear to be composed of quartz. (But since an overwhelming proportion of all the sand on the earth's surface is of quartz, this does not get us very far.)

Neither does the situation of the sand enter into its vocal property. I have found singing sand on the slip-faces of both seif and barchan dunes and of drifts formed under the shelter of cliffs.

The sound emitted by the vocal desert sand is much lower in frequency than the whistle of beach sands. Lewis measured it in the Kalahari Desert with tuned pitch pipes, and found that when induced by an artificial disturbance (a plank drawn through the sand) a plank speed of 15 cm./sec. gave a note whose frequency was about 132 cycles/sec., and a speed of 60 cm./sec. gave

[1] Lewis, A. D. (1936). *South African Geogr. J.*, Vol. XIX, p. 33.

[2] The booming sands which I have discovered here at different times all lie on or close to the Nubian Sandstone plateau of the Gilf Kebir (Lat. 23° N., Long. 26° E.).

a note higher by not more than one octave. At 120 cm./sec. the note changed to a swish. When allowed to avalanche by itself the sand had surface speed of about 15 cm./sec., and it then 'hummed' at about 264 cycles/sec. The mean grain diameter was 0·2 mm. In the Libyan Desert I had no means of exact measurement, but I put the note heard as somewhere around 132 cycles/sec., and my estimate of the steady speed of flow of the natural avalanche was 12 cm./sec. The mean size of the grains was larger, being about 0·35 mm.

The quality of the booming note of desert dunes has not been investigated with an oscillograph. It is certainly not as pure as the beach whistle. Lewis states that the determination of the note was difficult owing to noise, overtones, &c., and he confirms my notion of the sound as resembling that of an aeroplane in steady flight. As regards its intensity he states that at a distance of 600 yards it sounded like the rumble of thunder. He also confirms by a very convincing photograph (Fig. 5) and by his subsequent remarks that the motion of the sand within the natural avalanche is a rippling fluid flow with much individual movement between the grains.

Few experiments seem to have been made with the desert sand removed from its natural site. Lewis found that when the Kalahari sand was taken from its desert atmosphere to Pretoria it lost its vocal quality unless it was kept in airtight containers. The quality was quite restored by heating to 200° C. I once made a heap of the material close to its original site, and reproduced the sound by rocking a bottle to and fro about its base. I found that the sound could never be made to start on the first stroke, but only after several preliminary strokes had been made. It also appeared that a certain critical downward force was necessary. I estimated this as equivalent to the weight of a thickness of about 8 to 10 cm. of sand.

3. WHAT CONTROLS THE NOTE, AND HOW DOES THE SOUND ARISE?

Until we can predict from the examination of a small sample whether or no a given sand will whistle or boom, and if so the most favourable circumstances for it to do so, and what note it will emit, we cannot claim to understand much about singing sand. At present none of these questions can be answered. Certain deductions can, however, be drawn from the foregoing evidence, and certain physical principles can be applied.

(i) The oscillogram picture of the pressure variation within the sand indicates that all the grains vibrate in phase with one another. And the appearance of the avalanche in the case of the booming desert sand strongly suggests that all the grains are also in mutual movement like the molecules of a viscous liquid close to a boundary wall. (Were it not for the synchronism of the vibration the whole state of the sand might possibly be likened to that of a viscous gas.)

(ii) If this is correct the observed velocities of disturbance of the whole sand mass must be regarded as maximum velocities at the free surface of the fluid. The mean velocity of disturbance (as distinct from the vibration) should fall off progressively towards the bottom level where the motion ceases. On the analogy of the viscous fluid we might write $v = Vh/H$ for the velocity v of disturbance at any height h above this level, where V is the observed surface velocity, and H is the total height of the layer in motion.

(iii) Now the frequency multiplied by the repetition distance has the dimensions of a velocity. For instance, in the simple case of a fingernail being drawn across the corrugations of a book cover, the actual velocity of the finger is given by the product of the corrugation spacing and the frequency of the note emitted. Although in the case of musical sand it is very improbable that such a simple mechanism can exist, yet the product of the observed grain size and note frequency is likely to yield some kind of mean velocity of disturbance of all the grains which are combining to make the sound. Below are given in Column 3 the values of this hypothetical mean velocity $\bar{v}$ as calculated from the observed values of grain size and note frequency. These are compared in Column 4 with the observed velocity of the surface movement.

	Grain diameter d (cm.)	Frequency f (cycles per sec.)	Mean velocity $\bar{v} = f.d$	Observed surface velocity V	$\bar{v}/V$
Whistling sand from North Wales (Bagnold)	0·03	1,000	30	90	0·33
Booming sand, Kalahari (Lewis)	0·02	264	5·3	15	0·35
Booming sand, Gilf Kebir (Bagnold)	0·035	132	4·6	12	0·38

It will be seen that the ratio $\bar{v}/V$ is fairly constant over quite a wide range of values of diameter and frequency. The velocity $\bar{v} = f.d$ should give the actual velocity of disturbance at a certain depth below the surface, at which the vibration has its maximum intensity. And if the equation $v = Vh/H$ is even approximately true it appears that maximum vibration occurs at a depth of about two-thirds of the whole depth of the moving layer.

(iv) This idea, in conjunction with my experiment with the bottle, suggests that a definite steady external pressure, provided in nature by the weight of an overlying layer of sand, is necessary for the production of the vibration in addition to the force required to cause the actual disturbance of the sand mass.

(v) Since both the whistle and the booming are emitted by sands of the same grain diameter, it seems that the frequency of the sound is determined by the speed of the disturbance. But we know that a given sand is only set in vibration by a disturbance speed lying between fairly narrow limits. A whistling beach sand has never been made to yield the booming sound of the desert variety, and, as far as I am aware, the booming sand has not been made to whistle. Hence it seems that the disturbance speed which will set a given sand in vibration is determined by some unknown property of the grains themselves—some property, it is most likely, of their molecular surface structure.

One other piece of evidence may here be brought in. The whistle is produced by a very small quantity of sand in movement, close to the free surface. The booming on the other hand requires the movement of a far larger and deeper sand mass. The whistle can be made with a pencil end; but the minimum movement necessary to start the booming is that caused by a whole hand being scooped through the mass. Hence possibly the critical disturbance speed at which the sound occurs is itself some function of the whole mass of the sand disturbed, as well as of the structure of the grains composing it.

The vibration of any material body implies an alternating transformation of its energy between two different states. The body is at one phase of the vibration moving at its maximum speed; that is, its energy is all kinetic. Later on the motion of the body ceases, and the kinetic energy has then been converted into potential energy. It is stored either as gravitational energy (the raising of the body against gravity as in the simple pendulum) or as strain energy, such as that of a spring in tension or compression, or as that of the elastic distortion of a jelly.

When the potential energy is released the body again starts moving, and its energy becomes kinetic once more. At the end of this phase of the cycle the energy is again stored in the potential state, but this need not be of the same type as at first. A good example of such an asymmetrical vibration is given by the bouncing of a ball. The energy at the end of the rise is gravitational, and at the end of the fall, when the ball is in the act of striking the ground, the energy of the fall is stored momentarily as strain energy in the compression of the lower part of the ball against the ground.

The case of vibrating sand is far more complicated. The body as a whole consists of countless grains all vibrating in time with one another but not necessarily in the same direction; and further, unlike any other kind of vibration, sand only vibrates during a distortion of the whole mass; i.e., while the grains are changing their relative positions. The crux of the problem of the cause of the sand vibration can, however, to my mind be summed up in the one question: In what states is the energy of the vibrating grains stored at each of the two moments in the complete cycle of movement when all the grains are together momentarily at rest?

Only one serious answer has been put forward. Poynting and Thomson[1] suggested that the vibration is a pulsation of volume; that as a mass of uniform spherical grains is distorted it goes through alternate phases of loose ill-fitting grain piling when the volume of the interspaces is a maximum, and close compact piling when the volume is a minimum. As the volume rises to its maximum a partial vacuum is created between the grains, and at the moment of maximum volume the kinetic energy of the expanding mass is stored as negative pressure energy in the enclosed air. The excess atmospheric pressure outside then assists the mass to contract, and at the moment when it has collapsed to a state of minimum volume the enclosed air is compressed to a pressure greater than that of the atmosphere. The kinetic energy of the collapse is then stored as positive pressure energy in the enclosed air.

This answer is beautifully simple, but is open to several objections. It is very doubtful if even a collection of the best billiard balls, all spherical and all of equal size, would be sufficiently agile or sufficiently co-operative as to arrange themselves in perfect cannon-ball piling immediately after being dis-

[1] *Text Book of Physics* (*Sound*). (Ch. Griffin. London.) 1904.

turbed to such an extent that each finds itself amongst new neighbours. And the grains of singing sand are by no means round, and differ in size among themselves by at least one to two. But the most serious objection to this theory is that it entirely fails to account for the great rarity of the phenomenon, for the critical disturbance speed, or for the difference between the whistling and booming. At the same time I feel that the theory may well be partially correct, in that air pressure may enter considerably into the mechanism, even though the idea of alternate states of the piling arrangement of the grains is untenable. It would be interesting to observe how the true effect is modified by a reduction of the air pressure.[1]

Another theory is based on the idea that the disturbance of the sand mass is relieved by slipping along a series of instantaneous shear planes. Here the mean velocity $\bar{v}$ would be the velocity with which the shear jumped from one plane to the next in a direction at right angles to all the planes. A third theory which might be put forward is one based on the piezo-electric property of crystalline quartz. If a sphere of this material is rolled between two parallel pressure plates, electric charges appear whenever the pressure is applied to both ends of certain axes within the crystal. It is just possible that by continued rolling the grain axes might become so arranged that the tiny charges would accumulate.

The whole subject is very complicated, and the experimental difficulties are great, mainly because one cannot see what is going on inside the vibrating mass. Much more work will have to be done before the 'song of the sands' is understood.

[1] Presumably the sound could still be transmitted through the body of the sand and the walls of the containing vessel even if the air pressure were reduced to a vacuum.

INDEX

(*Page numbers in parentheses refer to Summary in Chapter* 8)

Lightning Source UK Ltd.
Milton Keynes UK
UKOW06f1110260416

272990UK00005B/192/P